CCLS

New York
Progress®
Mathematics

4

D1208715

Sadlier School

CCLS

Cover: *Series Design:* Studio Montage; *Title design:* Quarasan, Inc. **Photo Credits:** Cover: age fotostock/Rainer Martini: *right.* Getty Images/
Cameron Davidson: *bottom left.* Used under license from Shutterstock.com: kle555: *top left;* RoboLab: *background.* Interior: Alamy/Purestock/
Lisette Le Bon: 54 *top.* Blend Images/JGI: 124 *top;* KidStock: 8 *top,* 232 *top;* Somos: 302 *top.* Corbis/Patrick Giardino: 233. Dreamstime.com/
Steve Allen: 6 *bottom left;* 6 *top right.* Getty Images/Ming Tang-Evans: 55. Used under license from Shutterstock.com/Ilya Akinshin: 6 *bottom
right;* Jana Guothova: 8 *bottom,* 54 *bottom,* 124 *bottom,* 232 *bottom,* 302 *bottom;* kle555: 6 *center;* Levent Konuk: 9; koosen: 6 *top left;*
RoboLab: 1, 6 *background;* Ilya Ryabokon: 6 *top left.* SuperStock/SuperFusion/Ron Chapple Photography: 125; John Warden: 303.
Illustrator Credit: Dave Titus

For additional online resources, go to sadlierconnect.com.

William H. Sadlier, Inc.
9 Pine Street
New York, NY 10005-4700

Printed in the United States of America.
ISBN: 978-1-4217-3354-8
2 3 4 5 6 7 8 9 WEBC 19 18 17 16 15

Contents

NEW YORK
COMMON CORE
LEARNING STANDARDS

CCLS

continued next page

Unit 5   Focus on Geometry

Welcome

You have an exciting year ahead of you. You will be learning more about mathematics and the tools you will need to solve everyday problems.

Did you know that you solve problems and use math all the time? Think about your day. When you play sports after school, shop at your favorite store, cook delicious food, build something awesome like a tree house, or travel in a car, bus or train, you are using math and applying that understanding to make sense of the world around you.

Common Core Progress will help you improve problem-solving skills while becoming more confident in mathematics. That's why it's called *progress*.

Have a great year!

Progress Check

Look at how the Common Core standards you have learned and will learn connect.

It is very important for you to understand the standards from the prior grade level so that you will be able to develop an understanding of operations and algebraic thinking in this unit and be prepared for next year. To practice your skills, go to sadlierconnect.com.

GRADE 3	Before Unit 1	GRADE 4	After Unit 1	GRADE 5
I Can...		**Can I?**		**I Will...**
3.OA.1 Interpret products of whole numbers	☐ ☐	**4.OA.1** Interpret a multiplication equation as a comparison / Write multiplication equations to represent comparisons	☐ ☐	**5.OA.1** Write and evaluate expressions that use parentheses, brackets, or braces / **5.NF.5** Interpret multiplication as scaling (resizing)
3.OA.3 Multiply and divide within 100 to solve word problems	☐	**4.OA.2** Solve word problems involving multiplicative comparisons by multiplying or dividing	☐	**5.OA.2** Write simple expressions that record calculations with numbers
3.OA.8 Solve two-step word problems using the four operations / Represent two-step problems using equations	☐ ☐	**4.OA.3** Solve multistep word problems involving whole numbers using the four operations / Represent multistep problems using equations	☐ ☐	
3.OA.6 Find unknown factors to solve division problems	☐ ☐ ☐	**4.OA.4** Find all factor pairs for a whole number from 1 to 100 / Determine if a whole number from 1 to 100 is a multiple of a given one-digit number / Determine if a number from 1 to 100 is prime or composite	☐ ☐ ☐	
3.OA.9 Identify arithmetic patterns	☐ ☐	**4.OA.5** Generate a pattern that follows a given rule / Explore and explain features of patterns	☐ ☐	**5.OA.3** Generate two numerical patterns using two given rules, and explore how the two patterns are related

HOME◆CONNECT...

In this unit your child will:

- Interpret multiplication as comparison.

- Use multiplication and division to make comparisons.

- Use more than one step to solve problems.

- Find factors and multiples for whole numbers.

- Make and analyze number and shape patterns.

NOTE: All of these learning goals for your child are based on the Grade 4 Common Core State Standards for Mathematics.

Ways to Help Your Child

Help your child strengthen an interest in math by pointing out examples of math in your environment. You can look for patterns, take measurements, count together, and compare prices. A child who appreciates math and learning will look for connections and become a proficient problem solver.

Many mathematical concepts and skills that your child will learn are based on analyzing and applying patterns. Support your child by using the following Math vocabulary:

- A **pattern** follows a rule, called a **pattern rule**, which tells how the pattern will repeat or change in some way.

- A **number pattern** is an ordered list of numbers that follows a pattern rule. A **shape pattern** is an ordered sequence of shapes that follows a pattern rule.

- Each number or shape in a pattern is called a **term**.

- In a **repeating pattern**, the terms alternate.
  ○ ■ ○ ■ ○ ■

- In a **growing pattern**, each subsequent term increases by the same amount.
  5　　10　　15　　20　　25

Activity: Patterns are everywhere in the world around us. Look for patterns in the environment and use them to make a pattern book of number and shape patterns. For each pattern, show several repeating or growing terms. Ask your child to determine the pattern rule, and then follow the rule to extend each pattern using the appropriate terms.

ONLINE
For more Home Connect activities, continue online at sadlierconnect.com

Focus on Operations and Algebraic Thinking

Essential Question:
How are the operations of multiplication and division related?

Interpret Multiplication Equations as Comparisons

Guided Instruction

In this lesson you will learn about how a multiplication equation can represent comparisons.

Understand: How a multiplication equation represents two comparisons

The array below represents the multiplication equation $15 = 3 \times 5$.

A multiplication equation shows that:
factor × factor = product
$3 \times 5 = 15$
$5 \times 3 = 15$

Use the array to help you explain why the equation $15 = 3 \times 5$ represents these two comparison statements:

"15 is 5 times as many as 3."   "15 is 3 times as many as 5."

There are 3 dots in each column. There are 5 times that many dots in all five columns.
So, the array represents "15 is 5 times as many as 3."

There are 5 dots in each row. There are 3 times that many dots in all three rows.
So, the array represents "15 is 3 times as many as 5."

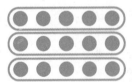

Jamie has 7 times as many pictures as Mary. Mary has 8 pictures. Write a multiplication equation that represents the comparison for this situation.

Guided Instruction

Connect: Multiplication equations and comparisons

Daniel is growing plants in science class. His shortest plant is 4 inches tall. His tallest plant is 20 inches tall.

Write a multiplication equation comparing the heights of Daniel's tallest and shortest plants.

Step 1

A comparison statement for this situation will be of the form:

height of tallest plant = unknown number × height of shortest plant

We know the heights of the tallest and shortest plants. We do not know the unknown number.

Step 2

Draw a model and use it to find the unknown information.

First represent 4 inches, the height of the shortest plant. Copy that model until you get 20 inches, the height of the tallest plant. You need 5 copies.

The height of the tallest plant is 5 times the height of the shortest plant.

Heights of Daniel's Plants

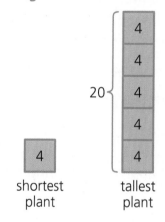

shortest plant

tallest plant

Step 3

Write a multiplication equation to represent the comparisons.

➡ 20 = 5 × 4 ← 20 inches is 5 times as much as 4 inches.
This equation shows that the height of the tallest plant is 5 times the height of the shortest plant.

✏ What other multiplication equation represents the comparison between Daniel's shortest and tallest plants?

Guided Practice

Complete exercises 1 and 2. Use the model at the right.

1. Complete the comparison statement to represent the model.

   12 is ___4___ times as many as 3.

2. Complete the multiplication equation to represent the model.

   12 = ___4___ × 3

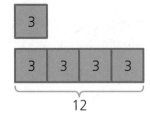

Complete exercises 3 and 4. Use the model at the right.

3. Complete the comparison statement to represent the model.

   __42__ is __6__ times as many as __7__.

4. Write a multiplication equation to represent the model.

   ___7×6=42___

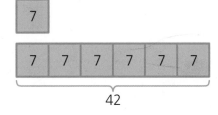

Solve the problem.

5. Lian has a new camera. She printed out 3 pictures for her album. Lian took 9 times as many pictures as she printed out. Write a multiplication equation comparing the number of pictures Lian took to the number she printed out.

   ___3×9=27___

✏ **Complete the model below to justify your answer.**

Lian's Pictures

27 total pictures

printed pictures 3

$27 \div 3 = 9$

Guided Practice

Use the model. Represent the comparison as a multiplication equation.

6. There are 7 girls and 35 boys on the team. Label the model to show the size of each equal group.

   Count the number of equal groups that make up the total number of boys. Use the information to complete the following sentence.

   There are __5__ times as many boys as girls.

   Compare the numbers of boys and girls. Write a multiplication equation.

   $$\underset{\text{boys}}{35} = \underset{}{5} \times \underset{\text{girls}}{7}$$

Students on the Team

girls | 7 |

boys | 7 | 7 | 7 | 7 | 7 |

Make a model to help you solve the problem.

7. Katie scored 6 points in the first basketball game of the season. In the second game, she scored 3 times as many points as she scored in the first game. Write a statement in words comparing the numbers of points Katie scored in the two games. Then, write an equation to represent the comparison.

   ✏️ **Show your work.**

   $$6 \times 3 = 18 \div 6 = 3$$

👏 Think • Pair • Share

MP7 8. Use a diagram or model to help you explain why 4 times as many as 3 is the same amount as 3 times as many as 4.

   It the same clames you Just
   did the ~~dist~~ commutive property

Independent Practice

Write a multiplication equation to represent the comparison shown in the model.

1. $4 \times 2 = 8$

8	
8	8

2. $3 \times 6 = 18$

3	3	3	3	3	3
3					

3. $7 \times 3 = 21$

7	7	7
7		

In exercises 4–6, complete the comparison statement that is represented by the equation.

4. $72 = 9 \times 8$

___72___ is ___9___ times as many as ___8___.

5. $49 = 7 \times 7$

___49___ is ___7___ times as many as ___7___.

6. $36 = 4 \times 9$

___36___ is ___4___ times as many as ___9___.

In exercises 7 and 8, solve the problem.

7. A sweater costs $40. This is 4 times the amount of money that Beth has. Write a multiplication equation to represent the comparison between the price of the sweater and the amount Beth has.

   Answer $40 \div 4 = 10 \times 4 = 40$

   ✏️ **Draw a model to justify your answer.**

   $40 \div 4 = 10$

8. Ramon has read 6 pages in his book. He needs to read 8 times as many pages to finish the book. Write a multiplication equation to represent the comparison between the number of pages Ramon has read and the number he has to read to finish the book.

   Answer $6 \times 8 = 48$

   ✏️ **Draw a model to justify your answer.**

   $6 \times 8 = 48$

Independent Practice

For exercises 9 and 10, use the model at the right to write a multiplication equation.

9. A large paint set has 2 times as many colors as a small set. A small paint set has 12 colors.

   Write a multiplication equation for the comparison.

   $24 = \underline{12 \times 2}$

   Paint Sets

   large | 12 | 12

   small | 12

10. Hassan lives 9 blocks from school. Jada lives 36 blocks from school. Complete the following sentence.

    Jada lives ___4___ times as far from school than Hassan does.

    Write a multiplication equation for the comparison.

    $\underline{9} \times \underline{4} = \underline{36}$

    Blocks from School

    Hassan | 9

    Jada | 9 | 9 | 9 | 9

11. The tree in Derrick's front yard is 8 times as old as the tree in his backyard. The tree in the front yard is 72 years old. Label the model to show the age of each tree.

    Derrick's Trees

    | 9 | 9 | 9 | 9 | 9 | 9 | 9 | 9 |

    | 9 |

For exercises 12–14, use the model above.

12. How old is the tree in Derrick's backyard?

    Answer $\underline{9 \times 8 = 72}$

13. How old is the tree in Derrick's front yard?

    a. 8 years   (b.) 9 years

    c. 10 years   d. 72 years

14. Which multiplication equation correctly compares the ages of the two trees?

    a. $10 \times 8 = 80$ (b.) $8 \times 9 = 72$

    c. $6 \times 12 = 72$ d. $9 \times 9 = 81$

Independent Practice

MP4 **15.** Give an example of a situation in which you would need to compare two amounts using multiplication. What multiplication equation shows the relationship between the numbers in your example?

MP7 **16.** In a multiplication equation, is it always important to know which amount represents the number of groups and which represents the size of each group? Give one example.

Solve the problems.

MP4 **17.** Last year, Ben's family went on vacation for 12 days. This year, the family is traveling for 5 times as many days as last year. Use your own method to find how long the family's trip will be.

> **Show your work.**

Answer _____

MP3 **18.** Nina draws the model at the right to represent the relationship 8 times as many as 4 is 32. Nina thinks she can label the model to represent $8 \times 2 = 16$. Is Nina correct?

4

4	4	4	4	4	4	4	4

> **Show your work.**

Answer _____

Independent Practice

Solve the problems.

MP6 **19.** One plant is 12 inches tall and another is 3 inches tall. Sam says "The height of the tall plant is 4 times as much as the height of the short plant." Meg says "The height of the tall plant is 9 inches more than the height of the small plant." Who is correct?

Answer _____

▸ **Justify your answer using words, drawings, or numbers.**

MP5 **20.** Huey walks neighborhood dogs to earn extra money. He walks 2 dogs each week. Huey says that he can walk 4 times *more* dogs each week. Is this the same as saying that Huey can walk 4 times *as many* dogs each week?

Answer _____

▸ **Justify your answer using words, drawings, or numbers.**

MP4 **21.** A summer camp has 5 cabins. There are 10 single beds in each cabin. So there are 10 times as many beds as cabins. If 55 campers sign up for camp, how many more beds will be needed?

▸ **Show your work.**

Answer _____

Problem Solving: Use Multiplication and Division to Make Comparisons

Guided Instruction

In this lesson you will learn how to solve problems involving multiplicative comparison.

Understand: Comparison with an unknown product

A board game costs $9. An electronic game costs 6 times as much as the board game. How much does the electronic game cost?

You can start by making a model of the problem, like the one shown at the right. Use a ■ for the unknown amount.

Next, write and solve a multiplication equation to find the cost of the electronic game.

Game Prices

board game $9

electronic game $9 $9 $9 $9 $9 $9

6 times as much as $9 = cost of electronic game

$6 \times \$9 = $ ■ ← Multiply to find the unknown product.

$6 \times \$9 = \$54$

➡ The electronic game costs $54.

Understand: Comparisons can involve addition

A board game costs $9. An electronic game costs $54. How much more does the electronic game cost than the board game?

A model of this problem is shown at the right.

Write and solve an equation.

$\$9 + $ ■ $ = \$54$ ← $9 *plus* unknown amount equals $54.

$\$54 - \$9 = $ ■ ← Write an equivalent subtraction equation.

$\$54 - \$9 = \$45$

➡ The electronic game cost $45 more than the board game.

✏ Compare these statements: $54 is *6 times as much as* $9.
$54 is *$45 more than* $9.

Guided Instruction

Understand: Comparison with an unknown factor

Tyler waits 21 minutes for the school bus. Tyler's waiting time is 3 times as long as Grace's waiting time. How long does Grace wait for the bus?

To find how long Grace waits for the bus, first model the problem. Then write and solve an equation. Use *g* to represent the unknown quantity, Grace's waiting time.

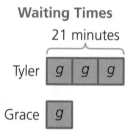

Waiting Times

Grace's waiting time is the amount being multiplied, or the size of each group in the model.

Write a multiplication equation for the comparison.

21 = 3 times as long as Grace's waiting time

$21 = 3 \times g$

Write and solve a related division equation to find *g*, the unknown factor.

$21 \div 3 = g$

$7 = g$

Remember!
Multiplication and division are opposite, or *inverse*, operations.

➡ Grace waits 7 minutes for the bus.

✏ Find how many minutes more Tyler waited than Grace waited.

Unit 1 ■ Focus on Operations and Algebraic Thinking   **19**

Guided Instruction

Connect: What you know about comparison and multiplication

> There are 32 students in an art contest. Only 4 prizes will be given.
> How many times the number of prizes is the number of students?

To solve, make a model and write an equation.

Step 1

Make a model to help you understand
the situation.

You need to find the factor that you must
multiply 4 by to get 32.

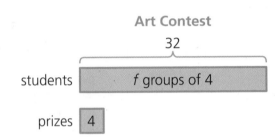

Step 2

Write an equation. Use *f* to represent the unknown factor.

32 is an unknown factor times as many as 4
$32 = f \times 4$

Step 3

Write a related division equation to find *f*.

$32 \div 4 = f$
$8 = f$

Remember!
factor × factor = product
product ÷ factor = factor

There are 8 times as many students as prizes.

In another contest, there are 42 students. There are 7 times as many
students as prizes. How many prizes are there?

Guided Practice

Use the model at the right to solve the problem.

1. An adult cat weighs 8 pounds, and is 4 times heavier than a kitten. How much does the kitten weigh?

   Cat's Weights

   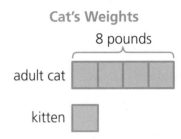

   a. Identify the numbers given in the problem.

   the greater amount, or product: _____ pounds

   the factor telling the number of groups in 8: _____

   b. What do you need to find? Describe the unknown factor.

   _____

   c. Write a letter to represent the unknown factor.

   _____

   Use this same letter for exercises d and e below.

   d. Write a multiplication equation for the comparison.

   $8 = \underline{\hspace{1cm}} \times \underline{\hspace{1cm}}$

   e. Write a related division equation to find the unknown factor.

   $\underline{\hspace{1cm}} \div \underline{\hspace{1cm}} = \underline{\hspace{1cm}}$

   f. Use your division equation to solve, and label the model above with your answer. Then complete the following sentence.

   The kitten weighs _____ pounds.

   g. How do you know that your answer is correct?

   _____

Think • Pair • Share

MP3 2. Why is it helpful to represent a multiplicative comparison problem with both a multiplication equation and a division equation? Explain.

Independent Practice

Write an equation you can use to solve for *u*, the unknown number. Then solve.

1. $2 \times u = 8$

    ___ ÷ ___ = *u*

    ___ = *u*

2. $u \times 7 = 49$

    _____ = *u*

    ___ = *u*

3. $9 \times 10 = u$

    _____ = *u*

    ___ = *u*

Describe the unknown number, *y*, in each problem. Then write the letter of the matching equation.

a. $6 \div 3 = y$

b. $6 - 3 = y$

c. $6 \times 3 = y$

d. $6 + 3 = y$

4. A fruit salad has 6 strawberries and 3 times as many blueberries. How many blueberries are there?

    y is _____

    Matching equation: ____

5. Diego orders 3 books online. The store mails him 6 books instead. How many more books does Diego have than he ordered?

    y is _____

    Matching equation: ____

6. A rectangular sign is 6 feet long. This is 3 times as long as the width of the sign. What is the width of the sign?

    y is _____

    Matching equation: ____

7. Emma's soccer team scores 3 goals. The winning team scores 6 goals. How many times as many goals does the winning team score as Emma's team?

    y is _____

    Matching equation: ____

Independent Practice

Write an equation with a letter for the unknown number. Then solve the problem. You can use the model to help.

8. Caleb's family has a car that is 3 years old. They also have a minivan that is 5 times as old as the car. How old is the minivan?

Equation _____

Answer _____

_____

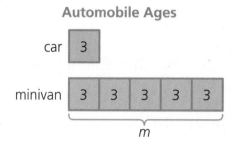

Automobile Ages

9. Houston gets about 48 inches of rain a year. Winslow gets about 8 inches of rain a year. How many times as much rain does Houston get as Winslow?

Equation _____

Answer _____

_____

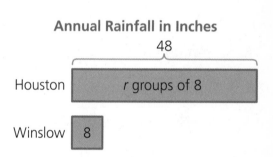

Annual Rainfall in Inches

10. Aliyah needs to bake 24 muffins. This is 4 times as many muffins as her muffin pan holds. How many muffins does Aliyah's pan hold?

Equation _____

Answer _____

_____

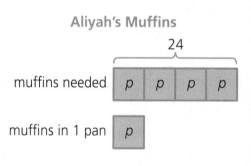

Aliyah's Muffins

Circle the correct answer.

11. Jin has a muffin pan that holds 12 muffins. He lends the pan to Aliyah, who needs to bake 24 muffins. How many times as many muffins are needed as Jin's pan can hold?

   a. 2 times as many   **b.** 3 times as many

   c. 4 times as many   **d.** 6 times as many

Independent Practice

Draw a model and write an equation to represent each problem. Then solve.

MP1 **12.** Dmitri has saved $9 to buy a skateboard. The one he wants costs 8 times as much as his savings. How much does the skateboard cost?

➤ **Show your work.**

Answer _____

MP2 **13.** An office building has 40 floors. It is 5 times as tall as the apartment building across the street. How many floors does the apartment building have?

➤ **Show your work.**

Answer _____

Answer each question in a complete sentence.

MP6 **14.** The deep end of a pool is 12 feet deep. The shallow end is 3 feet deep. Noah solved the equation $12 \div 3 = p$ to find that the deep end is 4 times as deep as the shallow end. Explain how Noah can check his answer.

MP3 **15.** Serena says that all multiplicative comparison problems are solved by multiplying the given numbers. Do you agree? Explain your answer.

Independent Practice

Solve the problems.

MP4 **16.** Eli collects stamps. He has 63 stamps from the United States. He also has 7 stamps from Canada. How many times as many U.S. stamps does Eli have as Canadian stamps?

➤ **Show your work.**

Answer _____

MP1 **17.** Olivia says that she used the computer for 9 hours this week. She thinks her brother Jack used it for 3 times as long as she did. Jack says he used it for 12 more hours than Olivia. Who counts a greater number of hours for Jack?

Answer _____

➤ **Justify your answer using words, drawings, or numbers.**

MP4 **18.** Olivia and Jack's father says that they used the computer for 30 hours altogether. He tells them that Jack used the computer for 2 times as long as Olivia. If this is true, did Olivia use the computer for 9 hours?

Answer _____

➤ **Justify your answer using words, drawings, or numbers.**

Problem Solving: Multistep Problems

Essential Question:
How can equations help you solve multistep problems?

4.OA.3

Words to Know:
remainder

Guided Instruction

In this lesson you will learn how to use equations to solve problems with more than one step.

Understand: Equations to solve multistep problems

The fourth graders are having a picnic. Two classes of 30 students each, 2 teachers, and 2 parents will be there. If 8 people sit at each table, how many tables are needed for all the people at the picnic?

To find the number of tables needed, you divide the total number of people by the number of people who can sit at each table.
To solve this problem, first write a statement or a word equation.

$$\text{number of tables needed} = \text{total number of people} \div \text{number who can sit at each table}$$

Next, think about the three quantities in the equation:
The number of tables needed is unknown. You can use t to represent this number. The total number of people is the number of students in the two classes plus the number of adults: $2 \times 30 + 2 + 2$
The number of people at each table is 8.

Use this information to rewrite an equation.

$$t = \underbrace{(2 \times 30 + 2 + 2)}_{\substack{\text{2 groups of 30 students} \\ \text{plus 2 teachers and 2 parents}}} \div 8$$

Use parentheses to show that the total number of people is calculated *before* dividing.

Now, solve the equation. Use the order of operations.

$t = (2 \times 30 + 2 + 2) \div 8$
$t = (60 + 2 + 2) \div 8$ Multiply within the parentheses.
$t = 64 \div 8$ Add within the parentheses.
$t = 8$ Divide.

Check that your answer is reasonable. You can use reasoning and mental math. Eight tables can hold 8×8, or 64 people. There will be 4 adults plus 2×30, or 60 students, which is a total of 64 people. The answer is correct.

➡ Eight picnic tables are needed for all the people at the picnic.

Understand: The meaning of a remainder

> Amanda collects old postcards. She had 71 postcards. Then, she sold 19 of them to another collector. She wants to put the postcards she has left in an album that fits 6 cards on each page. How many pages will Amanda need to hold the postcards she has left?

To find the number of pages Amanda needs, write a word equation for the problem.

number of pages = number of postcards ÷ number that fit on each page

You can use p to represent the unknown number of pages. Use the information from the problem to write the equation.

$p \quad = \quad (71 - 19) \quad \div \quad 6 \leftarrow$ Use parentheses to show that the subtraction is done *before* the division.

71 cards she started with minus the 19 she sold

Now, solve the equation.

$p = (71 - 19) \div 6$

$p = 52 \div 6$ Subtract within the parentheses.

$p = 52 \div 6 = 8 \text{ R4}$ Divide. Read as, "52 divided by 6 equals 8 remainder 4."

There are 8 groups of 6 in 52 with 4 left over. The amount left over after dividing is called the remainder. The remainder is written with an R before it.

Amanda can fill 8 whole pages. She will need 1 more page for the remaining 4 postcards. So, she needs 9 pages in all.

➡ Amanda will need 9 pages to hold the postcards she has left.

Guided Instruction

Connect: **Problem situations and reasonable solutions**

> On the first night of the school play, 371 tickets were sold. On the second night, 59 fewer tickets were sold than the first night. How many tickets were sold altogether for both nights of the play?

To find how many tickets were sold, write and solve an equation.

Step 1

Write a word equation to represent the problem.
total tickets sold = tickets sold the first night + tickets sold the second night

Step 2

Use the information from the problem to write an equation. You can use a model to help you understand how the quantities are related. Notice that you need to subtract to find the number of tickets sold on the second night.

t	
371	371 − 59

$$t = \quad 371 \quad + \quad \underbrace{(371 - 59)}_{\substack{\text{59 fewer tickets than} \\ \text{on the first night}}}$$

Step 3

Solve the equation.

$t = 371 + (371 - 59)$
$t = 371 + 312$ Subtract within parentheses.
$t = 683$ Add.

Step 4

Use rounding and estimation to check that the answer is reasonable. 371 is about 370 and 59 is about 60, so the answer should be about:
$370 + (370 - 60) = 370 + 310 = 680$

Remember!
An estimate is a number that is close to an exact amount.

The estimate 680 is close to the actual answer 683. So the answer is reasonable.

➡ A total of 683 tickets were sold altogether for both nights of the play.

For exercises 1–6, follow the steps to solve the problem. Use the model if it helps you.

There are 70 people waiting to tour a museum. The tour guide takes 4 groups with 16 people each. The remaining people will be in the last tour group. How many people are in the last tour group?

Museum Tour Groups

16	16	16	16	p

70

1. Use the following terms to make a word equation for this problem: *people in first 4 groups, people waiting, people in last group.*

   _____ = _____ – _____

2. There are ____ people waiting.

3. Show the number of people in the first four groups.

   ____ × 16

4. Use p to represent the number of people in the last group. Then write an equation to find how many people are in the last group using the information from the problem.

   $p =$ ____ – (_____)

5. Solve the equation.

   $p =$ ____ – (_____)

   $p =$ ____ – ____

   $p =$ ____

6. There are ____ people in the last tour group.

☆ **Think • Pair • Share**

MP2   7. Molly says that the answer for the problem above is the same as the remainder for 70 ÷ 16. Is Molly correct? You can use the model to help you explain your answer.

Independent Practice

Use the steps to model and solve each problem. Then estimate to check your answer.

1. Three hikers want to share the weight in their backpacks equally. Their backpacks weigh 32 pounds, 39 pounds, and 22 pounds. How much weight should each hiker carry?

   Write a word equation.

   weight each person carries = total weight ÷ _____

   Use b for the unknown. Use the information from the problem to rewrite the equation.

   $b =$ (_____ + _____ + _____) ÷ _____

   Solve the equation to find the answer.

   Answer _____

   Use estimation to check your answer.

2. Jacob has read 39 library books since school began. He plans to read another 2 books a week for the next 12 weeks. At the end of this time, how many books will he have read altogether?

   Write a word equation.

   _____ = books read so far + _____

   Use t for the unknown. Substitute the information from the problem.

   $t =$ _____ + _____

   Solve the equation to find the answer.

   Answer _____

   Use estimation to check your answer.

Independent Practice

In exercises 3–5, follow the steps to solve the problem. Use the model at the right if it helps you.

Tina has 6 packs of 8 colored markers to put into party gift bags. She splits the markers equally among 9 gift bags. How many markers can she put in each bag?

Party Gift Bags

m markers

3. Write an equation for this problem.

   $g =$ _____

4. Solve the equation.

5. Answer the question.

   Tina can put ____ markers in each bag.

6. Is the final answer in exercise 5 the same as the solution to your equation? Explain why or why not.

Circle the correct answer.

7. Peter practices the piano for 25 minutes 3 times a week. He also has a 55-minute piano lesson every Saturday. How much time does Peter spend playing the piano in one week?

   a. 80 minutes   **b.** 130 minutes

   c. 190 minutes   **d.** 240 minutes

8. Sixteen teams of 5 students each sign up for a sports tournament. The principal will combine the teams and then divide the students into 10 new teams. How many students will be on each of the new teams?

   a. 7   **b.** 7 R5

   c. 8   **d.** 10

Independent Practice

MP6 **9.** Haj solved the equation $w = 718 - (329 + 178)$. She got the solution $w = 567$. Use estimation to check Haj's solution. Do you think her solution is reasonable? Explain.

MP1 **10.** Consider this division problem: $27 \div 4 = 6$ R3. Describe a real-world problem that can be solved by finding $27 \div 4$. Give the solution to your problem. How did you think about the remainder when you found the solution?

Solve the problem.

MP4 **11.** A total of 96 students vote on two choices for a field trip. The zoo gets 2 times as many votes as the radio station. How many students vote to go to the zoo?

   ✏️ **Show your work.**

   Answer _____

Independent Practice

Solve the problems.

MP4 **12.** A soccer team orders 36 new jerseys for games. Half of the jerseys are red and the other half are white. Five of the white jerseys the team receives are the wrong size. How many white jerseys are the correct size?

▰▰▰▶ **Show your work.**

Answer _____

MP7 **13.** There are 29, 15, 31, and 25 people in four groups of volunteers. Colin wants to divide the volunteers into 5 equal teams to clean up different areas of the park. The following equation can be used to find the number of people on each team:

$$p = (29 + 15 + 31 + 25) \div 5$$

Rewrite this equation so it is easy to solve mentally. Then solve the problem in your head. Explain what you did.

Answer _____

▰▰▰▶ **Justify your answer using words, drawings, or numbers.**

MP6 **14.** A water faucet that drips 10 times a minute wastes 3 liters of water in 1 day. If 2 of the faucets in Charlotte's house drip at this rate, how many days will it take to waste 100 liters of water?

Answer _____

▰▰▰▶ **Justify your answer using words, drawings, or numbers.**

Find Factors and Multiples for Whole Numbers

Essential Question:
What are factors and multiples of whole numbers?

4.OA.4

Words to Know:
factor
factor pair
prime number
composite number
multiple

Guided Instruction

Understand: Factors and factor pairs

Mr. Yoo has 12 student worksheets to display. He wants to display them in rows. He wants the same number of worksheets in each row. How many different ways can Mr. Yoo display the worksheets?

Model all the ways that the 12 worksheets can be displayed in a rectangular array. To do this, find the pairs of whole numbers with a product of 12.

Factors are numbers that are multiplied together to make a product. A factor of a number can also be thought of as a number that divides evenly into that number, without a remainder.
The whole number factors of 12 are 1, 2, 3, 4, 6, and 12.

The factor pairs for 12 are: 1 and 12, 2 and 6, 3 and 4.
You can make two arrays for each factor pair.

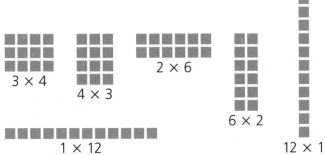

3×4 4×3 2×6 6×2 1×12 12×1

▶ Mr. Yoo can display the worksheets in 6 different ways.

Understand: Prime and Composite Numbers

Suppose Mr. Yoo has 13 pieces of student worksheets. In how many ways can Mr. Yoo display the worksheets in equal rows?

The only factor pair for 13 is 1 and 13. So Mr. Yoo can display the worksheets as a 1 × 13 array or as a 13 × 1 array.

The number 13 is an example of a prime number. A prime number is a number greater than 1 with only two factors, 1 and the number itself. The number 12 is a composite number. A composite number is a number greater than 1 that has more than two factors.

▶ Mr. Yoo can display the worksheets in 2 different ways.

Understand: Finding factors of a whole number

Find all the factors of 15. Tell whether 15 is prime or composite.

To find the factors of 15, divide 15 by whole numbers, starting with 1. If a number divides into 15 evenly, then both it and the quotient are factors of 15. Keep checking until the factors start to repeat.

Is 15 divisible by 1?	by 2?	by 3?	by 4?
Yes, 15 ÷ 1 = 15	No	Yes, 15 ÷ 3 = 5	No
1 and 15 are factors.		3 and 5 are factors.	

The next number to check is 5, but you already found that 5 is a factor of 15. You can stop checking. The factors of 15 are 1, 3, 5, and 15.

➡ The factors of 15 are 1, 3, 5, and 15. It is a composite number.

Understand: Finding multiples of a whole number

Students sign up for a competition in teams of 3. What are some possibilities for the total number of students in the competition?

1 team is $1 \times 3 = 3$ students   4 teams is $4 \times 3 = 12$ students
2 teams is $2 \times 3 = 6$ students   5 teams is $5 \times 3 = 15$ students
3 teams is $3 \times 3 = 9$ students   6 teams is $6 \times 3 = 18$ students

The numbers 3, 6, 9, 12, 15, and 18 are multiples of 3. A multiple of a whole number is the product of that number and another whole number. Notice that 3 is a factor of each of its multiples.

➡ The possible numbers of students are the multiples of 3: 3, 6, 9, 12, 15, 18, 21, 24, and so on.

✏ Find all the factors of 19 and 24. Tell whether each is prime or composite.

Guided Instruction

Connect: Factors and multiples

Juice boxes are sold in packs of 8. Snack bags of crackers are sold in packs of 6. Ms. Leone takes one of each in her lunch. What is the least number of packs of each Ms. Leone can buy to have the same number of juice boxes and bags of crackers?

To solve use multiples of 8 and 6.

Step 1

Use multiples to find the possible numbers of each item Ms. Leone can buy.

There are 8 juice boxes in each pack, so Ms. Leone can only buy juice boxes in multiples of 8. List the first several multiples of 8:

8	16	24	32	40	48	56	64
↑	↑	↑	↑	↑	↑	↑	↑
1×8	2×8	3×8	4×8	5×8	6×8	7×8	8×8

There are 6 bags of crackers in every pack, so Ms. Leone can only buy bags of crackers in multiplies of 6. List the first several multiples of 6:

6	12	18	24	30	36	42	48
↑	↑	↑	↑	↑	↑	↑	↑
1×6	2×6	3×6	4×6	5×6	6×6	7×6	8×6

Step 2

Find the least number that is both a multiple of 8 and a multiple of 6.

The least number that is both a multiple of 8 and a multiple of 6 is 24. Ms. Leone can buy exactly 24 boxes of juice and 24 bags of crackers.

$3 \times 8 = 24$, she must buy 3 packs of juice boxes to get 24 boxes.
$4 \times 6 = 24$, she must buy 4 packs of crackers to get 24 bags.

Notice the connection between factors and multiples:
24 is a multiple of 8 and 8 is a factor of 24.
Similarly, 24 is a multiple of 6 and 6 is a factor of 24.

> In general, a whole number is a multiple of each of its factors.

▶ The least number of packs Ms. Leone can buy is 3 packs of juice boxes and 4 packs of crackers.

Guided Practice

Make all the possible arrays for the number. Then, list the factors and circle *prime* or *composite*.

1. 10

Arrays:

Factors: ______________________________

prime or ***composite***

2. Complete this table to find the factors of 35. Use the first two rows as a guide. Some cells in the last column will be empty.

Is 35 divisible by 1?	Yes, 35 ÷ 1 = 35	1 and 35 are factors.
Is 35 divisible by 2?	No	
Is 35 divisible by 3?		
Is 35 divisible by 4?		
Is 35 divisible by 5?		
Is 35 divisible by 6?		

Why don't you need to check 7? ______________________________

List all the factors. ______________________________

Think • Pair • Share

MP2 3. Cole said, "All prime numbers are odd and all composite numbers are even." Do you agree with Cole? Explain.

Independent Practice

Make all the possible arrays for the number. Then, list the factors and circle *prime* or *composite*.

1. 11

   Arrays:

   Factors: _____

   prime or *composite*

2. 16

   Arrays:

   Factors: _____

   prime or *composite*

3. Complete this table to find the factors of 18. Use the first two rows as a guide. Some cells in the last column will be empty.

Is 18 divisible by 1?	Yes, 18 ÷ 1 = 18	_____ and _____ are factors.
Is 18 divisible by 2?		
Is 18 divisible by 3?		
Is 18 divisible by 4?		
Is 18 divisible by 5?		

Why don't you need to check 6? _____

the factors. _____

king

us on Operations and Algebraic Thinking

Independent Practice

For exercises 4–7, find all the factors of the number. Show your work. Then circle *prime* or *composite*.

4. 22

5. 23

Factors: _____

prime or *composite*

Factors: _____

prime or *composite*

6. 36

7. 50

Factors: _____

prime or *composite*

Factors: _____

prime or *composite*

For exercises 8 and 9, list the first six multiples of the number.

8. 7

9. 5

Multiples: _____

Multiples: _____

For exercises 10 and 11, circle the correct answer or answers.

10. Which of these numbers are multiples of 9?

a. 9

b. 38

c. 81

d. 84

11. Which of these numbers are prime numbers?

a. 2

b. 19

c. 52

d. 77

12. Mandy says that the factors of 20 are 2, 4, 5, and 10. What mistake did Mandy make?

_____

Independent Practice

MP7 **13.** Lily learns that all numbers that have 0 or 5 as the last digit have 5 as a factor. Explain why this is true.

MP7 **14.** David says that finding all the numbers that 28 is a multiple of is the same as finding the factors of 28. Is David correct? Explain.

Solve the problems.

MP7 **15.** Amelia says that 50 must have more factors than 40, since it is a greater number. Is Amelia correct? Find the factors of 50 and 40.

Show your work.

Answer _____

MP7 **16.** A multiplication table shows that 42 is a multiple of both 6 and 7. What other numbers have 42 as a multiple?

Show your work.

Answer _____

■ Focus on Operations and Algebraic Thinking

Independent Practice

Solve the problems.

MP6 **17.** A farmer has 96 apples to sell at the farmers market. She wants to bag the apples before going. How many ways can the farmer bag the apples so that:

• each bag has at least 4 apples

• each bag has no more than 10 apples

• all bags have the same number of apples?

Show your work.

Answer _____

MP4 **18.** A chef makes 88 ounces of jam. He wants to put the jam in 6-ounce jars. Can he use this size jar if each must be completely filled with jam, without any jam left over? If not, tell what sizes the chef can use.

Answer _____

Justify your answer using words, drawings, or numbers.

MP1 **19.** Andy set his computer to beep every 6 minutes and to chirp every 10 minutes. His computer just beeped and chirped at the same time. In how many minutes will it next make both sounds at the same time?

Answer _____

Justify your answer using words, drawings, or numbers.

5 Generate and Analyze Number and Shape Patterns

Essential Question:
How can you create and describe patterns?
4.OA.5

Words to Know:
number pattern
pattern rule
term
shape pattern

Guided Instruction

In this lesson you will learn how to make, analyze, and describe number and shape patterns.

Understand: Number patterns and pattern rules

> Maria is saving money for a new violin. She starts with $10 and saves $5 the first week and each week thereafter. How much money does Maria have each week for the first five weeks?

To find the money amounts, you can make a number pattern. A number pattern is an ordered list of numbers that follow a rule and repeat or change in some way. The pattern rule tells you how the pattern works.

To generate the pattern for Maria's savings, start at 10 and follow the rule *add* 5. Each number in a number pattern is called a term. This pattern tells you that each new term *increases* by 5, so this is a growing pattern.

	+5		+5		+5		+5		+5	
10		15		20		25		30		35
1st term		2nd term		3rd term		4th term		5th term		6th term

➤ For the first five weeks, Maria will have $15, $20, $25, $30, and $35.

✏️ Use the same rule to make a new number pattern that starts with 1 instead of 10. How does the pattern compare to Maria's pattern?

Guided Instruction

Understand: Growing shape patterns

> Maria uses parallelograms to make a pattern of growing shapes.
>
>
> 1st   2nd   3rd   4th
>
> What is the rule for Maria's pattern? What are the next two terms?

A shape pattern is an ordered sequence of shapes that follow a rule. Each shape in a shape pattern is called a term. Maria's shape pattern starts with one parallelogram and follows the rule *attach 1 parallelogram to the right side of the previous term*.

➡️ Here is Maria's pattern with two more terms.

Understand: Repeating shape patterns

> Start with the first term below and use the following rule to make a pattern: *If the term before is an ✕, make an ○. If the term before is an ○, make an ✕.*
>
>
> 1st

➡️ Start with ✕ and follow the rule. The pattern goes back and forth, or alternates, between ✕ and ○. Here are the first eight terms.

✕ ○ ✕ ○ ✕ ○ ✕ ○
1st 2nd 3rd 4th 5th 6th 7th 8th

In this pattern all the odd-numbered terms are ✕-shapes. All the even-numbered terms are circles.

Guided Instruction

Connect: Making patterns and analyzing terms

> Maria makes a new number pattern. She starts with 2 and uses the rule *multiply by 2*. What are the first six terms for Maria's pattern? Look for other patterns and relationships in the terms and record your observations.

To find the first six terms generate the pattern.

➡ To generate the first six terms, start with 2 and multiply the previous term by 2 to get the next term.

2, 4, 8, 16, 32, 64, . . .

Observation 1: The terms are all even numbers and increase by doubling.

Look at how the terms increase. Subtract each term from the next term to find their difference.

terms	2	4	8	16	32	64
difference		2	4	8	16	32

Observation 2: The difference between each two terms is the same as the lesser term. The same pattern is formed by the differences.

Look for a relationship between each term and its order in the pattern.

Terms

1st term	2	= 2
2nd term	4	= 2 × 2
3rd term	8	= 2 × 2 × 2
4th term	16	= 2 × 2 × 2 × 2
5th term	32	= 2 × 2 × 2 × 2 × 2
6th term	64	= 2 × 2 × 2 × 2 × 2 × 2

Observation 3: Each term's place in the pattern tells you the number of times 2 is multiplied by itself.

Use the rule to write or draw the missing terms in each pattern. Then complete the sentence below each exercise.

1. Start with 1 and follow the rule *add 2*.

   1, _____, 5, _____, 9, _____, . . .

   All of the terms are _____.
   <u>even or odd?</u>

2. Start with 50 and follow the rule *subtract 5*.

   _____, 45, _____, 35, _____, . . .

   All the terms are multiples of _____.

3. Start with a row of 2 unit squares and follow the rule *add a row of 2 unit squares on top of the shape*.

   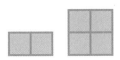

   This is a _____ shape pattern. The height of the shape
   <u>growing or repeating</u>

   increases by _____ unit with each term.

☗☗ Think • Pair • Share

MP7   4. Create a new pattern by adding the corresponding terms in the patterns from exercises 1 and 2. That is, add 1 and 50 to get the first term, add 3 and 45 to get the second term, and so on. The new pattern starts with 51. Show the pattern. What is the rule for the pattern? Explain why this rule makes sense?

Independent Practice

Identify the rule for the pattern. Write the letter of the correct rule.

1. 1, 5, 9, 13, 17, . . . ____

2. 3, 6, 12, 24, 48, 96, . . . ____

3. 1, 4, 16, 64, 256, . . . ____

4. 4, 7, 10, 13, 16, . . . ____

a. Multiply by 4

b. Add 2

c. Add 4

d. Add 3

e. Multiply by 2

Use the rule to write or draw the missing terms in each pattern.

5. Start with 10 and add 5.

   10, ____, 20, ____, 30, ____, . . .

6. Add the digits in each term in exercise 5 to make a new pattern.

   1, ____, ____, ____, ____, ____, . . .

7. Start with 1 and multiply by 3.

   1, ____, ____, ____, 81, . . .

8. Make a new pattern by finding the differences of consecutive terms for the pattern in exercise 7.

   2, ____, ____, ____, . . .

9. What is the rule for the new pattern in exercise 8?

   _____

10. Start with a triangle and follow this rule: *If the term before is a triangle, make a square. If the term before is a square, make a triangle.*

11. What pattern is shown by the number of sides in the shapes in exercise 10?

    _____

12. The pattern in exercises 10 and 11 are _____.
    growing or repeating

Independent Practice

For exercises 13–15, use the rule to generate the pattern. Then write at least two observations about the pattern.

MP7 **13.** Start with 6 and use the rule *add 3*.

6, ____, ____, ____, ____, ____, . . .

Observations

MP2 **14.** Continue the growing pattern of dots. How many dots will be in the bottom row of the 8th term?

1st term   2nd term   3rd term   4th term   5th term

Answer _____

Observations

MP6 **15.** Start with 3. Use the rule *multiply by 2 and then subtract 1*.

3, 5, ____, ____, ____, ____, . . .

Observations

MP4 **16.** Marley generated this pattern using an addition rule. One term in the pattern is incorrect.

7, 15, 25, 31, 39, 47, . . .

Which is the incorrect term?

a. 7   **b.** 25   **c.** 39   **d.** 47

▶ **Justify your answer using words, drawings, or numbers.**

Independent Practice

Solve the problems.

MP3 **17.** Tanya said, "If two patterns are generated using the same rule, then they must be the same." Is Tanya correct? Explain.

MP3 **18.** Michael says that number patterns cannot use subtraction. Do you agree? Give a simple example in your answer.

MP7 **19.** Haley is studying for a spelling bee. Her goal is to learn twice as many words each day as on the previous day. To show her study schedule for the next six days, she makes this number pattern for the number of words.

10, 20, 30, 40, 50, 60

If Haley learns this many words each day, will she meet her goal?

▭▭▶ **Show your work.**

Answer _____

MP8 **20.** Justin's neighbor hired him to mow her lawn each week for 6 weeks. She said she could either give him $10 per week, or she could give him $2 the first week and then double the amount each week. Write a number pattern for Justin's weekly earnings under the second plan. Which plan should Justin choose?

▭▭▶ **Show your work.**

Answer _____

Independent Practice

Solve the problems.

MP7 **21.** A roll of stickers starts with the three shapes shown below. The shapes repeat to make up the entire roll.

1st term   2nd term   3rd term

Which shape will be the hundredth sticker in the roll?

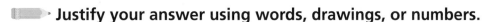 **Show your work.**

Answer _____

MP8 **22.** Simon said, "If the rule for a pattern is *add 2*, then the terms will either be all even numbers or all odd numbers." Is Simon correct?

Answer _____

▸ **Justify your answer using words, drawings, or numbers.**

MP7 **23.** The rule for the number pattern below is *add 8*, starting with 8.

   8, 16, 24, 32, 40, . . .

Find the 50th term of this pattern without finding all the terms in between.

Answer _____

▸ **Justify your answer using words, drawings, or numbers.**

1. Odell has 5 times as many crayons as Jason. Jason has 8 crayons. Label the model to show how many crayons each person has.

Number of Crayons

For exercises 2 and 3, use the model above.

2. How many crayons does Odell have?

   Answer _____

3. Which multiplication equation correctly compares the number of crayons the two boys have?

   a. $4 \times 8 = 32$ b. $5 \times 8 = 40$

   c. $2 \times 10 = 40$ d. $6 \times 8 = 48$

For exercises 4–6, circle the correct answer or answers.

4. Which of these numbers are multiples of 6?

   a. 10 b. 16

   c. 30 d. 48

5. At the library sale, a DVD costs $12. That is 3 times the cost of a book. Which equation can you use to find the cost of a book?

   a. $3 \times 12 = n$ b. $12 \times n = 3$

   c. $3 \times n = 12$ d. $12 \times 3 = n$

6. A small box holds 6 toy cars. A large box holds 18 toy cars. How many times as many cars can the large box hold as the small box?

   a. 2 times as many b. 3 times as many

   c. 4 times as many d. 6 times as many

For exercise 7, use the rule to generate the pattern. Then write at least two observations about the pattern.

MP8 **7.** Start with 3. Add 6.

3, ____, ____, ____, ____, ____

Observations

MP3 **8.** Chrissy estimates that if you add 20 + 31, then divide the sum by 7, the answer is about 12. Is this a reasonable estimate? Explain.

For exercises 9 and 10, find all the factors. Tell whether the number is *prime* or *composite*.

9. 56   **10.** 61

prime or *composite*? _____   *prime* or *composite*? _____

11. Draw the next two shapes in the pattern. Name the kind of pattern. Then write its rule.

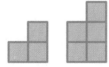

This is a _____ shape pattern.
      growing or repeating

Rule _____

Solve the problems.

MP1 **12.** Melinda is 3 times as old as Tom. Vihn is 4 times as old as Melinda. If Melinda is 9 years old, how old are Tom and Vihn?

➤ **Show your work.**

Answer _____

MP2 **13.** Franklin is packing his old toy trucks into boxes. He has 22 trucks. If each box holds 4 trucks, how many boxes will Franklin need?

> **Show your work.**

Answer _____

MP7 **14.** The rule for the number pattern below is to add 5, starting with 5. What is the hundredth number in the pattern?

5, 10, 15, 20, 25, . . .

> **Show your work.**

Answer _____

MP1 **15.** For the school carnival, Ms. Chen wants to bag 84 marbles to give away as prizes. How many ways can Ms. Chen bag the marbles so that:

• each bag has at least 3 marbles

• each bag has no more than 10 marbles

• all bags have the same number of marbles?

> **Show your work.**

Answer _____

Progress Check

UNIT 2

Look at how the Common Core standards you have learned and will learn connect.

It is very important for you to understand the standards from the prior grade level so that you will be able to develop an understanding of number and operations in base ten in this unit and be prepared for next year. To practice your skills, go to sadlierconnect.com.

GRADE 3 — I Can...	Before Unit 2	GRADE 4 — Can I ?	After Unit 2	GRADE 5 — I Will...
	☐	**4.NBT.1** Understand place value in whole numbers	☐	**5.NBT.1** Understand place value in whole numbers and decimal numbers **5.NBT.2** Explain patterns of zeros when multiplying by powers of 10 Use whole number exponents to show powers of 10
	☐	**4.NBT.2** Read and write whole numbers using numerals, number names, and expanded form	☐	**5.NBT.3** Read, write, and compare decimals to thousandths
	☐	Compare whole numbers	☐	
3.NBT.1 Round whole numbers to the nearest 10 or 100	☐	**4.NBT.3** Round multi-digit whole numbers to any place	☐	**5.NBT.4** Round decimals to any place
3.NBT.2 Add and subtract whole numbers within 1000	☐	**4.NBT.4** Add and subtract whole numbers within 1,000,000	☐	**5.NBT.7** Add and subtract decimals
3.NBT.3 Multiply one-digit numbers by multiples of 10	☐	**4.NBT.5** Multiply whole numbers by one-digit whole numbers	☐	**5.NBT.5** Multiply whole numbers
3.OA.7 Multiply and divide whole numbers within 100	☐	Multiply two 2-digit numbers	☐	**5.NBT.7** Multiply and divide decimal
	☐	**4.NBT.6** Divide whole numbers by one-digit divisors	☐	**5.NBT.6** Divide whole number two-digit divisors

HOME ◆ CONNECT...

Problem solving is an important skill for your child to master. Your child will make use of various problem-solving methods to solve word problems involving addition, subtraction, multiplication, and division. Support your child by using the following problem-solving model:

- **Read** Read the problem with your child. Focus on the facts and the questions. Ask: *What facts do you know? What do you need to find out?*

- **Plan** Outline a plan with your child. Plan how to solve the problem. Ask: *What operation* (addition, subtraction, multiplication, or division) *will you use? Do you need to use 1 step or 2 steps? Will you draw a picture? How have you solved similar problems?*

- **Solve** Follow the plan to solve the problem with your child. Ask: *Did you answer the question? Did you label ~~y~~our answer?*

~~Check~~ Test that the solution is reasonable. Ask: *How ~~can you so~~lve the problem a different way? Is the answer ~~reasonable? Ho~~w can you estimate to check your answer?*

Conversation Starter: Your child will need ~~an unde~~rstanding of both place value and ~~place~~ value by naming numbers for your ~~child. The p~~lace value of each digit in the ~~number in st~~andard form of *seven thousand ~~six hundred ~~seventy-two* is 7,672. It has seven thousands, ~~six hundreds, seventy, ~~two ones.

Number and Operations in Base Ten

In this unit your child will:

- Understand place value of whole numbers.

- Read, write, and compare whole numbers.

- Apply place value understanding to round whole numbers.

- Add and subtract fluently with whole numbers.

- Multiply and divide whole numbers using place value and properties of operations.

NOTE: All of these learning goals for your child are based on the Grade 4 Common Core State Standards for Mathematical Content.

Ways to Help Your Child

Make time to talk with your child's teacher about your child's level of progress. Discuss ways that you can assist with your child's learning at home. If your child needs extra practice, your support can really make a difference.

ONLINE

For more Home Connect activities, continue online at sadlierconnect.com

Focus on Number and Operations in Base Ten

Essential Question:
How does understanding place value help you with number relationships and computing efficiently?

Essential Question:
How does the place of a digit in a number affect its value?

4.NBT.1

Guided Instruction

In this lesson you will learn about place value relationships in whole numbers.

Understand: Place value and the value of a digit

> Kevin sees the digit 2 twice in the number 162,257. What is the value of each digit 2 in 162,257?

To find the value of each digit 2, use a place-value chart. The value of each digit in a whole number is shown by its place in the number. The value of the digit in each place is ten times greater than its value in the place to the right.

	× 10	× 10	× 10	× 10	× 10	
Place Value	100,000	10,000	1,000	100	10	1
	hundred thousands	ten thousands	thousands	hundreds	tens	ones
	÷ 10	÷ 10	÷ 10	÷ 10	÷ 10	

Use the place-value chart below to find the value of each 2 in 162,257.

hundred thousands	ten thousands	thousands	hundreds	tens	ones
1	6	2	2	5	7

place-value chart shows 2 in the thousands and
...ds places.

...ds = 2 × 1,000 = 2,000
... = 2 × 100   = 200

> To find the value of each digit 2, multiply it by its place value.

...times the value of 200, or

...alue of the digit 2 in the thousands place is 2,000 and
...2 in the hundreds place is 200.

...nship between 2,000 and 200 using division.

...mber and Operations in Base Ten

Guided Instruction

Understand: Place value and multiples of 10

> A mistake in a store ad shows the price of a digital notepad as $30. The correct price of the digital notepad is $300. How many times as much as $30 is $300?

To find how many times as much $300 is compared to $30, you can use place value. The value of the hundreds place is 10 times the value of the tens place: $100 = 10 \times 10$.

hundreds	tens	ones
3	0	0
	3	0

$30 = 3$ tens

$300 = 10 \times 3$ tens $= 3$ hundreds

$300 = 10 \times 30$

▶ $300 is ten times as much as $30.

Because 30 and 300 are multiples of 10, you can use a model to find the number of tens in 300.

Use place-value models to show that 300 is the same as 30×10.

$$300 = 3 \times 100$$
$$= 3 \times (10 \times 10)$$
$$= (3 \times 10) \times 10$$
$$= 30 \times 10$$

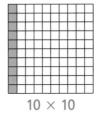 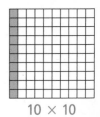

10×10 10×10 10×10

✏️ What number times 30 would move the digit 3 to the thousands place in a place-value chart? Explain your answer.

Guided Instruction

Connect: Relationships between place values

Abbie says that if you divide the value of each digit in 4,444 by the value of the digit to the right, the quotient will always be 10. Is Abbie correct?

Use place value.

Step 1

Start with the digits in the tens and the ones places.

4, 4 4 4.

40 ÷ 4 = 10.

Step 2

Continue with the digits in the hundreds and in the tens places.

4, 4 4 4.

400 ÷ 40 = 10.

Step 3

Then continue with the digits in the thousands and in the hundreds places.

4, 4 4 4.

4 000 ÷ 400 = 10.

Abbie is correct. If you divide the value of each digit in Abbie's
the value of the digit to the right, the quotient will always be 10.

ttern continue for 444,444? Explain.

Complete the place-value chart. Write the missing values and place names.

1.

Place Value	100,000		1,000		10	1
	hundred thousands	ten thousands			tens	ones

Complete the sentences for each underlined digit. You can use the place-value chart above to help.

2. 450,32**8**   The digit 8 is in the _____ place.

Its value is 8 × 1 = ____.

3. 450,3**2**8   The digit 2 is in the _____ place.

Its value is ____ × 10 = 20.

4. 450,**3**28   The digit 3 is in the _____ place.

Its value is 3 × _____ = _____.

5. 45**0**,328   The digit 0 is in the thousands place.

It shows that there are _____ thousands.

6. 4**5**0,328   The digit 5 is in the _____ place.

Its value is 5 × _____ = 50,000.

7. **4**50,328   The digit 4 is in the hundred thousands place.

Its value is ____ times the value of _____.

Think • Pair • Share

MP4 8. Use the place-value chart in exercise 1. Describe the rule for the pattern shown by the place values from right to left, starting with 1. How would you extend the place-value chart to show 1,000,000, or one million?

Independent Practice

Write 546,893 in the place-value chart. Then name the value of each digit in the number.

hundred thousands	ten thousands	thousands	hundreds	tens	ones

1. ____ ones = 3

2. ____ tens = ____

3. ____ hundreds = _____

4. ____ thousands = _____

5. ____ ten thousands = _____

6. ____ hundred thousands = _____

Write the place for the underlined digit. Then write the value of the digit.

7. 7,**4**45   place: _____

The digit 4 represents _____.

8. 16,2**3**8   place: _____

The digit 3 represents _____.

9. 4**8**,524   place: _____

The digit 8 represents _____.

10. **4**01,902   place: _____

The digit 4 represents _____.

̇e values of the digits in the given place. Circle the
̇ digit has the greater value.

572   614

14,308   22,563

63,450   275,029

̇ons in Base Te̷

̷r and Operations in Base Ten

Independent Practice

For exercises 14–16, use the model at the right.

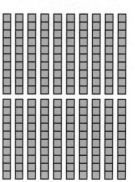

14. The model shows _____ tens.

15. The model shows _____ hundreds.

16. There are _____ times as many tens as hundreds.

**Write the value of the underlined digit.
Then regroup the value.**

17. <u>3</u>49   _____ = _____ tens

18. <u>2</u>,158   _____ = _____ hundreds

19. <u>1</u>6,331   _____ = _____ thousands

20. Look at the number shown below. Under each digit, write the letter of the matching description.

$$6 \quad 6 \quad 8 \; , \; 8 \quad 8 \quad 4$$

_____ _____ _____ _____ _____ _____

   a. The number of ones

   c. Represents 10 times the value of the tens

   e. Has a place value 10 times the value of the thousands place

   b. Has a value of 80

   d. The number of hundred thousands

   f. Represents 10 times the value of the hundreds

21. 80 × 10 = _____

22. 600 × 10 = _____

23. 5,000 ÷ 500 = _____

24. 7,500 ÷ 750 = _____

Independent Practice

MP6 **25.** John makes a mistake when he inputs the number 1,205. He inputs the number 2,105 instead. Use place value to explain John's mistake.

MP1 **26.** What number is represented by the model? Explain the value of each digit in the number.

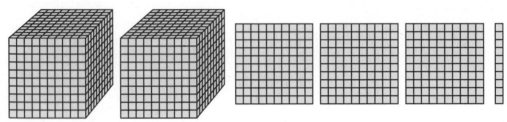

Solve the problems.

MP7 **27.** A cashier counts 25 ten-dollar bills and writes the total amount of money as a number. What is this number, and what is the place of the digit 2?

▭▬ **Show your work.**

_____

36,000 is the same as 360 hundreds. Is Tanya correct?

r **work.**

ns in Base Te

er and Operations in Base Ten

Independent Practice

MP6 **29.** Samantha is taking $2,000 out of her savings. She asks to have the money in 20-dollar bills. How many 20-dollar bills should Samantha receive?

✏️ **Show your work.**

Answer _____

MP7 **30.** Alejandro and Erin estimate the number of people at a football game. Alejandro thinks there are about 60,000 people in the stadium. Erin says there are about 6,000 people. How many times as much is Alejandro's estimate as Erin's estimate?

✏️ **Show your work.**

Answer _____

MP8 **31.** Briana says that $1,200 \div 12 = 10$. Is Briana's answer correct?

Answer _____

✏️ **Justify your answer using words, drawings, or numbers.**

MP6 **32.** Nicole and Micah are talking about the number 12,459. Micah says that the value of the thousands digit is 10 times the value of the hundreds digit. Nicole says this is not true, since the two digits are not the same. Who is correct?

Answer _____

✏️ **Justify your answer using words, drawings, or numbers.**

Read, Write, and Compare Whole Numbers

Essential Question:
How do you use place value to name and compare numbers?
4.NBT.2

Words to Know:
period
expanded form

Guided Instruction

In this lesson you will learn how to read, write, and compare whole numbers.

Understand: Names for whole numbers

> Kendra is reading her report about Mount Everest aloud. The height of Mount Everest is 29,035 feet. How should Kendra read this number?

To find how Kendra should read the number, write the number 29,035 in a place-value chart.

To read a number of thousands or greater, read each group of digits. A period is a group of 3 places. For example in the chart below, the periods are the thousands period, and the ones period. A comma usually separates periods.

Thousands			Ones		
hundreds	tens	ones	hundreds	tens	ones
	2	9	0	3	5

Read the total number of thousands written before the comma or in the thousands period:

...meral	number name
...35	*twenty-nine thousand*

...eriod groups the values less than 1,000. Read the total
...nes group of digits.
...rty five

...?9,035 as *twenty-nine thousand, thirty five*.

...for *six hundred fifteen thousand, two hundred one*
...wo thousand, forty-nine.

201   5,249

...ons in Base Te...

...er and Operations in Base Ten

Guided Instruction

Understand: Numbers in expanded form

You can think about the height of Mount Everest in another way.
Use the expanded form to see the value of each digit in 29,035.

You can also write a number in expanded form. The expanded form of
a number shows the value of each digit. Find the value of each digit
in 29,035.

2	9	,	0	3	5
↓	↓		↓	↓	↓
20,000	9,000		0	30	5

Remember!
Multiply a digit by its
place value to find
its value.

29,035 = 20,000 + 9,000 + 30 + 5

➡ The expanded form of 29,035 is 20,000 + 9,000 + 30 + 5.

Understand: Comparisons of whole numbers

The height of Mount McKinley is 20,320 feet. Which mountain is taller,
Mount McKinley or Mount Everest?

To compare numbers, first line up the digits by place value. You can use a
place-value chart to help.

29,035 > 20,320

29,035
20,320
+ 20,320
49,355

	Thousands			Ones		
	hundreds	tens	ones	hundreds	tens	ones
Mt. Everest		2	9	0	3	5
Mt. McKinley		2	0	3	2	0

Compare the digits in each place, starting with the greatest place.
Stop in the first place where the digits are different.
Ten thousands: 2 = 2
Thousands: 9 > 0

9 ⊝ 2   2 ⊝ 0
2 ⊝ 2

Remember!
= means *is equal to.*
< means *is less than.*
> means *is greater than.*

29,035 has the greater number of thousands,
so 29,035 > 20,320.

➡ Mount Everest is taller than Mount McKinley.

29,035 + 20,320
49,355

Unit 2 ■ Focus on Number and Opera...

Guided Instruction

Connect: Represent and compare whole numbers

A radio announcer says that two hundred fifteen thousand, four hundred seven people lost power in a storm. A news article reported that 215,470 people lost power. How do these numbers compare?

Write the numbers in the same form and then compare them.

Step 1

Write this number name in standard form:
two hundred fifteen thousand, four hundred seven.

215,407

Write the total number of thousands: 215.
Write the total number of ones given after the comma: 407.
Now write the full number with a comma: 215,407.
215,407 is not the same as 215,470, the number from the news article.

Step 2

To see why the numbers are different, write them in expanded form.
Find and list the values of the digits in each number.

215,407 200,000 + 10,000 + 5,000 + 400 + 0 + 7 = □
215,470 200,000 + 10,000 + 5,000 + 400 + 70 + 0 = □

There are different numbers of tens and ones. 215,407 < 215,470

the numbers. Line up the digits by place value and stop in the
here the digits are different.

215,407
+ 215,470
─────────
430,877

s is less than 7 tens: 0 < 7.

than 215,470.

number from the news article. Write the

407 + 215,470 = 430,877

and Operations in Base Ten

Guided Practice

Fill in the blanks to write the number in a different form.

1. 21,109

   number name: ___21___-one _thousand_, one _Hundred_ nine

2. 492,013

   number name: ___49___ hundred ___2___-___013___

   thousand, _____

3. sixty-three thousand, eight hundred fifty two

   numeral: _63,852_

4. five hundred fourteen thousand, three hundred three

   numeral: _63,82_

5. 89,780

   expanded form: _80,000_ + 9,000 + _700_ + _80_

6. 307,326

   expanded form: _30,000_ + ___0___ + _700_ + _30_ + _2_

Write < , =, or > to compare the numbers.

7. 6,**5**89 _<_ 6,**9**28

8. 2**1**,807 _<_ 2**0**,931

9. 37,146 _=_ 37,146

10. 458,923 _<_ 459,823

👑 Think • Pair • Share

MP1 11. Extend the place-value chart on page 64 to show 21,385,604. Be sure to label the millions period. Explain the value of each digit.

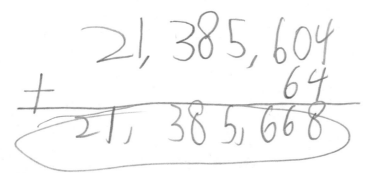

$$21,385,604$$
$$+ \quad\quad\quad\quad 64$$
$$\overline{21,385,668}$$

21,385,6

Independent Practice

Fill in the blanks to write each number in three forms. Look at all three forms to find the information you need.

1. 68,223

   sixty-___8___ thousand, two ___2___ twenty three

   ___66,000___ + 8,000 + 200 + ___20___ + 3

2. 104, ___10,000   40___

   one hundred ___and___ ___4___, eight hundred _____

   ___10___ + 4,000 + ___300___ + 10 + 6

3. 98 ___1___, ___8___ 31

   ___281,___ ___8___ eighty-five _____, thirty one

   _____ + _____ + 5,000 + ___ + 1

Circle the correct answer.

4. Which is the number name for 712,358?

   a. seven hundred thousand
      twelve, three fifty eight

   b. seventy one thousand,
      twenty-three hundred fifty-eight

   ~~c.~~ ven hundred twelve thousand,
      hundred fifty eight

   d. seven hundred twelve thousand,
      thirty-five hundred eight

   ~~e~~ is a different number from the others?

                                    b. 40,000 + 2,000 + 200 + 1

   2 thousands   d. forty-two thousand, two hundred one
   one

   e million?

                                    b. 100,000

                                    d. 100,000,000

and Operations in Base Ten

Write the given number in two other forms.

7. 33,410

   expanded form: _____ + _____ + _____ + _____

   number name: _____

8. 200,000 + 80,000 + 4,000 + 90 + 9

   numeral: _____

   number name: _____

Name the first place where the digits in both numbers are different. Then write < , =, or > to compare the numbers.

9. **4**9,603
   57,213

   _____

   49,603 ____ 57,213

10. 64,**8**19
    64,**5**47

    _____

    64,819 ____ 64,547

11. 12,213
    9,547

    _____

    12,213 ____ 9,547

12. 197,687
    861,070

    _____

    861,070 ____ 197,687

Write < , =, or > to compare the numbers. Circle the first digit that is different in the number pairs.

13. 3,526 ____ 3,526

14. 99,287 ____ 89,999

15. 28,843 ____ 28,871

16. 740,489 ____ 739,501

Independent Practice

Use place values in your explanation.

MP3 **17.** Colin is taking notes in class. The teacher says the number *eighty-five thousand, sixty two*. Colin writes *85,602* in his notebook. Explain the mistake Colin made.

MP6 **18.** Mara says that 28,597 is greater than 101,200 because 2 is greater than 1. Is Mara correct? Explain your answer.

Solve the problems.

MP8 **19.** James counts the number of times his heart beats in one minute. He figures out that his heart beats about 125,280 times in one day. What is 125,280 in expanded form?

   ✏ **Show your work.**

t sixteen thousand, two hundred seventeen has fewer tens
usand, one hundred forty eight. What is the difference
ns for these numbers?

ork.

Independent Practice

For exercises 21–24, use the table at the right.

Land Areas of Four States	
State	Land Area (square miles)
Arizona	113,634
California	155,959
Colorado	103,717
Kansas	81,815

MP2 21. Humberto writes the area of each state shown in the table in expanded form. Which two states have the same number of thousands in their expanded forms?

➤ **Show your work.**

Answer _____

MP6 22. Laurel reads the area of Arizona as *one hundred three thousand, six hundred thirty four* square miles. Which area has a greater number of ten thousands, Laurel's or the area in the table?

➤ **Show your work.**

Answer _____

MP7 23. Max knows that one state definitely has the least area, just by looking at the table. Which state is Max thinking of?

Answer _____

➤ **Justify your answer using words, drawings, or numbers.**

MP2 24. After Max identifies the state with the least area, he compares the areas of the three other states shown. Which place in the numbers will tell Max which state has the greatest area?

Answer place _____

state _____

➤ **Justify your answer using words, drawings, or numbers.**

Apply Place Value to Round Whole Numbers

Essential Question:
How can place value help you round to different places in a whole number?
4.NBT.3

Guided Instruction

In this lesson you will learn how to round to any place in a whole number.

Understand: The numbers you use to round

> In one day, 56,147 people watch a video of the baby panda at the zoo. Lily says that 56,147 is about 60,000 people. Is this a reasonable estimate?

To find an estimate for 56,147, you can round the number.

The greatest place in 56,147 is ten thousands. Between which two ten thousands is 56,147 the closest? You can make a number line to help.

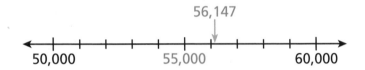

$50,000 < 56,147 < 60,000$

To find which ten thousand 56,147 is nearer to, you can use the number line or compare the digits.

Use the number line:
Mark the number that is exactly halfway between 50,000 and 60,000: 55,000. On the number line, 56,147 is to the right of 55,000, the halfway mark. Since 56,147 is nearer to 60,000 than to 50,000, round 56,147 up to 60,000.

Compare the digits: 56,147   6 > 5
                             55,000
Look at the digit to the right of the place to which you are rounding, in this case the thousands place. If it is 5 or greater, then round up.

Since 6 thousands is greater than 5 thousands, 56,147 is greater than 55,000. Then 56,147 is nearer to 60,000 than to 50,000.

➡ Yes. 60,000 is a reasonable estimate for 56,147 people.

✏ · What place can you round 56,147 to for a closer estimate?

Guided Instruction

Connect: What you know about rounding and closer estimates

The zoo gives a free panda poster to visitors each Saturday. Last Saturday, 4,532 people visited the zoo. If approximately the same number of people visit each Saturday, estimate the number of posters the zoo should have ready to give out this Saturday.

You can use place value to round a number to different places.

Step 1

For a first estimate, look at the digit in the greatest place in the number.

The 4 in 4,532 is in the thousands place. Round to the nearest thousand.

$$4,000 < 4,532 < 5,000$$

To find which thousand 4,532 is nearer to, compare it to the halfway mark. The number that is halfway between 4,000 and 5,000 is 4,500.

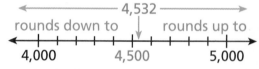

Step 2

To round to the nearest thousand, compare the hundreds digit in 4,532 to the hundreds digits in 4,500; 5 = 5

4,532 has the same number of hundreds as 4,500, the number halfway between 4,000 and 5,000.

So 4,532 rounds up to 5,000.

Remember!
If the digit to the right of the place to which you are rounding is 5 or greater, round up.

Step 3

To find a closer estimate, you can round 4,532 to the hundreds place.

The next closest hundred to 4,500 is 4,600. 4,550 is the number halfway between 4,500 and 4,600.

To round to the nearest hundred, compare the tens digit in 4,532 to the tens digit in 4,550: 3 < 5

So rounding to the nearest hundred, 4,532 rounds down to 4,500.

Depending on which place value you estimated to, the zoo should have about 5,000 or 4,500 posters ready to give out on Saturday.

Guided Practice

Round each number to the underlined place. You can use the number line to help.

1. 2**3**,485

23,000   23,500   24,000

3 is in the _____ place.

The closest thousands are _____ and 24,000.

Compare the hundreds digit in 23,485 to the 5 hundreds in _____.

   4 ___ 5

23,485 rounds _____ to _____.

2. 23,**4**85

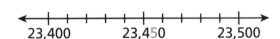

23,400   23,450   23,500

4 is in the _____ place.

_____ < 23,485 < _____

Compare the _____ digit in 23,485 to the ___ tens in _____.

   8 ___ 5

23,485 rounds _____ to _____.

For exercises 3–5, use the number line at the right.

3. What number is exactly halfway
   between 190,000 and 200,000?

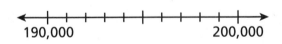

190,000   200,000

   _____

4. Write four numbers that can be rounded up to 200,000.

   _____ _____ _____ _____

5. Write four numbers that can be rounded down to 190,000.

   _____ _____ _____ _____

Round each number to the underlined place. Write the numbers you can round to. Then circle the correct rounded number.

6. _____ < **6**,742 < 7,000

7. _____ < **1**2,099 < 20,000

8. _____ < 3**8**,250 < 39,000

9. _____ < 54**5**,123 < _____

For exercises 10 and 11, you can use a number line.

10. Ross is going to Australia to visit his grandparents. The airline says the distance between Boston and Brisbane is 9,773 miles. What is a reasonable estimate for this distance? Explain your answer.

11. Audrey read that the area of a new shopping mall is 57,600 square feet. What are the greatest and least possible actual areas of the mall if 58,000 square feet is an estimate to the nearest thousand?

Think • Pair • Share

MP4 12. Toni draws a number line and uses it to round 83,768 to the nearest ten thousand. Then she decides to round 83,768 to the nearest thousand. Show how Toni can use the same number line to do this?

Independent Practice

Round the number to the underlined place. You can use the number line to help.

1. 5<u>2</u>,143

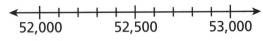

2 is in the _____ place.

The closest thousands are _____ and _____.

Compare the _____ digit in 52,143 to the _____

in _____.

1 ____ 5

52,143 rounds _____ to _____.

Round each number to the underlined place. Label the number line to show the numbers you are using.

2. <u>3</u>,325

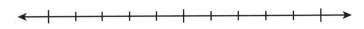

Answer _____

3. <u>4</u>5,918

Answer _____

4. 6<u>7</u>,472

Answer _____

5. 2<u>0</u>8,366

Answer _____

Independent Practice

Match the number with the estimate rounded to the underlined place. Write the letter of the correct estimate.

Estimates

6. <u>7</u>16,549 _____

7. 7<u>1</u>6,549 _____

8. 71<u>6</u>,549 _____

9. 716,<u>5</u>49 _____

a. 717,000

b. 720,000

c. 700,000

d. 716,500

Round each number to the given place.

10. 10,401 to the thousands place

_____

11. 26,792 to the ten thousands place

_____

12. 48,638 to the thousands place

_____

13. 84,151 to the hundreds place

_____

14. 447,950 to the hundred thousands place

_____

15. 625,099 to the ten thousands place

_____

16. 773,646 to the thousands place

_____

17. 998,979 to the hundreds place

_____

Solve the problems.

18. A restaurant owner is ordering supplies for the week. Last week, she ordered 1,458 pounds of potatoes. Which is the best estimate for this number?

   a. 1,000 pounds

   b. 1,400 pounds

   c. 1,500 pounds

   d. 2,000 pounds

19. Chung's family is hiking all 2,184 miles of the Appalachian Trail. He estimates the trail length as 2,000 miles. Which estimate will better help the family make sure that they bring enough supplies?

   a. 1,000 miles

   b. 2,100 miles

   c. 2,200 miles

   d. 3,000 miles

Independent Practice

MP5 **20.** The local news says that ticket sales for a new movie were $256,500 on Friday night, $421,000 on Saturday, and $301,850 on Sunday. Do you think these numbers are estimates or exact amounts? Explain.

MP6 **21.** Does it make sense to round a six-digit number to the tens place? Explain your answer with an example.

Solve the problems.

MP2 **22.** At a carnival, Jenn correctly guesses the exact number of pennies in a jar as 124,983. The closest guess the day before was 124,983 rounded to the hundreds place. What was this guess?

✏️ **Show your work.**

Answer _____

MP8 **23.** A store owner is adding $5,641 and $5,238 to find his total sales for the past two days. He rounds each amount to the nearest hundred dollars and then adds the rounded numbers. What is the store owner's estimated total sales amount?

✏️ **Show your work.**

Answer _____

Independent Practice

MP1 **24.** Victor estimates the sum of 289 and 532 in two ways. First he rounds both numbers and then adds them. Then he adds the exact numbers and rounds the sum. Both methods give him the same final number, but he gets a different answer when he rounds to a different place. What two estimated sums does Victor find?

➤ **Show your work.**

Answer _____

MP7 **25.** Ben and Lisa round the same number to different places. Ben rounds to the nearest ten thousand and gets 70,000. Lisa rounds to the nearest thousand and gets 68,000. If they both rounded correctly, what are the greatest and least possible numbers they could have rounded?

➤ **Show your work.**

Answer _____

MP3 **26.** An Arctic tern can fly more than 43,496 miles as it migrates each year. Round this number to the nearest ten thousand miles. Then round 43,496 miles to the place of your choice for a better estimate.

Answer _____

➤ **Justify your answer using words, drawings, or numbers.**

MP8 **27.** Owen incorrectly rounds 384,478 to the thousands place by rounding in three steps. He rounds to the nearest ten first, and then rounds two more times until he reaches 385,000. Is it possible that Owen rounded correctly at each step, even though his final estimate is wrong?

Answer _____

➤ **Justify your answer using words, drawings, or numbers.**

Add and Subtract Fluently with Whole Numbers

Guided Instruction

In this lesson you will learn the standard algorithms for adding and subtracting using place value.

Understand: Place value and addition

One report states that scientists have discovered 307,674 different kinds of plants and 64,283 kinds of vertebrates, or animals with a backbone. How many different kinds of plants and vertebrates are there altogether?

To find the sum of 307,674 and 64,283, you can add. Align the digits by place value.

Add the ones: $4 + 3 = 7$.
Add the tens: $7 + 8 = 15$.
15 tens is the same as
1 hundred 5 tens.
Regroup 15 tens as 1 hundred 5 tens.
Write the 1 hundred above the
hundreds place, and write the 5 tens
in the sum.

Remember!
You can only write one digit for each place of the sum.

$$
\begin{array}{r}
1 \\
307{,}674 \\
+\ \ 64{,}283 \\
\hline
57
\end{array}
$$

Keep adding the digits in each place, regrouping whenever the sum for that place is 10 or greater.

Add the hundreds: $1 + 6 + 2 = 9$
Add the thousands: $7 + 4 = 11$.
11 thousands is the same as
1 ten thousands 1 thousand.
Regroup 11 thousands as 1 ten thousand
1 thousand.

$$
\begin{array}{r}
1\ \ 1 \\
307{,}674 \\
+\ \ 64{,}283 \\
\hline
1{,}957
\end{array}
$$

Add the ten thousands: $1 + 0 + 6 = 7$
There is nothing to add to the 3 hundred thousands, so write 3 in the sum.

$$
\begin{array}{r}
1\ \ 1 \\
307{,}674 \\
+\downarrow 64{,}283 \\
\hline
371{,}957
\end{array}
$$

➡ There are 371,957 different kinds of plants and vertebrates altogether.

Understand: Subtraction and regrouping

> Spiders, scorpions, and other animals with eight legs are called *arachnids*. The report also states that there are 102,248 kinds of arachnids. How many more kinds of arachnids are there than the 64,283 kinds of vertebrates?

To find how many more kinds of arachnids there are, start by estimating the difference. This estimate will allow you to judge the reasonableness of your exact answer.

$$102,248 - 64,283$$
$$100,000 - 64,000 = 36,000$$

Next align the digits by place value. Subtract in each place.

Start with the ones: $8 - 3 = 5$.
To subtract 4 tens − 8 tens, more tens are needed. Regroup.

```
  102,248
−  64,283
───────────
       ? 5
```

Regroup 2 hundreds 4 tens as 1 hundred 14 tens.
Then subtract: $14 - 8 = 6$.

```
        1  14
  102,248
−  64,283
───────────
        6 5
```

Since you must subtract 1 hundred − 2 hundreds, regroup the thousands:
2 thousands 1 hundred as 1 thousand 11 hundreds.
Then subtract the hundreds. $11 - 2 = 9$

```
      1 11 14
  102,248
−  64,283
───────────
      9 6 5
```

To subtract 1 thousand − 4 thousands, regroup ten thousands:
10 ten thousands 1 thousand as 9 ten thousand 11 thousands.
Subtract the thousands. $11 - 4 = 7$

```
    9 11 11 14
  102,248
−  64,283
───────────
    7,9 6 5
```

Now subtract the ten thousands. $9 - 6 = 3$

```
   9 11 11 14
  102,248
−  64,283
───────────
  3 7,9 6 5
```

37,965 is close to the estimate of 36,000 so the exact answer is reasonable.

➡ There are exactly 37,965 more kinds of arachnids than vertebrates.

Guided Instruction

Connect: Subtraction and addition

Sometimes scientists disagree over their findings. One report says that there are 310,129 kinds of plants instead of 307,674. What is the difference between the number of plants?

Subtract to find the difference between the number of plants. Then add to check.

Step 1

To subtract, align the digits by place value.
Subtract the ones: 9 − 4 = 5.
Regroup hundreds and tens.
Subtract the tens.

$$\begin{array}{r} 0\ 12 \\ 3\,1\,0,\cancel{1}\,\cancel{2}\,9 \\ -\,3\,0\,7,6\,7\,4 \\ \hline 5\,5 \end{array}$$

Regroup thousands and hundreds as needed.
Subtract the hundreds.

$$\begin{array}{r} 0\ 9\ 10\,12 \\ 3\,\cancel{1}\,\cancel{0},\cancel{1}\,\cancel{2}\,9 \\ -\,3\,0\,7,6\,7\,4 \\ \hline 4\,5\,5 \end{array}$$

Subtract the thousands.
Subtract the ten thousands.
Subtract the hundred thousands.
310,129 − 307,674 = 2,455

$$\begin{array}{r} 0\ 9\ 10\,12 \\ 3\,\cancel{1}\,\cancel{0},\cancel{1}\,\cancel{2}\,9 \\ -\,3\,0\,7,6\,7\,4 \\ \hline 2,4\,5\,5 \end{array}$$

Remember!

The expanded form of a number shows the values of all its digits.
310,129 = 300,000 + 10,000 + 100 + 20 + 9

Step 2

You can add to check your answer.
If the sum is the number you started with, then you subtracted correctly.

$$\begin{array}{r} 1\ 1\ 1 \\ 3\,0\,7,6\,7\,4 \\ +\ \ \ \ \ 2,4\,5\,5 \\ \hline 3\,1\,0,1\,2\,9 \end{array}$$

Remember!

Addition and subtraction are inverse operations.

➡ The difference between the number of plants is 2,455.

✏ You know that 10,000 − 1 = 9,999. Show the regrouping that is needed to find the answer.

Guided Practice

For each step in exercises 1–4, write the missing digits to add or subtract.

1.
```
      [ ]
  3, 5 8 4
+ 2, 4 5 6
     [ ]
```

```
      [ ]
        1
  3, 5 8 4
+ 2, 4 5 6
    [ ][ ]
```

```
      [ ]
       1 1
  3, 5 8 4
+ 2, 4 5 6
  6, [ ] 4 0
```

2.
```
       [ ]
  4 6, 1 7 9
+ 3 8, 6 4 4
       [ ]
```

```
       [ ]
          1
  4 6, 1 7 9
+ 3 8, 6 4 4
      [ ] 3
```

```
       [ ]
        1 1
  4 6, 1 7 9
+ 3 8, 6 4 4
 [ ][ ],[ ] 2 3
```

3.
```
      [ ][ ]
  5 3, 7 8 5
- 1 4, 3 8 1
       [ ]
```

```
            6  15
  5 3, 7  8  5
- 1 4, 3  8  1
      [ ] 7 4
```

```
      [ ][ ]
            6  15
  5 3, 7  8  5
- 1 4, 3  8  1
      [ ] 9, 3 7 4
```

4.
```
  8 0, 0 9 2
- 6 6, 5 7 1
     [ ][ ]
```

Regroup to make hundreds.

$80{,}000 = 70{,}000 + \underline{\hphantom{xxxxxx}}$

$10{,}000 = 9{,}000 + \underline{\hphantom{xxxxxx}}$

$1{,}000 = \underline{\hphantom{xx}}$ hundreds

```
  [ ][ ][ ][ ]
  8 0, 0 9 2
- 6 6, 5 7 1
  [ ][ ],[ ] 2 1
```

☆ Think • Pair • Share

MP4 5. To understand the problem at the right, Hunter writes the numbers in expanded form. How can Hunter regroup to keep subtracting and finish the problem?

```
  7, 0 3 4          7,000 + [ ] + 30 + 4
- 5, 6 5 3   →    - 5,000 + 600 + 50 + 3
      1                            1
```

Independent Practice

Write the missing digits to complete each exercise.

1.
```
      □
   7, 3 6 0
 + 1, 4 5 9
 ───────────
   8, □ 1 □
```

2.
```
     □ □
   8, 5 4 8
 + 8, 9 3 4
 ───────────
 □ □ , 4 □ 2
```

3.
```
     □ 1 □
  5 2, 7 2 6
 + 4 4, 9 7 6
 ─────────────
 □ □ □ , □ □ 2
```

4.
```
   □ 13
  6, 7 3̶ 9
 − 2, 6 8 3
 ───────────
  4, 0 □ □
```

5.
```
     □ □
  9, 2 9̶ 7̶
 − 2, 1 4 8
 ───────────
  7, □ 4 □
```

6.
```
   □ □ 4 □10
  4̶ 7̶, 8̶ 2̶ 0
 − 1 5, 4 6 1
 ─────────────
  2 □, 0 □ 9
```

Add or subtract to check your answers.

7.
```
       □
   7, 1 4 9
 + 2, 1 4 8
 ───────────
   9, 2 □ □
```

8.
```
  □ □ □ □
  7̶ 7̶, 4̶ 8̶ 2̶
 −   8, 9 3 4
 ─────────────
  □ , 5 □ 8
```

9.
```
  □ □ □ □
  9 7̶, 7̶ 0̶ 2̶
 − 4 4, 9 7 6
 ─────────────
  5 □, 7 □ 6
```

Estimate each sum. Then find the actual sum. Show how you regroup.

10. Estimate:

_____

```
   3 8, 4 3 4
 +  2, 5 7 5
```

11. Estimate:

_____

```
   5 9, 1 4 9
 + 5 2, 6 1 2
```

12. Estimate:

_____

```
   2 2 3, 4 5 8
 + 1 9 8, 8 3 7
```

13. Estimate:

_____

```
   4 6 4, 7 7 2
 + 2 5 7, 4 3 2
```

Independent Practice

Estimate each difference. Then find the actual difference. Show how you regroup.

14. Estimate: _____

$$
\begin{array}{r}
9,185 \\
-3,964 \\
\hline
\end{array}
$$

15. Estimate: _____

$$
\begin{array}{r}
17,268 \\
-12,970 \\
\hline
\end{array}
$$

16. Estimate: _____

$$
\begin{array}{r}
640,593 \\
-286,406 \\
\hline
\end{array}
$$

17. Estimate: _____

$$
\begin{array}{r}
500,642 \\
-371,351 \\
\hline
\end{array}
$$

For problems 18–19, use the table at the right.

Greatest Known Ocean Depths	
Ocean	Depth in feet
Pacific	36,198
Atlantic	30,246
Southern	23,736
Arctic	18,456

MP1 **18.** Naomi says the combined depth of the Southern Ocean and Artic Ocean is less than the depth of the Pacific Ocean. Estimate and then find the combined depth. Is Naomi correct?

Answer _____

MP2 **19.** Vince wants to know how much deeper the Atlantic Ocean is than the Southern Ocean. What is the difference between the greatest depths of the two oceans?

Answer _____

MP7 **20.** Naomi rounds the greatest depth of the Pacific Ocean to 36,200 feet. The deepest a scuba diver has gone underwater is 1,044 feet. What is the difference between the two depths?

Answer _____

Independent Practice

MP7 **21.** Michael made a mistake while subtracting. What mistake did Michael make?

$$\begin{array}{r} 5,543 \\ -4,895 \\ \hline 1,352 \end{array}$$

MP6 **22.** Rosie says that when you regroup while adding, the amount that you add to the next place to the left will always be 1. Is Rosie correct? Explain.

For problems 23–26, use the table at the right. Use addition or subtraction to check your answer.

Aquarium Visitors	
Month	Number of Visitors
May	85,628
June	97,134
July	101,942
August	123,291
September	64,417

MP1 **23.** How many people visited the aquarium in May and June?

▭▭▶ **Show your work.**

Answer _____

MP1 **24.** How many visitors went to the aquarium in June, July, and August?

▭▭▶ **Show your work.**

Answer _____

Independent Practice

MP1 **25.** How many more visitors went to the aquarium in August than in June?

✏️ **Show your work.**

Answer _____

MP2 **26.** What is the difference between the greatest and least numbers of visitors to the aquarium in one month?

✏️ **Show your work.**

Answer _____

MP6 **27.** Trey is teaching his brother how to add.
Here is how his brother added.
Is Trey's brother's work correct?
If not, what mistake did Trey's brother make?

$$\begin{array}{r} {\scriptstyle 1\ 1\ 1\ 1\ 1\ 1} \\ 1\,2\,3{,}4\,5\,6 \\ +\ 1\,2\,3{,}4\,5\,6 \\ \hline 3\,5\,7{,}9\,1\,3 \end{array}$$

Answer _____

✏️ **Justify your answer using words, drawings, or numbers.**

MP3 **28.** Trey says that before you subtract, you can regroup all of the values that you need to at once. Does this method give you the same difference as when you regroup one place at a time, while you subtract?

Answer _____

✏️ **Justify your answer using words, drawings, or numbers.**

Multiply Whole Numbers: Use Place Value

Essential Question:
How can you use place value and patterns to multiply?
4.NBT.5

Words to Know:
partial products

Guided Instruction

In this lesson you will learn how to use place value to multiply greater factors.

Understand: Products of tens, hundreds, and thousands

> At a swimming pool guests are charged $5 to swim for the day. How much money does the pool receive if 20, 200, or 2,000 people swim?

To find each product, use the fact 5×2 and place-value patterns.

Remember!
Each place in a number is 10 times the value of the place to its right.

5×20
$= 5 \times 2$ tens
$= 10$ tens
$= 100$

5×200
$= 5 \times 2$ hundreds
$= 10$ hundreds
$= 1,000$

$5 \times 2,000$
$= 5 \times 2$ thousands
$= 10$ thousands
$= 10,000$

➡ The pool receives $100 for 20 people, $1,000 for 200 people, and $10,000 for 2,000 people.

You can also multiply the nonzero digits, $5 \times 2 = 10$ and then compare the number of zeros in the factors with the number of zeros after the 10 in each product. You can use this pattern with zeros to multiply.

$5 \times 20 = 100$
$5 \times 200 = 1,000$
$5 \times 2,000 = 10,000$

Note that it works in other problems. Look at the problem 10×20. There are two zeros in the factors.
Multiply the nonzero digits: $1 \times 2 = 2$.
Then write the number of zeros in the factors to the end of that product, to show the correct place value.

$10 \times 20 = 1$ ten $\times 2$ tens
$= 2$ hundreds
$= 200$

This pattern helps you when you multiply tens, hundreds, and thousands.

Understand: Place value and partial products

> Rob is using a garden hose to fill a swimming pool. In one hour there will be 924 gallons of water. How many gallons of water will the pool have in it after 6 hours?

To find the total number of gallons, you can multiply 6 times the value of each digit in 924. Partial products are formed by multiplying the value of each digit by a factor.

Find the partial products.

Multiply the ones first. Multiply 6 times the value of the digit 4. Write the product below.	Next, multiply 6 times the value of the digit 2.	Then multiply 6 times the value of the digit 9.
$\begin{array}{r} 924 \\ \times\quad 6 \\ \hline 24 \end{array}$ ← 6 × 4 ones	$\begin{array}{r} 924 \\ \times\quad 6 \\ \hline 24 \\ 120 \end{array}$ ← 6 × 4 ones ← 6 × 2 tens	$\begin{array}{r} 924 \\ \times\quad 6 \\ \hline 24 \\ 120 \\ 5400 \end{array}$ ← 6 × 4 ones ← 6 × 2 tens ← 6 × 9 hundreds

Now add all the partial products.
924 × 6 = 24 + 120 + 5,400 = 5,544

$$\begin{array}{r} 924 \\ \times\quad 6 \\ \hline 24 \\ 120 \\ +\,5400 \\ \hline 5,544 \end{array}$$

You can use an area model to show the partial products in the final product. Use the value of the digits in each factor as the side lengths of the area model.

	900	+	20	+	4	= 924
6	6 × 900 = 5,400		6 × 20 = 120		6 × 4 = 24	

➡ The pool will have 5,544 gallons of water in it after 6 hours.

Guided Instruction

Connect: What you know about multiplication and partial products

> A lifeguard works at a pool for 28 hours each week. How many hours will the lifeguard work in 12 weeks?

To multiply two 2-digit numbers, use the expanded form of each factor to find partial products. Begin by estimating to judge the reasonableness of your exact answer.

Step 1

Estimate the product. You can round down 12 and round up 28.

$12 \times 28 \rightarrow 10 \times 30 = 300$.

> Find the products of the nonzero factors. Count the zeros in the factors. Write the total number of zeros at the end of the product.

Step 2

Make an area model to show the partial products you need to find. In the area model the sides represent the 12 weeks, $12 = 10 + 2$, and the 28 hours, $28 = 20 + 8$, worked each week.

The sum of the areas of each part is the total product. Side lengths of the rectangle:

$12 = 10 + 2 \qquad 28 = 20 + 8$

	20	+ 8
10	10×20 = 200	10×8 = 80
+ 2	2×20 = 40	2×8 = 16

Step 3

Now multiply to find each partial product.

```
    2 8              2 8              2 8              2 8
  × 1 2            × 1 2            × 1 2            × 1 2
  ─────            ─────            ─────            ─────
   1 6 ← 2 × 8      1 6 ← 2 × 8      1 6 ← 2 × 8      1 6 ← 2 × 8
                    4 0 ← 2 × 20     4 0 ← 2 × 20     4 0 ← 2 × 20
                                     8 0 ← 10 × 8     8 0 ← 10 × 8
                                                    2 0 0 ← 10 × 20
```

Step 4

Add the partial products to find the total product. How does this compare to your estimate?

The exact answer, 336, is reasonably close to the estimate of 300.

➤ The lifeguard will work 336 hours in 12 weeks.

```
      2 8
    × 1 2
    ─────
      1 6
      4 0
      8 0
  + 2 0 0
    ─────
    3 3 6
```

Guided Practice

Use place value to find each product.

1. 4×700

$= 4 \times \underline{\quad}$ hundreds

$= \underline{\quad}$ hundreds

$= 2,800$

2. $9 \times 5,000$

$= 9 \times \underline{\quad}$ thousands

$= \underline{\quad}$ thousands

$= \underline{\qquad\qquad}$

Complete the multiplication pattern.

3. $8 \times 3 = \underline{\quad}$

$8 \times 30 = 240$

$8 \times 300 = \underline{\qquad\qquad}$

$8 \times 3,000 = \underline{\qquad\qquad}$

4. $5 \times 6 = \underline{\quad}$

$5 \times 60 = \underline{\qquad\qquad}$

$5 \times \underline{\qquad\qquad} = 3,000$

$5 \times 6,000 = \underline{\qquad\qquad}$

Use the area model to multiply. Label the model with the partial products. Then complete the multiplication.

5. $300 \quad + \quad 10 \quad + \quad 8 \ = 318$

| | $4 \times 300 =$ | $4 \times 10 =$ | $4 \times 8 =$ |

4

318
$\times \quad 4$
_____
$\leftarrow 4 \times 8$ ones
$\leftarrow 4 \times 1$ ten
$+ \underline{\qquad} \leftarrow 4 \times 3$ hundreds

6. $4,000 \quad + 200 + 50 + 6 = 4,256$

8

$4,256$
$\times \qquad 8$

$+ \underline{\qquad\qquad}$

Think • Pair • Share

MP2 **7.** Mia says the product of 21 and 53 is about the same as 2×500. Is Mia correct? Explain her method for estimating, and why it does or does not work.

Independent Practice

Use multiplication patterns to multiply.

1. 200 × 4 =

   ___ ___ ___

2. 3,000 × 4 =

   ___ ___ ___ ___ ___

3. 20 × 30 =

   ___ ___ ___

4. 9 × 500 =

   _____

5. 8 × 7,000 =

   _____

6. 50 × 40 =

   _____

Use the area model to multiply. Label the model with the partial products. Then complete the multiplication.

7.

| | 200 | + | 30 | + | 9 | = 239 |

| 6 | 6 × 200 = | 6 × 30 = | 6 × 9 = |

6 × 239 = _____ + _____ + ___

     = _____

8.
   5,804
×   7

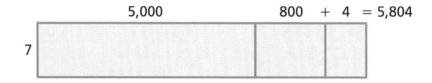

5,000   800 + 4 = 5,804

7

+ _____

9.
   67
×   59

+ _____

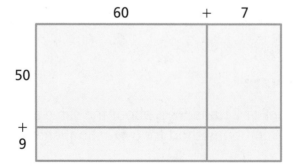

60   +   7

50

+ 9

Independent Practice

Multiply. Use the area model to help you.

10. A store at the beach sells 9,586 bottles of sunscreen in one summer. Each bottle costs $8. How much does the store receive for sunscreen?

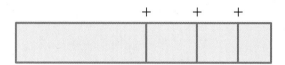

$9,586 \times \$8 =$ _____

11. Crystal is training for a swimming competition. She swims 72 feet in 1 minute. If Crystal could keep up this pace, how far would she swim in 85 minutes?

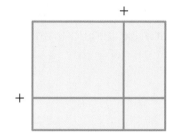

$72 \times 85 =$ _____

Solve the problem.

12. Oscar uses the expanded form of the factors to find and record partial products without a model. Use Oscar's method to multiply 8,954 by 9.

$8,000 + 900 + 50 + 4 \rightarrow 8,954$

$\times \qquad\qquad 9 \qquad \times \qquad 9$

8,1

$+ \qquad 36$

Estimate each product. Then multiply.

13. $3,362 \times 5$

14. 77×43

Independent Practice

MP2 **15.** George multiplies 3 times 3,519. His work is shown to the right. What mistake does George make?

$$
\begin{array}{r}
3,519 \\
\times \quad 3 \\
\hline
27 \\
30 \\
150 \\
+\,9,000 \\
\hline
9,207
\end{array}
$$

MP7 **16.** Robin is multiplying 80 times 42. How many partial products will Robin have to add? Explain your answer.

Solve the problems.

MP1 **17.** An airline has planes in two sizes. The small planes have 135 seats, and the larger planes have 172 seats. What is the total number of seats on 5 small planes and 4 large planes?

 **Show your work.**

Answer _____

MP2 **18.** A large, older airplane uses 1,193 gallons of fuel each hour that it is flying. How many gallons of fuel will the plane use for a 6-hour flight?

 **Show your work.**

Answer _____

Independent Practice

MP2 **19.** Mr. Roberts is enrolled in a frequent flyer program. He earns a point for each air mile he travels. If Mr. Roberts travels 4,254 air miles each month for 3 months, how many points would Mr. Roberts earn altogether?

✏️ **Show your work.**

Answer _____

MP1 **20.** A group of 55 tourists order a special meal at a restaurant. The cost of each person's meal is $38. Each person will pay a $7 tip. What is the total restaurant bill for the group?

✏️ **Show your work.**

Answer _____

MP4 **21.** Jessica uses a number line to find the product 4 × 15. She skip-counts by 15 four times, and reaches a product of 60.

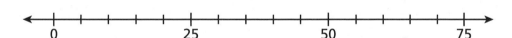

Miles says this is not the best method for multiplying greater numbers. Do you agree with Miles? Give one example.

Answer _____

✏️ **Justify your answer using words, drawings, or numbers.**

11 Multiply Whole Numbers: Use Properties of Operations

Guided Instruction

In this lesson you will learn how to multiply greater whole numbers using the Distributive and other properties.

Understand: The Distributive Property and expanded form

> To raise money, a school will have a concert and it will charge $5 for each ticket to the concert. How much will the school receive if the school sells 384 tickets?

To find how much the school will receive you can use the Distributive Property to multiply 5 × 384.

First, decompose 384, the greater factor.
Write 384 in expanded form, to break it into a sum of hundreds, tens, and ones.

$$5 \times 384 = 5 \times (300 + 80 + 4)$$

Multiply each addend by 5, the lesser factor.
Then add the partial products.

$$5 \times (300 + 80 + 4) = (5 \times 300) + (5 \times 80) + (5 \times 4)$$
$$= 1,500 + 400 + 20$$
$$= 1,920$$

You use the Distributive Property when you multiply the addends in the expanded form of one factor by the other factor.

➡ The school will receive $1,920 from the sale of 384 tickets.

Use an area model to represent the partial products.

	300	+ 80	+ 4	= 384
5	5 × 300 = 1,500	5 × 80 = 400	5 × 4 = 20	

The area model can be helpful when using the Distributive Property. It shows how multiplying 5 times the hundreds, tens, and ones in 384 is the same as multiplying 5 × 384.

✏ What are some other ways you can break apart 384?

Guided Instruction

Understand: The Distributive Property and two-digit factors

> There are 64 fourth graders at the school. If each fourth grader sells 15 concert tickets, how many tickets will the fourth graders sell altogether?

To find how many tickets will be sold, multiply 64 × 15.

Write the multiplication using the expanded form of both factors.
Use the Commutative Property to change the order of the factors.
15 × 64 = (10 + 5) × (60 + 4)

You can use an area model to help you. Use the value of the digits in each factor as the side lengths of the area model.

You can use the Distributive Property more than once. To distribute, multiply *each addend* for 64 by *each addend* for 15.

First, multiply by 5, the ones digit in 15.

$$5 \times (60 + 4) = (5 \times 60) + (5 \times 4)$$

Next, multiply by 10, the tens digit in 15.

$$10 \times (60 + 4) = (10 \times 60) + (10 \times 4)$$

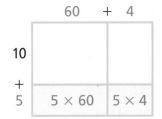

Then, write an equation showing the sum of the four partial products and solve.

$$
\begin{aligned}
(10 + 5) \times (60 + 4) &= (10 \times 60) + (10 \times 4) + (5 \times 60) + (5 \times 4) \\
&= 600 + 40 + 300 + 20 \\
&= (600 + 300) + (40 + 20) \\
&= 900 + 60 \\
&= 960
\end{aligned}
$$

Remember!
You can use the Commutative and Associative properties to help you add.

➤ The fourth graders will sell 960 concert tickets altogether.

Look at the highlighted digits to the right. How are they related to the partial products that you found above?

$$
\begin{array}{r} 64 \\ \times 15 \\ \hline \end{array}
\qquad
\begin{array}{r} 64 \\ \times 15 \\ \hline \end{array}
$$

Guided Instruction

Connect: **What you know about the Distributive Property and other multiplication strategies**

Ruby and Omar both multiply 1,296 × 3. Ruby uses the expanded form of 1,296 and the Distributive Property. Omar multiplies a number close to 1,296 and uses other properties. Can both Ruby and Omar find the correct product using their different methods?

Try each method to compare Ruby and Omar's work.

Step 1

Ruby's Method

Write the problem using the expanded form of 1,296.
Multiply each addend for 1,296 by 3.
Multiply inside the parentheses.
Add the partial products.

$$1{,}296 \times 3$$
$$= (1{,}000 + 200 + 90 + 6) \times 3$$
$$= (1{,}000 \times 3) + (200 \times 3) + (90 \times 3) + (6 \times 3)$$
$$= 3{,}000 + 600 + 270 + 18$$
$$= 3{,}888$$

Step 2

Omar's Method

Omar uses an estimate.
1,296 is almost 1,300, or 13 hundreds.
He uses the Commutative Property to reorder the factors.

$$1{,}300 \times 3 = 13 \times 100 \times 3$$
$$= 13 \times 3 \times 100$$

Omar uses the Associative Property to group 13 and 3.
Then he uses multiplication patterns with zero to multiply.

$$= (13 \times 3) \times 100$$
$$= 39 \times 100$$
$$= 3{,}900$$

Since 1,300 − 1,296 = 4, he compensates for the difference. There are 3 groups of 1,300 in 3,900, so he subtracts 4 three times.

$$1{,}296 \times 3 = 3{,}900 - (4 \times 3)$$
$$= 3{,}900 - 12$$
$$= 3{,}888$$

▷ Yes, Ruby and Omar can both find the correct product using their different methods.

Use the Distributive Property to multiply. You can use the area model to help.

1. 6×573

$= 6 \times (\underline{\quad} + 70 + \underline{\quad})$

$= (\underline{\quad} \times \underline{\quad}) + (6 \times 70) + (\underline{\quad} \times \underline{\quad})$

$= \underline{\quad\quad\quad} + 420 + \underline{\quad}$

$= \underline{\quad\quad\quad}$

	500	+ 70	+ 3
6	6×500	6×70	6×3

2. 32×29

$= (\underline{\quad} + 2) \times (\underline{\quad} + 9)$

$= (30 \times \underline{\quad}) + (30 \times \underline{\quad}) + (2 \times \underline{\quad}) + (2 \times \underline{\quad})$

$= \underline{\quad} + 270 + 40 + \underline{\quad}$

$= \underline{\quad}$

	20	+ 9
30	30×20	30×9
+ 2	2×20	2×9

Use the Distributive Property and expanded form to multiply.

3. $4 \times 6{,}725 = \underline{\quad} \times (6{,}000 + \underline{\quad} + \underline{\quad} + 5)$

$= (4 \times 6{,}000) + (\underline{\quad\quad\quad}) + (\underline{\quad\quad\quad}) + (4 \times 5)$

$= \underline{\quad\quad\quad} + 2{,}800 + \underline{\quad} + \underline{\quad}$

$= \underline{\quad\quad\quad}$

⚊ Think • Pair • Share

MP6 4. Leo multiplies 4×285 as shown below.

$4 \times (250 + 30 + 5) = 1{,}000 + 120 + 20 = 1{,}140$

Does Leo use the Distributive Property? Does he find the correct product? Explain why or why not.

Independent Practice

Use the Distributive Property and expanded form to multiply.

1. $5 \times 468 = 5 \times (\underline{\hspace{1cm}} + \underline{\hspace{1cm}} + 8)$

        $= (5 \times 400) + (\underline{\hspace{2cm}}) + (\underline{\hspace{2cm}})$

        $= \underline{\hspace{2cm}} + 300 + \underline{\hspace{1cm}}$

        $= \underline{\hspace{2cm}}$

2. $7 \times 5{,}619 = 7 \times (\underline{\hspace{2cm}} + \underline{\hspace{1cm}} + 10 + \underline{\hspace{1cm}})$

        $= (\underline{\hspace{2cm}}) + (\underline{\hspace{2cm}}) + (7 \times 10) + (7 \times 9)$

        $= \underline{\hspace{2cm}} + \underline{\hspace{2cm}} + \underline{\hspace{1cm}} + \underline{\hspace{1cm}}$

        $= \underline{\hspace{2cm}}$

Use the Distributive Property and area model to multiply. Label the model with the partial products to help you.

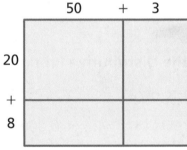

3. 28×53

$28 \times 53 = (\underline{\hspace{1cm}} + 8) \times (\underline{\hspace{1cm}} + 3)$

        $= (20 \times \underline{\hspace{1cm}}) + (\underline{\hspace{1cm}} \times 3) + (8 \times \underline{\hspace{1cm}}) + (\underline{\hspace{1cm}} \times 3)$

        $= \underline{\hspace{2cm}} + 60 + \underline{\hspace{1cm}} + 24$

        $= \underline{\hspace{2cm}}$

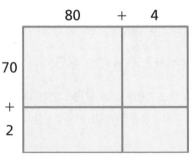

4. 72×84

$72 \times 84 = (\underline{\hspace{2cm}}) \times (\underline{\hspace{2cm}})$

        $= (\underline{\hspace{2cm}}) + (\underline{\hspace{2cm}}) + (\underline{\hspace{2cm}}) + (\underline{\hspace{2cm}})$

        $= \underline{\hspace{1.5cm}} + \underline{\hspace{1.5cm}} + \underline{\hspace{1.5cm}} + \underline{\hspace{1.5cm}}$

        $= \underline{\hspace{2cm}}$

Independent Practice

Circle the correct answer.

5. Each equation below shows a different method for multiplying 40×48. Which equation is incorrect?

   a. $40 \times 48 = 40 \times (40 + 8)$ b. $40 \times 48 = (20 + 20) \times (40 + 8)$

   c. $40 \times 48 = 10 \times 4 \times (40 + 8)$ d. $40 \times 48 = (2 \times 20) + (40 + 8)$

   ✏️ **Justify your answer using words, drawings, or numbers.**

Match each equation with the correct product.   **Products**

6. $8 \times 198 = 8 \times (100 + 90 + 8)$ _____   a. 972

7. $3 \times 325 = 3 \times (300 + 20 + 5)$ _____   b. 975

8. $5 \times 264 = 5 \times (200 + 60 + 4)$ _____   c. 1,200

9. $16 \times 75 = (10 + 6) \times (70 + 5)$ _____   d. 1,320

10. $27 \times 36 = (20 + 7) \times (30 + 6)$ _____   e. 1,584

Estimate the product. Then multiply using the properties of operations. Show your work.

11. $4,462 \times 9$

    Estimate: _____

    Answer _____

12. 34×56

    Estimate: _____

    Answer _____

Independent Practice

MP6 **13.** Compare your work for exercises 11 and 12. How is multiplying by a factor with one digit different from multiplying two factors with two digits?

MP2 **14.** Jenny multiplies $9,059 \times 6$ as shown below.

$$
\begin{array}{r}
9,059 \\
\times \quad 6 \\
\hline
54,000 \\
0 \\
300 \\
+ \quad\quad 54 \\
\hline
54,354
\end{array}
$$

$6 \times 9,000$

6×0

6×50

6×9

How is Jenny using the Distributive Property with this method? Explain.

Solve the problems using the method of your choice.

MP4 **15.** The students are helping to set up chairs for their school's concert. They make 24 rows with 32 chairs in each row. How many chairs do the students set up altogether?

✏️ **Show your work.**

Answer _____

MP2 **16.** A grocery store uses 3,452 plastic bags in one week. If the store uses 5 times as many bags for the whole month, how many bags does the store use that month?

✏️ **Show your work.**

Answer _____

Independent Practice

MP1 **17.** An athlete training for the Olympics eats 9,655 calories of food each day for 7 days in a row. What is the total number of calories the athlete eats that week?

✏️ **Show your work.**

Answer _____

MP4 **18.** The soccer field at the park is 48 yards wide and 75 yards long. There are 36 inches in 1 yard. What are the width and length of the field in inches?

✏️ **Show your work.**

Answer _____

MP8 **19.** Brian says that the product of two whole numbers with 2 digits each will always have 4 digits. Do you agree? Give at least one example to support your answer.

Answer _____

✏️ **Justify your answer using words, drawings, or numbers.**

Lesson 12

Divide Whole Numbers: Use Place Value

Essential Question:
How can place value and estimation help you divide?
4.NBT.6

Words to Know:
dividend
divisor
quotient
compatible numbers

Guided Instruction

In this lesson you will learn how to use place value to estimate quotients and divide greater whole numbers.

Understand: Quotients of tens, hundreds, and thousands

> An article in a magazine states that scientists estimate that lightning strikes about 200 times around the world every 5 seconds. Following this pattern, find the number of times lightning strikes each second.

To find the number of lightning strikes in 1 second, divide 200 by 5.

In this division 200 represents the dividend, the number you divide; 5 represents the divisor, the number you divide by in the division to find a quotient, the unknown number that is the answer to the problem.

$$
\underset{\text{dividend}}{200} \quad \underset{}{\div} \quad \underset{\text{divisor}}{5} \quad = \quad \underset{\text{quotient}}{n}
$$

Use the fact $20 \div 5 = 4$ and the pattern of zeros to find the quotient, n.

$20 \div 5 = 4$ $200 \div 5 = n$

20 tens $\div\ 5 = 4$ tens ⟶ $200 \div 5 = 40$, so $n = 40$

➡ Lightning strikes about 40 times each second.

You can use a number line to show a model of $200 \div 5 = 40$.

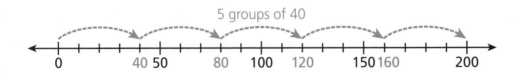

5 groups of 40

0   40 50   80 100 120 150 160   200

✏ Continue the pattern of zeros to find $2,000 \div 5$. How can you change the number line to model $2,000 \div 5$?

Guided Instruction

Understand: Place value and regrouping

Julia will drive 324 miles to go camping. If Julia drives the same number of miles each hour, how many miles should Julia drive each hour to reach the camp in 6 hours?

To find the number of miles that Julia has to drive each hour, divide 324 by 6. Use place value models to represent the miles. Divide 3 hundreds, 2 tens, 4 ones into 6 equal groups.

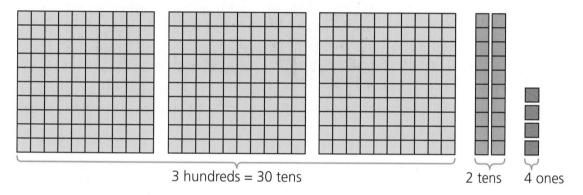

3 hundreds = 30 tens   2 tens   4 ones

To find 324 ÷ 6, find the partial quotients. Then add them.
Look at the model. Regroup 3 hundreds as 30 tens.
30 tens + 2 tens = 32 tens total to share equally in groups.

Divide 32 tens into 6 equal groups.
32 tens ÷ 6 = 5 tens in each group
and 2 tens left over.

2 tens left over is not enough to make 6 groups of ten.

Regroup the 2 left over tens as 20 ones.
20 ones + 4 ones = 24 ones to share

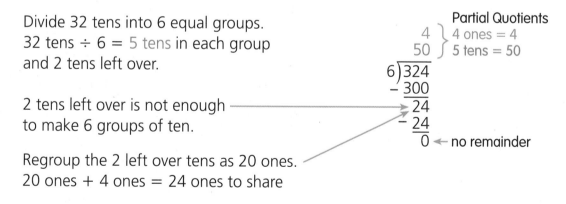

Partial Quotients
4   } 4 ones = 4
50 } 5 tens = 50

6)324
 − 300
    24
  − 24
     0 ← no remainder

Divide the 24 ones into 6 equal groups.
24 ones ÷ 6 = 4 ones in each group.

Add the partial quotients.
324 ÷ 6 = 50 + 4 = 54

➡ Julia should drive 54 miles each hour to reach the camp in 6 hours.

Guided Instruction

Connect: **What you know about regrouping to divide whole numbers into equal groups**

A television manufacturer puts 4 batteries in each remote controller. The manufacturer has 1,217 batteries. How many remote controllers can the manufacturer fill with batteries?

To find the number of remote controllers, divide 1 thousand, 2 hundreds, 1 ten, 7 ones by 4. $1,217 \div 4$

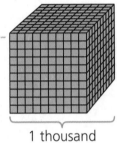 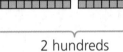

1 thousand   2 hundreds   1 ten   7 ones

Step 1

Regroup 1 thousand as 10 hundreds.
10 hundreds + 2 hundreds
= 12 hundreds
Divide 12 hundreds by 4.
12 hundreds ÷ 4 = 3 hundred groups of 4.

Step 2

There are no hundreds left to divide.
Regroup 1 ten as 10 ones.
10 ones + 7 ones = 17 ones; Divide 17 ones by 4.
17 ones ÷ 4 = 4 groups of 4 and 1 one left over.

Partial Quotients

$$\begin{array}{r} 4 \\ 300 \\ \hline 4)\overline{1,217} \\ -1,200 \\ \hline 17 \\ -16 \\ \hline 1 \end{array}$$

4 ones = 4
3 hundreds = 300

← Remainder

Step 3

Add the partial quotients.
$1,217 \div 4 = 304$ groups of 4 batteries and 1 battery left over.

The 1 battery left over does not make another group of 4.

$1217 \div 4 = 304 \text{ R}1$

Remember!
A remainder (R) is the amount left over after dividing.

Step 4

You can estimate to make sure that the answer is reasonable. Use a number that is close to 1,217 and easy to divide by 4.

Estimate $1,200 \div 4 = 300$; about 300 groups
Answer $1,217 \div 4 = 304 \text{ R}1$

1,200 and 4 are compatible numbers. Compatible numbers are those that are easy to compute mentally.

The estimate 300 is close to 304 R1, so 304 R1 is a reasonable answer.

➡ The manufacturer can fill 304 remote controllers with 1,216 batteries.

Guided Practice

Complete exercises 1 and 2 to solve the problem. Show your work.

Arly's Movie Triplex has a total of 825 seats in 3 theaters that are the same size. How many seats are in each theater?

1. Estimate the number of seats in each theater. Use compatible numbers.

Estimate 825 ÷ 3. ____________

2. Divide 825 to find the actual quotient.
825 = 8 hundreds + 2 tens + 5 ones

a. Divide the hundreds. 8 hundreds ÷ 3

There are 3 groups of ____ hundreds in 825.

____ hundreds represent seats shared equally among the 3 theaters. ____ hundreds are left over.

b. Regroup the hundreds that are left over.

2 hundreds = ____ tens

____ tens + 2 tens = ____ tens

c. Divide the tens.

There are 3 groups of ____ tens in 22 tens.

____ tens are shared equally among the 3 theaters.

____ ten is left over.

d. Regroup the 1 ten left over with the 5 ones.

1 ten = ____ ones

____ ones + ____ ones = ____ ones to share equally among the 3 theaters.

e. 15 ones = 3 groups of ____ ones.
There are 275 seats in each theater.

$$\begin{array}{r} 5 \\ 70 \\ 200 \\ 3\overline{)825} \\ -\ 600 \\ \hline 225 \\ -\ 210 \\ \hline 15 \\ -\ 15 \\ \hline 0 \end{array} \quad \left.\begin{array}{l} \\ \\ \\ \end{array}\right\} 275$$

Think • Pair • Share

MP7 **3.** Is the actual quotient close to the estimated quotient? Explain why it is helpful to estimate before solving the problem.

Independent Practice

Use division patterns with zeros to find each quotient.

1. $500 \div 5 =$

___ ___ ___

2. $6,000 \div 3 =$

___ ___ ___ ___

3. $200 \div 4 =$

___ ___

4. $2,400 \div 8 =$

_____

5. $1,800 \div 9 =$

_____

6. $4,000 \div 5 =$

_____

Find each quotient. You can use a model to help.

7. $620 \div 5 =$

_____

8. $337 \div 9 =$

___ R ___

9. $2,908 \div 4 =$

_____

10. $2,909 \div 4 =$

_____ R ___

11. $197 \div 8 =$

___ R ___

12. $508 \div 5 =$

_____ R ___

13. $1,344 \div 6 =$

_____

14. $7,249 \div 8 =$

_____ R ___

15. $5,320 \div 7 =$

_____

16. $4,545 \div 3 =$

_____

Independent Practice

Estimate each quotient. Use compatible numbers.

17. 71 ÷ 3

Estimate: _____

18. 409 ÷ 8

Estimate: _____

19. 3,514 ÷ 9

Estimate: _____

20. 5,247 ÷ 5

Estimate: _____

Divide. Then estimate to find if your quotient is reasonable. Show your work.

21. 421 ÷ 3 = _____

Estimate: _____

_____

Is your quotient reasonable?

_____

22. 4,298 ÷ 7 _____

Estimate: _____

_____

Is your quotient reasonable?

_____

Circle the correct answer.

23. Which quotient below has a remainder?

    a. 248 ÷ 9

    b. 700 ÷ 4

    c. 2,905 ÷ 5

    d. 6,332 ÷ 4

Independent Practice

MP6 **24.** A music store is selling all of its CDs for $9 each. Jordan has a gift card worth $110. He divides $110 by 9 correctly, and says that he can buy 12 R2 CDs with the gift card. Why is Jordan's statement incorrect?

MP5 **25.** Lucy divides 7,062 by 8 as shown at the right. The correct quotient is 882 R6. What mistakes might Lucy have made? Explain at least two mistakes.

$$7{,}062 \div 8 = 95 \text{ R2}$$

Solve the problems.

MP2 **26.** A garden has 4 rain barrels. When the 4 barrels are full, they hold 255 gallons of rain water altogether. If all 4 barrels are the same size, how many gallons of rain water does each barrel hold?

▪▬▶ **Show your work.**

Answer _____

MP1 **27.** A farm offers horseback trail rides on weekends. The riding trail is 3 miles long. If the horses covered 1,221 miles altogether in one month, how many trail rides were taken at the farm?

▪▬▶ **Show your work.**

Answer _____

Independent Practice

MP2 **28.** A statue at an art museum is 8 times as old as a famous painting. If the statue is 2,376 years old, how old is the painting?

✏️➤ **Show your work.**

Answer _____

MP1 **29.** The Water Warehouse store sells 6,093 bottles of water on Friday. The bottles come in packs of 9 bottles each. On Monday, the store sells 215 fewer packs of water than it sells on Friday. How many packs of water does the store sell on Monday?

✏️➤ **Show your work.**

Answer _____

MP2 **30.** Carmen knows that when you use an area model, you multiply the side lengths to find the area. She says that if the area of the rectangle is 1,800 square feet, then its length must be 200 feet. Is Carmen correct?

```
                              ?
9 feet │ area = 1,800 square feet │
```

Answer _____

✏️➤ **Justify your answer using words, drawings, or numbers.**

MP6 **31.** The bowling league allows no more than 5 people on a team. Is it possible to have 28 teams if there are 142 people?

Answer _____

✏️➤ **Justify your answer using words, drawings, or numbers.**

Divide Whole Numbers: Use Properties of Operations

Essential Question:
How can breaking apart whole numbers make them easier to divide?
4.NBT.6

Guided Instruction

In this lesson you will learn how to divide using properties and the relationship between multiplication and division.

Understand: Division and multiples of the divisor

> There are 9 innings in a baseball game. Last season Tom pitched all complete games. If he pitched 765 innings, how many games did Tom pitch last season?

To find how many games Tom pitched, divide the number of games he pitched by the number of innings in a game. You can use an area model to represent 765 divided by 9. In the area model at the right, the quotient 765 ÷ 9 is the unknown side length.

Remember!
Use basic facts and patterns with 0 to find the products.

Find a multiple of 9 that is close to but not greater than 765.

$9 \times 100 = 900 \qquad 9 \times 90 = 810 \qquad 9 \times 80 = 720$

720 is easy to divide: $720 \div 9 = 80$.

80 is part of the unknown side length of the area model. Show 720 as the area of the 9 × 80 region. Subtract this area from 765:
$765 - 720 = 45$.
Draw another region to show 45 as the remaining area. Divide by 9 to find the other part of the unknown side length.

45 is a multiple of 9. Divide to find the side length of the new region: $45 \div 9 = 5$.
Subtract: $45 - 45 = 0$. There is nothing left over.
Look at the completed model of 765 ÷ 9 below.

To find the quotient, add the side lengths you found.
$80 + 5 = 85$

➡ Tom pitched 85 games last season.

✏ What happens if you break 765 into smaller multiples of 9?

Guided Instruction

Understand: Division and the Distributive Property

A new high-speed train in Japan will travel 2,280 feet in 5 seconds. How many feet will the high-speed train travel in 1 second?

You can break apart a dividend to divide. The Distributive Property states that to divide a sum by a number, you can divide each addend of the sum by that number and add the partial quotients.

Remember! The dividend is the number you divide.

To find how many feet the train will travel in 1 second, divide 2,280 by 5. Break apart 2,280.

Choose a hundreds number that when multiplied by 5 would be close to 2,280.
$5 \times 400 = 2,000$

Subtract.

$$
\begin{array}{r}
2,280 \\
-2,000 \leftarrow 5 \times 400 \\
\hline
280 \\
-250 \leftarrow 5 \times 50 \\
\hline
30 \\
-30 \leftarrow 5 \times 6 \\
\hline
0
\end{array}
$$

Next choose a tens number that when multiplied by 5 would be close to 280.

$5 \times 50 = 250$. Subtract.

Now choose a ones number that when multiplied by 5 would be close to 30.

$5 \times 6 = 30$. Subtract.

Remember! The divisor is the number you divide by in a division problem.

Write 2,280 as a sum of $2,000 + 250 + 30$.

You can distribute the divisor, 5, the same way you distributed a factor when using the Distributive Property of multiplication.

When dividing 2,280, each addend is divided by 5. Add these partial quotients to find the answer.

$$
\begin{aligned}
2,280 \div 5 &= (2,000 \div 5) + (250 \div 5) + (30 \div 5) \\
&= 400 + 50 + 6 \leftarrow \text{partial quotients} \\
&= 456
\end{aligned}
$$

➡ The high-speed train will travel 456 feet in 1 second.

Guided Instruction

Connect: Multiples and partial quotients

Marco uses a pedometer to count the steps he takes. He takes 2,207 steps in 3 hours. If he takes the same number of steps each hour, how many steps does Marco take in one hour?

To find how many steps Marco takes in one hour, divide 2,207 by 3.
Use the Distributive Property to find 2,207 ÷ 3.

Break apart 2,207. Divide each addend by 3 and add the partial products.
Use basic facts and patterns with 0.
    3 × 800 = 2,400   3 × 700 = 2,100   3 × 6 = 1,800

You can use 2,100 as the first addend.
Find the first partial quotient:
2,100 ÷ 3 = 700

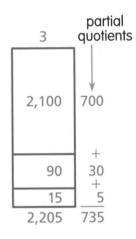

Subtract. Find the other partial products.
You can record your work either
way shown.

```
    2,2 0 7
  − 2,1 0 0  ← 3 × 700
      1 0 7
  −     9 0  ← 3 × 30
        1 7
  −     1 5  ← 3 × 5
          2    remainder
```

Look at the area model.
Add the partial quotients to find 2,205 ÷ 3.
    2205 ÷ 3 = (2,100 ÷ 3) + (90 ÷ 3) + (15 ÷ 3) ← Distributive Property of Division
           = (700 + 30 + 5)
           = 735

Note that the quotient for the full quantity has a remainder of 2.
    2,207 ÷ 3 = 735 R2
    735 R2 ⟶ (2,100 ÷ 3) + (90 ÷ 3) + (15 ÷ 3) + 2

Since Marco takes 1 extra step for 2 of the 3 hours, increase the quotient by 1 to include the remainder 2 as part of your answer.

➤ Marco takes about 736 steps in one hour.

✏ Look at the area model again. Why is the remainder not shown as part of the rectangle?

Guided Practice

Complete each area model. Write the unknown side lengths to find the partial quotients. Then add to find the quotient.

1.

+

5 | 300 | 25

$325 \div 5 =$ ___ + ___

= ___

2.

+	+

4 | 400 | 120 | 32

$552 \div 4 =$ ___ + ___ + ___

= ___

Complete each area model. Then write the quotient below.

3.   100   +

8 | | 72

$872 \div 8 =$ ___

4.   + 80 +

6 | 1,200 | | 12

$1,692 \div 6 =$ ___

Complete each division.

5. $496 \div 2 = ($___$\div 2) + (80 \div 2) + ($___$\div 2)$
     $= 200 + 40 + 8$

     $=$ ___

6. $2,189 \div 7 =$ _____

2,189
−_____ ←7 × 300
  89
−_____ ←7 × 10
  19
−_____ ←7 × 2

Think•Pair•Share

MP2

7. A snack company has 1,102 granola bars to give out as samples. A sample pack has 4 bars. Use the Distributive Property to find out how many sample packs the company can make. Then explain your answer.

Independent Practice

Use the area model and the Distributive Property to divide. Complete the model and equations.

1. $434 \div 7$

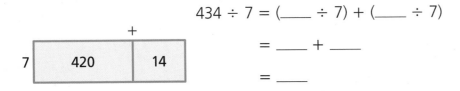

$434 \div 7 = (\underline{\quad} \div 7) + (\underline{\quad} \div 7)$

$= \underline{\quad} + \underline{\quad}$

$= \underline{\quad}$

2. $3,605 \div 5$

| 5 | 3,500 | | |

$3,605 \div 5 = (\underline{\qquad}) + (\underline{\qquad}) + (\underline{\qquad})$

$= \underline{\quad} + \underline{\quad} + \underline{\quad}$

$= \underline{\quad}$

Use the Distributive Property to divide. Complete the equation to represent the problem. Then solve.

3. $476 \div 2 = (\underline{\qquad}) + (60 \div 2) + (\underline{\qquad})$

$= \underline{\quad} + \underline{\quad} + 8$

$= \underline{\quad}$

4. $728 \div 4 = (\underline{\qquad}) + (\underline{\qquad}) + (8 \div 4)$

$= \underline{\quad} + 80 + \underline{\quad}$

$= \underline{\quad}$

5. $1,932 \div 6 = (\underline{\qquad}) + (120 \div 6) + (\underline{\qquad})$

$= 300 + \underline{\quad} + \underline{\quad}$

$= \underline{\quad}$

Independent Practice

Divide. Show the partial quotients. Use a strategy that works for you.

6. $830 ÷ 2 = $ ____

7. $675 ÷ 3 = $ ____

8. $2,072 ÷ 4 = $ ____

9. $1,968 ÷ 6 = $ ____

Match each of the following.

10. $(800 ÷ 4) + (28 ÷ 4)$ ____

a. $855 ÷ 5$

11. $(5 × 100) + (5 × 30) + (5 × 2) + 1$ ____

b. $661 ÷ 5$

12. $(500 ÷ 5) + (300 ÷ 5) + (55 ÷ 5)$ ____

c. $774 ÷ 4$

13. $(4 × 100) + (4 × 90) + (4 × 3) + 2$ ____

d. $828 ÷ 4$

Independent Practice

MP7 **14.** Look at exercises 10–13. Which of the quotients have a remainder? Explain how you know. Use the words *dividend*, *divisor*, and *addend* in your answer.

MP8 **15.** To divide 144 by 3, Pranav subtracts 3 from 144 until he has a difference of 0. Then he counts the number of times he subtracted 3. How can Pranav divide more efficiently? Use your method to find the quotient.

Solve the problems. You may use any method to divide.

MP4 **16.** Laura joins a walkathon to help raise money for a charity. The walkathon distance is 80 blocks. If you assume that 80 blocks is the same as 5 miles, how many blocks are in 1 mile?

Show your work.

Answer _____

MP2 **17.** Ben has 769 songs on his computer that he wants to save on CDs. He has 6 blank CDs and wants to save the same number of songs on each CD. How many songs can Ben save on each CD?

Show your work.

Answer _____

MP8 **18.** A 7-night vacation package costs $2,583 altogether. What is the cost for each night?

✏️ **Show your work.**

Answer _____

MP2 **19.** Yuna says that 9 times as many people are at the football game as at the basketball game. The ticket office sold 7,052 tickets to the football game. If Yuna is correct, about how many people are at the basketball game?

✏️ **Show your work.**

Answer _____

MP4 **20.** Carrie divides 4,981 by 4 and finds the correct quotient, 1,245 R1. Then she represents the problem with the equation below.

$4,981 \div 4 = (4,400 \div 4) + (400 \div 4) + (160 \div 4) + (20 \div 4) + 1$

Is Carrie's equation correct?

Answer _____

✏️ **Justify your answer using words, drawings, or numbers.**

MP3 **21.** Sean uses place value to find $5,672 \div 8$ with the method shown at the right. He says that he also uses the Distributive Property with this method. Do you agree with Sean?

$$\begin{array}{r} 709 \\ 8\overline{)5,672} \\ -56\downarrow\downarrow \\ \hline 072 \\ -72 \\ \hline 0 \end{array}$$

Answer _____

✏️ **Justify your answer using words, drawings, or numbers.**

1. What number is represented by the model below? Explain the value of each digit in the number.

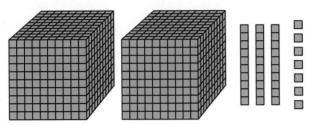

2. Draw a point on the number line to show 7,352. Then round 7,352 to the nearest hundred.

7,000   8,000

Answer To the nearest hundred, 7,352 rounds to _____.

Estimate. Then add or subtract.

3. 4,389
   +7,915

4. 112,075
   + 38,472

5. 581,227
   +378,978

6. 9,302
   −1,842

7. 53,891
   −48,089

8. 827,354
   −609,378

Circle the correct answer.

9. Which is the number name for 805,392?

   a. eight hundred thousand five, three nine two

   b. eight hundred fifty thousand, three hundred ninety-two

   c. eight hundred five thousand, three hundred ninety-two

   d. eight hundred five thousand, thirty-nine two

10. Which of these is a different number from the others?

   a. 30,000 + 7,000 + 40 + 5

   b. 3 ten thousands + 7 thousands + 4 tens + 5 ones

   c. 37,045

   d. thirty-seven thousand, four hundred five

11. Complete the area model at the right. Then multiply.

$43 \times 48 = $ _____

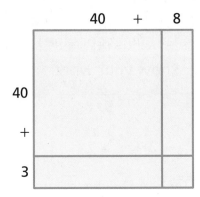

12. Use the Distributive Property and expanded form to multiply.

$4 \times 3{,}725 = 4 \times ($ _____ $+$ _____ $+$ _____ $+$ _____ $)$

$= ($ _____ $) + ($ _____ $) + ($ _____ $) + ($ _____ $)$

$= $ _____ $+$ _____ $+$ _____ $+$ _____

$= $ _____

Use division patterns with zeros to find each quotient.

13. $600 \div 6 = $ _____   **14.** $9{,}000 \div 3 = $ _____   **15.** $2{,}400 \div 8 = $ _____

16. For a report on the world's longest rivers, Justine finds that the Lena River in Russia is 2,734 miles long and the Amur River in northeast Asia is 2,744 miles long. Which river is longer? _____

Solve the problems.

MP4 **17.** The Obricki family is buying a computer for $765. To pay for it, they will make 9 monthly payments of the same amount. How much will one month's payment be?

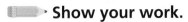 **Show your work.**

Answer _____

MP1 **18.** The ruby-throated hummingbird beats its wings 52 times per second. How many times does the hummingbird beat its wings per minute?

✎▸ **Show your work.**

Answer _____

MP3 **19.** Lennon found the sum of the following two numbers.

```
    1
  57,024
+ 38,983
  95,907
```

What is Lennon's mistake? What is the correct sum?

✎▸ **Justify your answer using words, drawings, or numbers.**

Answer _____

MP2 **20.** Charlotte and Finn round the same number to different places. Charlotte rounds to the nearest thousand and gets 0. Finn rounds to the nearest hundred and gets 400. If they both rounded correctly, what are the greatest and least possible numbers they could have rounded?

✎▸ **Justify your answer using words, drawings, or numbers.**

least number _____

greatest number _____

Progress Check

UNIT 3

Look at how the Common Core standards you have learned and will learn connect.

It is very important for you to understand the standards from the prior grade level so that you will be able to develop an understanding of fractions in this unit and be prepared for next year. To practice your skills, go to sadlierconnect.com.

GRADE 3	Before Unit 3	GRADE 4	After Unit 3	GRADE 5
I Can...		**Can I ?**		**I Will...**
3.NF.3 Find equivalent fractions	☐	**4.NF.1** Explain why fractions are equivalent	☐	
3.NF.3 Compare fractions with the same numerator or denominator	☐	**4.NF.2** Compare fractions with different numerators and denominators	☐	
3.NF.1 Understand the meaning of the numerator of a fraction Understand the meaning of the denominator of a fraction	☐ ☐	**4.NF.3** Add and subtract fractions and mixed numbers with like denominators Solve word problems involving addition and subtraction of fractions with like denominators	☐ ☐	**5.NF.1** Add and subtract fractions and mixed numbers **5.NF.2** Solve word problems involving addition and subtraction of fractions
3.NF.2 Represent unit fractions on a number line Represent fractions on a number line	☐ ☐ ☐	**4.NF.4** Multiply a unit fraction by a whole number Multiply a fraction by a whole number Solve word problems involving multiplication of fractions by whole numbers	☐ ☐ ☐	**5.NF.4** Multiply a fraction or whole number by a fraction **5.NF.6** Solve word problems involving multiplication of fractions and mixed numbers **5.NF.7** Divide with unit fractions
3.NF.3 Find equivalent fractions	☐	**4.NF.5** Add two fractions with denominators of 10 and 100	☐	**5.NBT.7** Add and subtract decimals to hundredths
	☐	**4.NF.6** Express as decimals, fractions with denominators of 10 or 100	☐	**5.NBT.3** Read and write decimals to thousandths
	☐	**4.NF.7** Compare two decimals to hundredths using >, =, or <	☐	**5.NBT.3** Compare two decimals to thousandths

HOME ◆ CONNECT...

odels can help your child to visualize and solve problems. Visuals model are effective tools that can help your child to better understand fraction concepts. A visual model of a fraction should show the number of equal parts as indicated by the denominator of the fraction.

numerator   number of equal parts you are talking about
denominator   total number of equal parts in the whole

Support your child by using visual models such as the following when solving problems involving fractions.

Sarah has a watercolor paint set with 8 colors. She uses $\frac{1}{8}$ of the colors first. Then she uses another $\frac{5}{8}$ of the colors. How much of the paint set is left?

1 paint set = $\frac{8}{8}$ The $\frac{1}{8}$ and $\frac{5}{8}$ $\frac{2}{8}$ left
Sarah uses

Activity: Coins values are fractional parts of a dollar. A dime is $\frac{1}{10}$ of a dollar and a penny is $\frac{1}{100}$ of a dollar. While you are shopping with your child, find prices that are less than one dollar. Ask your child to tell you how many dimes and/or pennies each price represents. Then ask your child to name each price as a fraction with either 10 or 100 as the denominator.

In this unit your child will:

- Understand and write equivalent fractions.

- Compare fractions.

- Add and subtract fractions with like denominators.

- Add and subtract mixed numbers with like denominators.

- Multiply fractions by whole numbers.

- Write and compare decimal fractions.

NOTE: All of these learning goals for your child are based on the Grade 4 Common Core State Standards for Mathematics.

Ways to Help Your Child

Manipulatives are objects that students can use to see relationships and solve problems. Virtual manipulatives exist digitally. They can also be a great tool to help your child visualize concepts. Libraries of virtual manipulatives are available online.

ONLINE
For more Home Connect activities, continue online at sadlierconnect.com

Focus on Number and Operations—Fractions

Essential Question:
How can writing fractions more than one way help you to compare and compute fractions?

14 Understand Equivalent Fractions

Essential Question:
Why can different fractions name the same amount?

4.NF.1

Words to Know:
unit fraction
fraction
equivalent fractions

Guided Instruction

In this lesson you will learn how to model and recognize equivalent fractions.

Understand: Model equivalent fractions

> Dina's mother says that one of her plants is $\frac{1}{3}$-foot taller than last year. Dina agrees, since she measured the plant growth as $\frac{4}{12}$ foot. Are $\frac{1}{3}$ and $\frac{4}{12}$ equivalent fractions?

You can model $\frac{1}{3}$ and $\frac{4}{12}$ to decide whether they are equivalent fractions. To compare fractions, they must have the same whole.
When a whole is partitioned, or divided, into equal parts, one of those parts is a unit fraction.
A number formed by putting together unit fractions is a fraction.
Fractions that describe the same amount are equivalent fractions.

Draw 2 same-size rectangles to represent the whole.

Divide one into 3 equal-size parts.
Color 1 part to represent $\frac{1}{3}$.

Divide the other into 12 equal-size parts.
Color 4 parts to represent $\frac{4}{12}$.

$\frac{1}{3}$ ← parts colored in → $\frac{4}{12}$
total parts

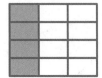

Compare the areas that you colored in. Both cover the same area of the rectangle, so the fractions they represent are equivalent.

➡ The models show that $\frac{1}{3}$ and $\frac{4}{12}$ are equivalent fractions.

Look at the area models above.

You can see that the whole with 12 equal parts has 4 times as many total parts as the whole with 3 equal parts.

$$\text{numerator} \longrightarrow \frac{1}{3} = \frac{4 \times 1}{4 \times 3} = \frac{4}{12} \longleftarrow \text{denominator}$$

You can see that to cover the same area as $\frac{1}{3}$ with the smaller twelfths unit fractions, you colored in 4 times as many twelfths as thirds.

When you multiply both the numerator and the denominator by the same number you get an equivalent fraction.

Guided Instruction

Connect: Recognize and identify equivalent fractions

> Jay, Will, and Nasir have cherries for a snack. Jay has $\frac{2}{5}$ pound, Will has $\frac{1}{3}$ pound, and Nasir has $\frac{4}{10}$ pound. Which friends have the same amount of cherries?

To find which amounts are the same, you can use a number line to decide whether any of the fractions are equivalent.

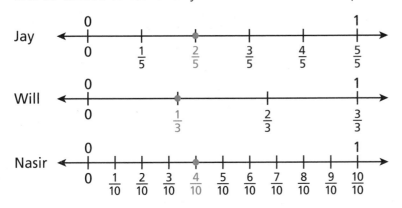

Look at the number line models.
The distance from 0 to 1 is the whole.

Use the model to identify the equivalent fractions.

$\frac{2}{5}$ and $\frac{4}{10}$ are the same distance from 0. They name the same point on the number line, so they are equivalent fractions.

$\frac{1}{3}$ is a different point on the number line. It is closer to 0 than both $\frac{2}{5}$ and $\frac{4}{10}$, so it is not equivalent to the other two fractions.

equivalent fractions
$\frac{2}{5} = \frac{4}{10}$
not equivalent fractions
$\frac{1}{3} \neq \frac{2}{5}, \frac{1}{3} \neq \frac{4}{10}$

▶ Jay and Nasir have the same amount of cherries, because $\frac{2}{5}$ and $\frac{4}{10}$ are equivalent fractions.

Use the number line to look at the relationship between unit fractions of $\frac{1}{5}$ and unit fractions of $\frac{1}{10}$. The whole has 2 times as many $\frac{1}{10}$ unit fractions as $\frac{1}{5}$ unit fractions, so 1 unit fraction of $\frac{1}{5}$ is equal to 2 unit fractions of $\frac{1}{10}$. So, $\frac{1}{5} = \frac{2}{10}$.

The two fractions are equivalent if you can multiply both the numerator and the denominator of one fraction by the same number to get the other fraction.

Look at $\frac{4}{5}$ and $\frac{8}{10}$. Recall that $10 = 2 \times 5$. Multiplying the numerator and denominator of $\frac{4}{5}$ by 2 you get $\frac{8}{10}$, so $\frac{4}{5}$ and $\frac{8}{10}$ are equivalent fractions.

$\frac{4}{5} = \frac{2 \times 4}{2 \times 5} = \frac{8}{10}$

Guided Practice

For exercises 1–4, use the model at the right.

1. Each model represents 1 whole.
   Color the models to show $\frac{2}{3}$ and $\frac{4}{6}$.

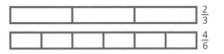

2. Write = or ≠ to tell if the fractions are equivalent.

   $\frac{2}{3}$ _____ $\frac{4}{6}$

3. Complete the sentences to explain the relationship.

   The fractions name the _____ area.

   One whole has _____ times as many $\frac{1}{6}$ unit fractions as $\frac{1}{3}$ unit fractions.

   Each $\frac{1}{3}$-unit fraction is equal to _____ $\frac{1}{6}$-unit fractions.

4. Write the number you can use to show that $\frac{2}{3}$ and $\frac{4}{6}$ are equivalent.

   $\frac{2}{3} = \frac{\times 2}{\times 3} = -$

For exercises 5–8, use the number lines at the right.

5. Place points on the number lines to show $\frac{2}{5}$ and $\frac{3}{8}$.

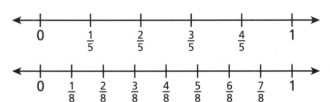

6. Write = or ≠ to tell whether the fractions are equivalent.

   $\frac{2}{5}$ _____ $\frac{3}{8}$

7. Complete the sentences.

   The fractions name _____ points on the number line.

   There is no whole number of _____ that equal $\frac{2}{5}$.

   There is no whole number of _____ that equal $\frac{3}{8}$.

8. Is there a whole number, n, that you can use to find an equivalent fraction?

   $\frac{2}{5} = \frac{n \times 2}{n \times 5} = \frac{3}{8}$

   Try some whole numbers.

   Answer _____

Model the fractions. Write = or ≠. If the fractions are equivalent, write the number you can use to show they are equivalent.

9. $\dfrac{2}{3}$ ——— $\dfrac{8}{12}$

$$\dfrac{2}{3} = \dfrac{\times\,2}{\times\,3} = \dfrac{8}{12}$$

10. $\dfrac{3}{4}$ ——— $\dfrac{2}{5}$

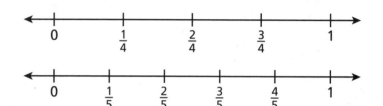

$$\dfrac{2}{5} = \dfrac{\times\,2}{\times\,3} = \dfrac{3}{4}$$

11. $\dfrac{1}{4}$ ——— $\dfrac{2}{6}$

$$\dfrac{1}{4} = \dfrac{\times\,1}{\times\,4} = \dfrac{2}{6}$$

 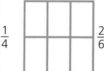

Write = or ≠. If the fractions are equivalent, write the number you can use to show they are equivalent. You can use models to help.

12. $\dfrac{1}{2}$ ——— $\dfrac{3}{6}$

$$\dfrac{1}{2} = \dfrac{\times\,1}{\times\,2} = \dfrac{3}{6}$$

13. $\dfrac{5}{4}$ ——— $\dfrac{10}{8}$

$$\dfrac{5}{4} = \dfrac{\times}{\times} = \dfrac{10}{8}$$

 **Think • Pair • Share**

MP3 **14.** Pick a pair of fractions from the previous exercises that are not equivalent. Explain why the fractions are not equivalent.

Independent Practice

Use the models to show the fractions. Write = or ≠. If the fractions are equivalent, write the number you can use to show they are equivalent.

1. $\frac{1}{2}$ _____ $\frac{4}{8}$

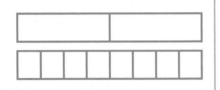

$\frac{1}{2} = \frac{\times\,1}{\times\,2} = \frac{4}{8}$

2. $\frac{2}{4}$ _____ $\frac{4}{10}$

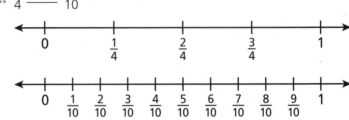

$\frac{2}{4} = \frac{\times\,2}{\times\,4} = \frac{4}{10}$

3. $\frac{1}{3}$ _____ $\frac{2}{6}$

$\frac{1}{3} = \frac{\times\,1}{\times\,3} = \frac{2}{6}$

4. $\frac{4}{5}$ _____ $\frac{9}{10}$

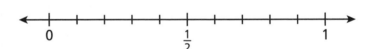

$\frac{4}{5} = \frac{\times\,4}{\times\,5} = \frac{9}{10}$

5. $\frac{8}{6}$ _____ $\frac{16}{12}$

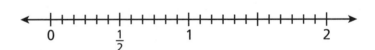

$\frac{8}{6} = \frac{\times\,8}{\times\,6} = \frac{16}{12}$

Write = or ≠. If the fractions are equivalent, write the number you can use to show they are equivalent. You can use models to help.

6. $\frac{2}{4}$ _____ $\frac{2}{5}$

$\frac{2}{4} = \frac{\times\,2}{\times\,4} = \frac{2}{5}$

7. $\frac{2}{10}$ _____ $\frac{1}{5}$

$\frac{1}{5} = \frac{\times\,1}{\times\,5} = \frac{2}{10}$

8. $\frac{1}{4}$ _____ $\frac{3}{12}$

$\frac{1}{4} = \frac{\times}{\times} = \frac{}{}$

Independent Practice

Write = or ≠. If the fractions are equivalent, write the number you can use to show they are equivalent. You can use models to help.

9. $\dfrac{2}{6}$ ___ $\dfrac{4}{5}$

10. $\dfrac{6}{5}$ ___ $\dfrac{12}{10}$

11. $\dfrac{5}{10}$ ___ $\dfrac{5}{12}$

$\dfrac{2}{6} = \dfrac{\times 2}{\times 6} = \dfrac{4}{5}$

$\dfrac{6}{5} = \dfrac{\times 6}{\times 5} = \dfrac{12}{10}$

$\dfrac{5}{10} = \dfrac{\times 5}{\times 10} = \dfrac{5}{12}$

For exercises 12–14, use the model. Each model represents 1 whole.

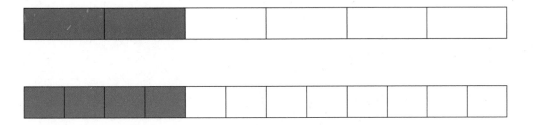

12. Which pair of equivalent fractions is shown in the model?

   a. $\dfrac{2}{4}$ and $\dfrac{1}{2}$ **b.** $\dfrac{2}{6}$ and $\dfrac{4}{12}$

   c. $\dfrac{2}{4}$ and $\dfrac{4}{8}$ **d.** $\dfrac{6}{2}$ and $\dfrac{12}{2}$

13. Which sentence does NOT help to explain why the two fractions shown are equivalent?

   a. The fractions represent the same area.

   b. The fractions would share the same point on the number line.

   c. There are two unit fractions of $\dfrac{1}{12}$ for each unit fraction of $\dfrac{1}{6}$.

   d. One whole has more equal parts than the other.

14. Which of the fractions below are equivalent to the fractions shown in the model?

   a. $\dfrac{1}{3}$ **b.** $\dfrac{2}{4}$

   c. $\dfrac{2}{6}$ **d.** $\dfrac{1}{2}$

Independent Practice

MP2 **15.** Zach needs $\frac{3}{4}$ cup of sugar for a recipe. He does not have a $\frac{1}{4}$-cup measuring cup, so he fills a different measuring cup more times. What must be true about the size of the measuring cup Zach uses, compared to a $\frac{1}{4}$-cup? Explain.

MP6 **16.** The number line shows two equivalent fractions, $\frac{1}{2}$ and $\frac{5}{10}$.

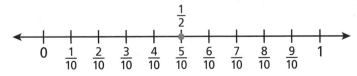

What is the relationship between the unit fractions, $\frac{1}{2}$ and $\frac{1}{10}$? Describe both the number and size of the parts.

Solve the problems.

MP7 **17.** The students have $\frac{5}{6}$ hour for recess. Vinh says this is the same as $\frac{10}{12}$ hour. Is Vinh's thinking correct? Write = or ≠.

✏️ **Show your work.**

$$\frac{5}{6} \quad\underline{\quad\quad}\quad \frac{10}{12}$$

Answer _____

MP4 **18.** An egg carton holds 12 eggs. Lucy uses 5 of the eggs and says there is $\frac{2}{3}$ of a carton left. Is Lucy's thinking correct?

✏️ **Show your work.**

Answer _____

Independent Practice

MP1 **19.** One lap around the track at Dennis's school is $\frac{1}{8}$ mile. When Dennis runs, he stops to rest only when he has completed one or more $\frac{1}{4}$-mile distances. Would Dennis stop to rest when he reaches $\frac{14}{8}$ miles?

Answer _____

✏ **Justify your answer using words, drawings, or numbers.**

MP7 **20.** Tracy says that $\frac{30}{100}$ must be a greater amount than $\frac{3}{10}$, since 30 is greater than 3. Do you agree? You can use the model of 100 below to justify your answer.

Answer _____

✏ **Justify your answer using words, drawings, or numbers.**

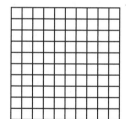

MP3 **21.** Holly says that you cannot write equivalent fractions that have 3 and 5 as denominators. Susan says that $\frac{6}{3}$ and $\frac{10}{5}$ are equivalent fractions because they both equal 2 wholes. Whose reasoning is correct?

✏ **Show your work.**

Answer _____

Essential Question:
How can you multiply to write equivalent fractions?

4.NF.1

Guided Instruction

In this lesson you will learn how to write equivalent fractions.

Understand: Multiply to write equivalent fractions

> An apple bread recipe calls for $\frac{3}{4}$ cup of apple sauce. Cheng only has an $\frac{1}{8}$-cup measuring cup. How many times does Cheng need to fill the $\frac{1}{8}$ cup to measure $\frac{3}{4}$ cup?

To answer this question, find an equivalent fraction with a denominator of 8.

Draw an area model.
$\frac{3}{4}$ is 3 of 4 equal parts, or fourths.
To have a denominator of 8, you need to partition, or divide, the whole into 8 equal parts, or eighths.

$\frac{3}{4}$

Draw lines in the model to make 8 equal parts.
There are 2 eighths for each of the 1 fourths.
The 3 blue fourths equal 6 eighths.

$\frac{6}{8}$

Since $\frac{3}{4}$ and $\frac{6}{8}$ cover the same area, they are equivalent.

➡ Cheng needs to fill the $\frac{1}{8}$ cup 6 times to measure $\frac{3}{4}$ cup.

Another way to write an equivalent fraction is to use multiplication.

Since $8 = 2 \times 4$, the equivalent fraction has 2 times the total number of equal parts in $\frac{3}{4}$. $\longrightarrow \quad \frac{3}{4} = \frac{3}{2 \times 4} = \frac{}{8}$

There are 2 eighths for each fourth.
Multiply 3, the number of fourths, by 2 to find the number of eighths in the equivalent fraction. $\longrightarrow \quad \frac{3}{4} = \frac{2 \times 3}{2 \times 4} = \frac{6}{8}$

✏ In the area model above, suppose you made 8 equal parts in a different way. Explain why the model will still show that $\frac{3}{4} = \frac{6}{8}$.

Understand: Divide to write fractions

Grace wants to see 4 of the 10 movies at the theater. She tells Zena she wants to see $\frac{4}{10}$ of the movies. Zena wants to see the same movies, but she wants to use a fraction with a smaller denominator to describe the number of movies. How can Zena do this?

You can model $\frac{4}{10}$ to see whether you can find a smaller denominator.

Draw a number line with tenths. Place a point to show $\frac{4}{10}$.

Think: $10 \div 2 = 5$. Using the same whole unit, draw another number line with fifths.

You can see that $\frac{4}{10}$ and $\frac{2}{5}$ are at the same point on the number line. It is possible to write an equivalent fraction for $\frac{4}{10}$ that has a smaller denominator.

➡ Zena can use the number lines to write $\frac{2}{5}$ to show the number of movies she wants to see.

Another way to write an equivalent fraction is to use division.

Since $5 = 10 \div 2$, the number of equal parts in the fraction equivalent to $\frac{4}{10}$ is 5. You start by dividing the denominator 10 by 2.

$$\frac{4}{10} = \frac{4}{10 \div 2} = \frac{4}{5}$$

There is 1 fifth for every 2 tenths. You find the numerator of the equivalent fraction, which represents the number of fifths, by dividing the numerator 4 by 2. By dividing the numerator and the denominator by the same number, you see that $\frac{4}{10} = \frac{2}{5}$.

$$\frac{4}{10} = \frac{4 \div 2}{10 \div 2} = \frac{2}{5}$$

✏ Compare writing equivalent fractions by multiplying and by dividing.

Guided Instruction

Connect: What you know about equivalent fractions

Cheng wants to give away $\frac{4}{6}$ of his apple bread. He can give bigger pieces to fewer people or smaller pieces to more people. What equivalent fractions can represent these two ways for Cheng to share the bread?

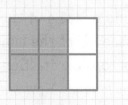

To find the answer, use models or multiply or divide both the numerator and the denominator by the same number.

If Cheng gives away $\frac{4}{6}$ of the bread which he cut into 6 pieces, he will give pieces of bread to 4 people.

Suppose he decides to give bread to fewer people. He can divide 6 by 2 and cut the bread into only 3 pieces. To find the equivalent fraction, divide the numerator and the denominator of $\frac{4}{6}$ by 2.

$$\frac{4}{6} = \frac{4 \div 2}{6 \div 2} = \frac{2}{3}$$

If Cheng gives away the same amount of bread but cuts it into 3 pieces, he will give pieces of bread to 2 people.

Suppose he decides to give bread to more people. He can multiply 6 by 2 and cut the bread into 12 pieces. To find the equivalent fraction, multiply the numerator and the denominator of $\frac{4}{6}$ by 2.

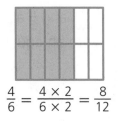

$$\frac{4}{6} = \frac{4 \times 2}{6 \times 2} = \frac{8}{12}$$

If Cheng gives away the same amount of bread but cuts it into 12 pieces, he will give pieces of bread to 8 people.

➡ Equivalent fractions representing two other ways for Cheng to share the apple bread are $\frac{2}{3}$ and $\frac{8}{12}$.

✏ Why is it important to use the same operation with the same number on both the numerator and the denominator when you want to find an equivalent fraction?

Remember!

You must multiply or divide both the numerator and the denominator by the same number.

Guided Practice

Draw on the area model to make an equivalent fraction with the given denominator. Then show what number to use to write the equivalent fraction.

1. $\frac{1}{3} = \frac{\times 1}{\times 3} = \frac{}{6}$

2. $\frac{3}{6} = \frac{\times 3}{\times 6} = \frac{}{12}$

3. $\frac{2}{4} = \frac{2 \div}{4 \div} = \frac{}{2}$

4. $\frac{2}{8} = \frac{2 \div}{8 \div} = \frac{}{4}$

For exercises 5–8, use the number line.

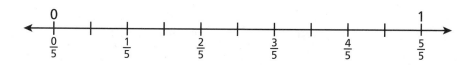

5. Write an equivalent fraction for $\frac{3}{5}$.

   $\frac{3}{5} = \frac{}{10}$

6. Label the number line to show the fraction you wrote for exercise 5.

7. Write an equivalent fraction for $\frac{4}{10}$.

   $\frac{4}{10} = \frac{}{5}$

8. Circle any equivalent fractions.

   $\frac{1}{5}$ $\frac{1}{10}$ $\frac{2}{5}$ $\frac{2}{10}$

⛹ Think • Pair • Share

MP6 9. You used a number line to write an equivalent fraction for exercise 7. Explain how to use two other methods to write the equivalent fraction.

Independent Practice

Draw on the model to make an equivalent fraction with the given denominator. For 1 and 2, show what number to use to write the equivalent fraction. For 3 and 4, complete the equation.

1.

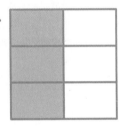

$$\frac{1}{3} = \frac{\times 1}{\times 3} = \frac{}{12}$$

2.

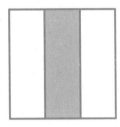

$$\frac{2}{5} = \frac{\times 2}{\times 5} = \frac{}{15}$$

3.

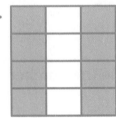

$$\frac{3}{6} = \frac{}{2}$$

4.

$$\frac{8}{12} = \frac{}{3}$$

Write an equivalent fraction. You can use the number line to help.

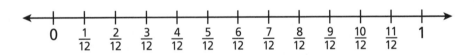

5. $\dfrac{6}{12} = -$

6. $\dfrac{8}{12} = -$

7. $\dfrac{5}{6} = \dfrac{}{12}$

8. $\dfrac{2}{6} = \dfrac{4}{}$

9. One point on the number line shows that three fractions are equivalent. What are the three equivalent fractions?

Independent Practice

Model the fraction. Then write an equivalent fraction.

10.  $\dfrac{4}{8} = -$

11.  $\dfrac{6}{8} = -$

12.  $\dfrac{2}{12} = -$

13.  $\dfrac{2}{4} = -$

14.  $\dfrac{4}{6} = -$

15. 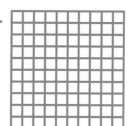 $\dfrac{70}{100} = \underline{\quad}$

Show how to write an equivalent fraction. You can draw models to help.

16. $\dfrac{1}{5} = \underline{\quad\quad} = -$ 17. $\dfrac{6}{10} = \underline{\quad\quad} = -$ 18. $\dfrac{5}{4} = \underline{\quad\quad} = -$

Write an equivalent fraction.

19. $\dfrac{10}{12} = -$ 20. $\dfrac{3}{12} = -$ 21. $\dfrac{8}{10} = -$

22. $\dfrac{2}{5} = \underline{\quad}$ 23. $\dfrac{9}{12} = -$ 24. $\dfrac{4}{10} = -$

25. $\dfrac{2}{6} = -$ 26. $\dfrac{2}{3} = -$ 27. $\dfrac{5}{6} = \underline{\quad}$

Independent Practice

MP7 **28.** Stan says that when you multiply to get an equivalent fraction, the equivalent fraction is greater than the other fraction. Explain the error in Stan's thinking.

MP3 **29.** Dylan says that when you rename $\frac{5}{10}$ as $\frac{1}{2}$, you change the situation you are working with. Do you agree? Explain your thinking.

For exercises 30 and 31, use the table.

MP6 **30.** What fraction of the total number of goals did Kim score?

Show your work.

Soccer Goals Scored	
Player	Number of Goals
Angie	1
Kim	4
Mateo	2
Pete	3
Ricky	0
Sabrina	2

Answer _____

MP3 **31.** Sabrina scored $\frac{1}{6}$ of the total goals. Pete scored $\frac{1}{4}$ of the total goals. Explain why these two fractions do not have the same denominator even though they describe fractions of the same whole.

Show your work.

Answer _____

Independent Practice

Solve the problems.

MP4 **32.** Curtis draws a model of the fraction $\frac{5}{6}$. Then he divides each equal part into 2 smaller equal parts to help him write an equivalent fraction for $\frac{5}{6}$. What is the equivalent fraction?

➤ **Show your work.**

Answer _____

MP2 **33.** Karl says that when you write an equivalent fraction, the size of each equal part in the equivalent fraction will always be greater than in the original fraction. Meg says this is not true, since you can multiply the numerator and denominator in a fraction to write an equivalent fraction. Whose reasoning is correct?

Answer _____

➤ **Justify your answer using words, drawings, or numbers.**

MP6 **34.** Jack and Louise have equal-size gardens. Jack lays out his garden in 6 spaces and plants melons in 2 spaces. Louise lays out her garden in 12 spaces and plants melons in 4 spaces. Is the fraction of the garden planted with melons the same for both gardens?

Answer _____

➤ **Justify your answer using words, drawings, or numbers.**

16 Compare Two Fractions

Essential Question:
How can you use equivalent fractions to compare fractions?
4.NF.2

Words to Know:
 benchmark

Guided Instruction

In this lesson you will learn how to compare fractions that have different numerators and different denominators.

Understand: **Using benchmarks to make comparisons**

Clint and Jason are meeting at the park. Clint is $\frac{5}{8}$ mile away, and Jason is $\frac{9}{10}$ mile away. If the boys ride their bicycles at the same speed, who will reach the park first?

A benchmark is an amount that you know and can use to compare or estimate other amounts.

To compare $\frac{5}{8}$ and $\frac{9}{10}$, you can use $\frac{1}{2}$ and 1 as benchmarks.

Look at the models. Compare the fractions to $\frac{1}{2}$ and 1.

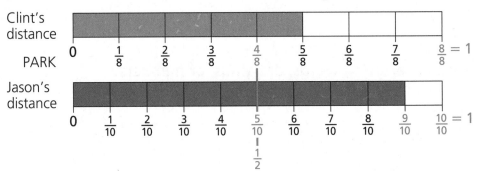

Notice that $\frac{4}{8} = \frac{1}{2}$, and $\frac{5}{8}$ is greater than $\frac{4}{8}$ by 1 eighth.

Clint's distance: $\frac{5}{8} = \frac{1}{2} + \frac{1}{8}$. So $\frac{5}{8}$ is much closer to $\frac{1}{2}$ than $\frac{8}{8}$, or 1.

Notice that $\frac{10}{10} = 1$, and $\frac{9}{10}$ is less than 1 by 1 tenth.

Jason's distance: $\frac{9}{10} = \frac{10}{10} - \frac{1}{10}$. So $\frac{9}{10}$ is much closer to 1 than to $\frac{1}{2}$.

$\frac{9}{10}$ is closer to 1 on the number line than $\frac{5}{8}$ is, so $\frac{9}{10} > \frac{5}{8}$.

Remember!
When fractions have the same denominator, compare the numerators to see which is greater.

➡ Jason is farther from the park, so Clint will reach the park first.

You can compare the fractions in this problem because both distances are fractions of a mile. They refer to the same whole amount, 1 mile.

✏ Suppose that Clint is $\frac{7}{8}$ mile away and Jason is $\frac{9}{10}$ mile away and both travel at the same speed. Who will reach the park first?

Understand: Using equivalent fractions to make comparisons

> Allison has to buy clay for her art class. She is choosing between two pieces of clay. One piece is $\frac{2}{3}$ pound, and the other piece is $\frac{3}{4}$ pound. The pieces feel about the same weight. Which piece is heavier?

To decide which piece is heavier, use equivalent fractions to find the greater fraction. You can compare $\frac{2}{3}$ and $\frac{3}{4}$ because they are parts of the same whole, 1 pound.

One way to compare the fractions is to write equivalent fractions with the same denominator. Use the product of the two denominators as the denominator of the equivalent fractions: $\frac{2}{3}$ and $\frac{3}{4}$; $3 \times 4 = 12$

Write equivalent fractions for $\frac{2}{3}$ and $\frac{3}{4}$ with 12 as the denominator.

$$\frac{2}{3} = \frac{2 \times 4}{3 \times 4} = \frac{8}{12} \qquad\qquad \frac{3}{4} = \frac{3 \times 3}{4 \times 3} = \frac{9}{12}$$

Compare the numerators to compare the fractions.

$$\frac{8}{12} < \frac{9}{12}, \text{ so } \frac{2}{3} < \frac{3}{4} \text{ and } \frac{3}{4} > \frac{2}{3}$$

➡ The $\frac{3}{4}$ pound piece of clay is heavier.

Another way to compare the fractions is to write equivalent fractions with the same numerator. Use the product of the numerators as the numerator of the equivalent fractions: $\frac{2}{3}$ and $\frac{3}{4}$; $2 \times 3 = 6$.

Write equivalent fractions for $\frac{2}{3}$ and $\frac{3}{4}$ with 6 as the numerator.

$$\frac{2}{3} = \frac{2 \times 3}{3 \times 3} = \frac{6}{9} \qquad\qquad \frac{3}{4} = \frac{3 \times 2}{4 \times 2} = \frac{6}{8}$$

To compare the fractions, compare the denominators. Recall that unit fractions of $\frac{1}{9}$ are smaller than unit fractions of $\frac{1}{8}$.

$$\frac{1}{9} < \frac{1}{8}, \text{ so } \frac{6}{9} < \frac{6}{8}. \text{ This means } \frac{2}{3} < \frac{3}{4} \text{ and } \frac{3}{4} > \frac{2}{3}.$$

Guided Instruction

Connect: Benchmarks and equivalent fractions

> Kevin needs to buy poster board before the stores close. The drugstore closes in $\frac{3}{4}$ hour. The office supply store closes in $\frac{8}{12}$ hour. Which store is open longer?

You can use models or the same denominator to compare the fractions $\frac{3}{4}$ and $\frac{8}{12}$.

Notice that $12 = 3 \times 4$. You can use 12 as the denominator for the fractions. This means you only need to find one equivalent fraction.

Method 1 Compare with Models
Draw models of the fractions.

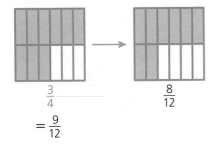

$$\frac{3}{4}$$
$$= \frac{9}{12}$$

$$\frac{8}{12}$$

$\frac{9}{12}$ covers more area than $\frac{8}{12}$.

This means $\frac{9}{12} > \frac{8}{12}$, so $\frac{3}{4} > \frac{8}{12}$.

Method 2 Compare with the Same Denominator
Use 12 as the denominator to compare $\frac{3}{4}$ and $\frac{8}{12}$.
Write an equivalent fraction for $\frac{3}{4}$.

$$\frac{3}{4} = \frac{3 \times 3}{3 \times 4} = \frac{9}{12}$$

$$\frac{9}{12} > \frac{8}{12}, \text{ so } \frac{3}{4} > \frac{8}{12}.$$

➡ The drugstore is open a little longer than the office supply store.

✏ Why can you compare the two fractions to compare the amounts of time?

Guided Practice

For exercises 1–3, use the models.

1. Label the model to show:
   - $\frac{6}{10}$ and $\frac{4}{6}$
   - equivalent fractions for $\frac{1}{2}$
   - equivalent fractions for 1
   - the unit from $\frac{1}{2}$ to $\frac{6}{10}$
   - the unit from $\frac{1}{2}$ to $\frac{4}{6}$

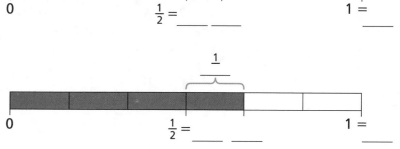

$0 \qquad\qquad \frac{1}{2} = \underline{\quad}\ \underline{\quad} \qquad 1 = \underline{\quad}$

$0 \qquad\qquad \frac{1}{2} = \underline{\quad}\ \underline{\quad} \qquad 1 = \underline{\quad}$

2. Circle the fraction that is farther from $\frac{1}{2}$.

   $\frac{6}{10} \qquad \frac{4}{6}$

3. Write <, =, or > to compare the fractions.

   $\frac{6}{10} \underline{\quad} \frac{4}{6}$

Use the models to compare the fractions. Label the models to show any benchmarks you use. Then write >, =, or <.

4. $\frac{2}{6} \underline{\quad} \frac{3}{12}$

5. $\frac{4}{10} \underline{\quad} \frac{5}{8}$

Use equivalent fractions to compare.

6. Use the same numerator to compare $\frac{1}{4}$ and $\frac{2}{10}$.

   $\frac{1}{4} = \frac{\times 1}{\times 4} = \frac{}{8} \qquad \frac{2}{10} = \frac{\times 2}{\times 10} = \frac{}{}$

   $\frac{}{\underline{\quad}} \underline{\quad} \frac{}{}$, so $\frac{1}{4} \underline{\quad} \frac{2}{10}$

7. Use the same denominator to compare $\frac{9}{12}$ and $\frac{4}{5}$.

   $\frac{9}{12} = \frac{\times 9}{\times 12} = \frac{45}{} \qquad \frac{4}{5} = \frac{\times 4}{\times 5} = \frac{48}{}$

   $\frac{45}{\underline{\quad}} \underline{\quad} \frac{48}{}$, so $\frac{9}{12} \underline{\quad} \frac{4}{5}$

 **Think ● Pair ● Share**

MP8 8. Which pair of fractions from exercises 1–7 could you easily compare using a different method? Discuss your choice with a partner and explain your reasoning below.

Independent Practice

Write >, =, or < to compare each fraction to $\frac{1}{2}$.

1. $\frac{8}{10}$ _____ $\frac{1}{2}$

2. $\frac{6}{12}$ _____ $\frac{1}{2}$

3. $\frac{45}{100}$ _____ $\frac{1}{2}$

4. $\frac{1}{1}$ _____ $\frac{1}{2}$

Color or label the models to show the fractions and any benchmarks you use. Then write >, =, or < to compare.

5. $\frac{6}{8}$ _____ $\frac{3}{4}$

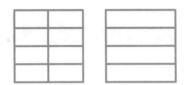

6. $\frac{1}{4}$ _____ $\frac{2}{6}$

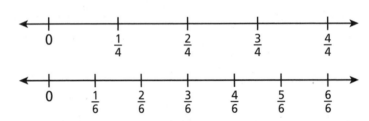

7. $\frac{9}{12}$ _____ $\frac{7}{10}$

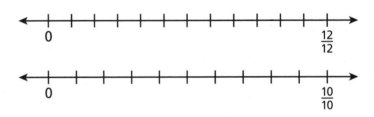

Draw a model to show the fractions. Then write >, =, or < to compare.

8. $\frac{1}{6}$ _____ $\frac{2}{5}$

9. $\frac{2}{8}$ _____ $\frac{3}{4}$

Independent Practice

Write equivalent fractions with the same denominator or numerator to compare the fractions. Show your work.

10. Compare $\frac{5}{6}$ and $\frac{7}{12}$.

$$\frac{5}{6} = \frac{\times 5}{\times 6} = \underline{}$$

$\underline{}$ $\frac{7}{12}$ $\frac{5}{6}$ $\underline{}$ $\frac{7}{12}$

11. Compare $\frac{3}{8}$ and $\frac{1}{3}$.

$\frac{3}{8}$ $\underline{}$ $\frac{1}{3}$

12. Compare $\frac{11}{12}$ and $\frac{3}{4}$.

$\frac{11}{12}$ $\underline{}$ $\frac{3}{4}$

13. Compare $\frac{5}{4}$ and $\frac{7}{5}$.

$\frac{5}{4}$ $\underline{}$ $\frac{7}{5}$

Write >, =, or < to compare the fractions. You can use models to help.

14. $\frac{2}{4}$ $\underline{}$ $\frac{5}{10}$

15. $\frac{3}{5}$ $\underline{}$ $\frac{8}{10}$

16. $\frac{6}{8}$ $\underline{}$ $\frac{4}{6}$

17. $\frac{4}{12}$ $\underline{}$ $\frac{2}{5}$

18. $\frac{2}{2}$ $\underline{}$ $\frac{1}{3}$

19. $\frac{9}{12}$ $\underline{}$ $\frac{9}{8}$

For exercises 20 and 21, circle the correct answer.

20. Tricia has $\frac{5}{6}$ hour before she has to go to bed. How much time can she spend reading before she goes to bed?

a. $\frac{3}{4}$ hour

b. $\frac{7}{8}$ hour

c. $\frac{9}{10}$ hour

d. $\frac{11}{12}$ hour

21. Adam needs red balloons for a party. In a package of long balloons, $\frac{1}{3}$ of the balloons are red. In a package of jumbo balloons, $\frac{2}{5}$ of the balloons are red and $\frac{3}{5}$ are white. Which of these statements is true?

a. The package of jumbo balloons has more red balloons.

b. The package of long balloons has more red balloons.

c. The fractions cannot be compared without knowing the number of balloons in each package.

d. The total number of red balloons is less than the number of white jumbo balloons.

Independent Practice

MP6 **22.** Kelly uses 30 as a denominator for equivalent fractions to compare $\frac{3}{10}$ and $\frac{1}{3}$. Is this easier than using 3 as a numerator for equivalent fractions to compare $\frac{3}{10}$ and $\frac{1}{3}$? Explain.

MP1 **23.** When can writing equivalent fractions be more helpful for comparing fractions than visual models? Give one example.

Solve the problems.

MP2 **24.** In art class, Amber uses $\frac{7}{12}$ pound of modeling clay and Cole uses $\frac{5}{8}$ pound. Who uses more clay, Amber or Cole?

 Show your work.

Answer _____

MP7 **25.** Two cereal boxes are the same size. The box of corn flakes is $\frac{11}{12}$ full. The box of wheat puffs is $\frac{9}{10}$ full. Which cereal box has more cereal?

 Show your work.

Answer _____

Independent Practice

MP6 **26.** Jeff has $\frac{200}{100}$ dollars in pennies, and Michelle has $\frac{25}{10}$ dollars in dimes. Who has more money, Jeff or Michelle?

➤ **Show your work.**

Answer _____

MP3 **27.** Sam says that you cannot use $\frac{1}{2}$ as a benchmark when you are comparing fractions with odd denominators, like $\frac{2}{5}$. Do you agree? Use this example to support your answer.

Answer _____

➤ **Justify your answer using words, drawings, or numbers.**

MP1 **28.** Donna and her brother are raking leaves. Donna rakes $\frac{1}{4}$ of her yard and her brother rakes $\frac{1}{2}$ of her neighbor's yard. Donna's brother says he has raked more than Donna, because $\frac{1}{2} > \frac{1}{4}$. Is this always true?

Answer _____

➤ **Justify your answer using words, drawings, or numbers.**

Add and Subtract Fractions with Like Denominators

Essential Question:
What happens when you find a sum or difference of fractions?

4.NF.3a

Words to Know:
like denominators

Guided Instruction

In this lesson you will learn why you can add and subtract fractions of the same whole.

Understand: **Addition of fractions with like denominators**

Tanya cuts a pan of brownies into 12 equal pieces. She puts 1 piece on a plate for her mother. Then she adds 1 piece for herself, and 1 piece for her sister. What fraction of the brownies does Tanya put on the plate?

To find the fraction of the brownies Tanya put on the pan, think of each brownie as one twelfth, or $\frac{1}{12}$, of the whole pan.

Write the number of twelfths and a fraction for each number of twelfths. Then add the numerators to find the total number of twelfths.

Remember!
The numerator is the number of equal parts in a fraction.

Mother		Tanya		Sister		Total on Plate
1 twelfth	+	1 twelfth	+	1 twelfth	=	3 twelfths
$\frac{1}{12}$	+	$\frac{1}{12}$	+	$\frac{1}{12}$	=	$\frac{3}{12}$

➡ Tanya puts $\frac{3}{12}$ of the brownies on the plate.

In this problem, the addends and the sum have like denominators. This means that the denominators are alike or the same. Fractions with like denominators are made up by putting together the same unit fractions.

✏ Write an equation to show Tanya putting 1 more brownie on the plate.

Understand: Adding unit fractions to add fractions

> Tanya and her sister drink milk with their brownies. Tanya drinks $\frac{3}{4}$ pint of milk. Her sister drinks $\frac{2}{4}$ pint of milk. How much milk do Tania and her sister drink in all?

To find the amount of milk Tania and her sister drink, add the fractions $\frac{3}{4}$ and $\frac{2}{4}$.

$$\frac{3}{4} + \frac{2}{4} = \overbrace{\frac{1}{4} + \frac{1}{4} + \frac{1}{4}}^{\frac{3}{4}} + \overbrace{\frac{1}{4} + \frac{1}{4}}^{\frac{2}{4}}$$ Decompose the fractions into unit fractions.

$$= \frac{1 + 1 + 1 + 1 + 1}{4}$$ Add the numerators.

$$= \frac{5}{4}$$ Notice that 5 is the sum of 3 + 2.

➡ Tania and her sister drink $\frac{5}{4}$ pints of milk in all.

Understand: Subtraction of fractions with like denominators

> Tanya has put a total of $\frac{4}{12}$ of the pan of brownies on a plate. What fraction of the brownies does Tanya leave in the pan?

A whole pan of brownies is $\frac{12}{12}$. Subtract $\frac{4}{12}$ from $\frac{12}{12}$ to find the number of twelfths left in the pan.

When fractions have like denominators, you can subtract the numerators to find the difference.

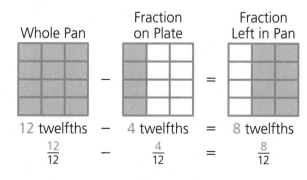

Whole Pan		Fraction on Plate		Fraction Left in Pan
12 twelfths	−	4 twelfths	=	8 twelfths
$\frac{12}{12}$	−	$\frac{4}{12}$	=	$\frac{8}{12}$

➡ Tanya leaves $\frac{8}{12}$ of the brownies in the pan.

Guided Instruction

Connect: Add and subtract fractions with the same denominator

> Gavin has a wood board that is $\frac{7}{8}$ yard long. If he uses only $\frac{5}{8}$ yard for his project, how much wood does Gavin have left over?

To find the length of wood left over, subtract $\frac{5}{8}$ from $\frac{7}{8}$. You can use number lines and fraction bars as models.

Identify the whole: 1 yard. Show the board length on the models.

The blue point locates $\frac{7}{8}$.

The blue bar shows $\frac{7}{8}$.

Find the number of unit fractions in the amount to subtract:

$$\frac{5}{8} = \frac{1}{8} + \frac{1}{8} + \frac{1}{8} + \frac{1}{8} + \frac{1}{8}$$

Use the number line to subtract.
Count back 5 unit fractions of $\frac{1}{8}$.

Use the fraction bar to subtract.
Cross out 5 unit fractions of $\frac{1}{8}$.

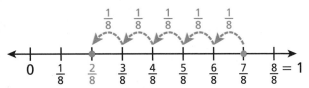

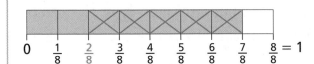

The red point locates $\frac{2}{8}$, the amount left over. The difference is $\frac{2}{8}$. $\frac{7}{8} - \frac{5}{8} = \frac{2}{8}$

The red fraction $\frac{2}{8}$ shows the amount left over.

Add to check the difference, just like with whole numbers. Start at $\frac{5}{8}$.

From $\frac{5}{8}$, count up 2 unit fractions of $\frac{1}{8}$.

From $\frac{5}{8}$, add on 2 unit fractions of $\frac{1}{8}$.

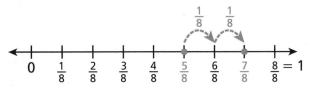

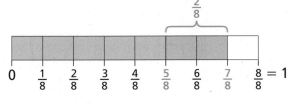

The sum is $\frac{7}{8}$.

The sum is $\frac{7}{8}$.

➡ Gavin has $\frac{2}{8}$ yard of wood left over.

Complete the equation to represent the problem. Add or subtract to solve.

1.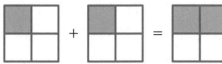

$$\frac{}{4} + \frac{}{4} = \frac{}{}$$

1 fourth + 1 fourth = _____ fourths

2.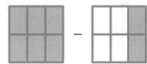

$$\frac{}{6} - \frac{}{6} = \frac{}{}$$

6 sixths − 2 sixths = _____ sixths

3.

0   1

$$\frac{}{5} + \frac{1}{5} = \frac{}{}$$

4.

0   1

$$\frac{}{10} - \frac{}{10} = \frac{}{}$$

Color or draw on the model to represent the problem. Then add or subtract to solve.

5.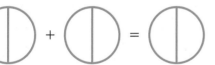

$$\frac{1}{2} + \frac{1}{2} = \frac{}{}$$

6.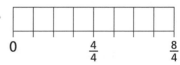

0          $\frac{4}{4}$ $\frac{8}{4}$

$$\frac{6}{4} - \frac{3}{4} = \frac{}{}$$

Find the sum or difference.

7. $\frac{5}{3} - \frac{1}{3} = \frac{}{}$

8. $\frac{5}{12} + \frac{9}{12} = \frac{}{}$

 Think • Pair • Share

MP4 9. Lisa drew the model at the right to add $\frac{1}{3} + \frac{1}{3}$. What sum did she find? Explain Lisa's mistake.

Independent Practice

Color or draw on the model to represent the problem. Then add or subtract to solve.

1. ☐☐☐ + ☐☐☐ = ☐☐☐   2. ☐☐☐☐☐☐

$\frac{1}{3} + \frac{1}{3} = -$ $\frac{5}{6} - \frac{2}{6} = -$

Color or draw on the model to find the sum or difference. Then write an equation to represent the problem.

3.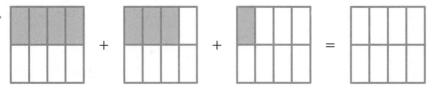

_____

4.

_____

5.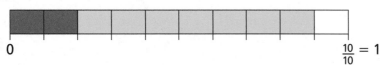

0 $\frac{10}{10} = 1$

_____

6. Which difference is modeled below?

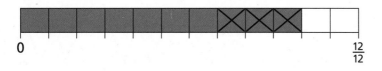

0 $\frac{12}{12}$

a. $\frac{7}{12} - \frac{3}{12} = \frac{4}{12}$ b. $\frac{10}{12} - \frac{3}{12} = \frac{7}{12}$

c. $\frac{12}{12} - \frac{2}{12} = \frac{10}{12}$ d. $\frac{10}{12} - \frac{7}{12} = \frac{3}{12}$

Independent Practice

Add or subtract. Draw a model to support your answer.

7. $\frac{3}{4} - \frac{2}{4} = -$

8. $\frac{2}{2} + \frac{1}{2} = -$

9. $\frac{4}{5} + \frac{3}{5} = -$

10. $\frac{12}{10} - \frac{5}{10} = \underline{\quad}$

Write a fraction to complete the equation. You can use models to help.

11. $\frac{5}{6} + - = \frac{6}{6}$

12. $- - \frac{3}{8} = \frac{3}{8}$

13. $\underline{\quad} + \frac{5}{12} = \frac{13}{12}$

14. $\frac{7}{3} - - = \frac{2}{3}$

Independent Practice

MP6 **15.** Write an addition word problem that involves fractions. Then solve your problem.

MP2 **16.** Jack buys a package of gum that has 4 packs. He gives 1 pack of gum to his friend and 1 pack to his father. Explain why the equation below represents this problem.

$$\frac{4}{4} - \frac{2}{4} = \frac{2}{4}$$

Solve the problems.

MP4 **17.** There are 8 books in Audrey's favorite book series. Audrey reads 5 of the books over the winter vacation. What fraction of the series does Audrey have left to read?

➤ **Show your work.**

Answer _____

MP6 **18.** Kenneth walks $\frac{1}{5}$ mile to his friend's house. Then they walk $\frac{3}{5}$ mile to the ice cream store, and $\frac{2}{5}$ mile back to Kenneth's house. How far does Kenneth walk altogether?

➤ **Show your work.**

Answer _____

Independent Practice

MP1 **19.** Mikayla makes smoothies with $\frac{3}{4}$ pound of blueberries and $\frac{2}{4}$ pound of strawberries. Carly makes smoothies with $\frac{1}{6}$ pound of banana and $\frac{4}{6}$ pound of strawberries. Whose smoothies have more than 1 whole pound of fruit?

✏️ **Show your work.**

Answer _____

MP2 **20.** Jordan answers $\frac{8}{10}$ of the questions on a quiz correctly. On her second quiz, Jordan answers $\frac{9}{10}$ of the questions correctly. If both quizzes have the same number of questions, on which quiz did Jordan have more answers wrong?

Answer _____

✏️ **Justify your answer using words, drawings, or numbers.**

MP7 **21.** Oliver is choosing between two packs of baseball cards. In one pack, $\frac{8}{12}$ of the cards are for his favorite teams. In the other pack, $\frac{10}{12}$ of the cards are for his favorite teams. Oliver says he will get more cards that he likes with the second pack. Is Oliver correct?

Answer _____

✏️ **Justify your answer using words, drawings, or numbers.**

Decompose a Fraction as a Sum of Fractions

Essential Question:

How can you decompose a fraction or mixed number into a sum of fractions with the same denominator?

4.NF.3b

Words to Know:
   decompose
   mixed number

Guided Instruction

In this lesson you will learn how to decompose fractions and mixed numbers and write them as sums of other fractions.

Understand: Ways to break apart a whole

> Sydney collects quarters. She arranges them in rows of 4 quarters. She arranges the quarters in each row in a different way. Then she writes an equation to describe the arrangement. What are some equations she writes?

To find the equations she writes, recall that 1 quarter is $\frac{1}{4}$ of 1 dollar. This means that 4 quarters are $\frac{4}{4}$ of 1 dollar.

She makes a row with 4 groups of 1 quarter each.

Remember!
$\frac{4}{4} = 1$, because 4 unit fractions of $\frac{1}{4}$ equal 1 whole.

She writes $\frac{4}{4} = \frac{1}{4} + \frac{1}{4} + \frac{1}{4} + \frac{1}{4}$.

She makes a row with 2 groups of 1 quarter and 1 group of 2 quarters.

She writes $\frac{4}{4} = \frac{1}{4} + \frac{1}{4} + \frac{2}{4}$.

She makes a row with 1 group of 1 quarter and 1 group of 3 quarters.

She writes $\frac{4}{4} = \frac{1}{4} + \frac{3}{4}$.

➤ Some equations Sydney writes are $\frac{4}{4} = \frac{1}{4} + \frac{1}{4} + \frac{1}{4} + \frac{1}{4}$, $\frac{4}{4} = \frac{1}{4} + \frac{1}{4} + \frac{2}{4}$, and $\frac{4}{4} = \frac{1}{4} + \frac{3}{4}$.

✏️ Compare the equations that Sydney wrote.

Understand: Ways to decompose a fraction

> For Fred's math and art project, he draws identical rectangles with
> 8 equal sections. He uses 6 sections in each rectangle to represent $\frac{6}{8}$ and
> paints them to show ways to decompose $\frac{6}{8}$. Then he writes equations to
> describe his work. What kinds of sums do Fred's equations describe?

You can decompose, or break apart, a fraction by writing it as the sum of
other fractions with the same denominator.

One way to decompose $\frac{6}{8}$
is to write it as the sum of
unit fractions.

$$\frac{6}{8} = \frac{1}{8} + \frac{1}{8} + \frac{1}{8} + \frac{1}{8} + \frac{1}{8} + \frac{1}{8}$$

Another way to decompose
$\frac{6}{8}$ is to write it as the sum
of unit fractions and
other fractions.

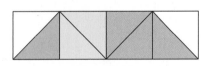

$$\frac{6}{8} = \frac{1}{8} + \frac{2}{8} + \frac{3}{8}$$

A third way to decompose
$\frac{6}{8}$ is to write it as the sum
of fractions that are not
unit fractions.

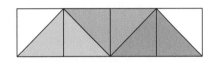

$$\frac{6}{8} = \frac{2}{8} + \frac{2}{8} + \frac{2}{8}$$

➥ Fred's equations describe sums of unit fractions, of unit fractions and
other fractions, and of fractions that are not unit fractions.

✏️ Color the rectangle to show another way to decompose $\frac{6}{8}$. Then write
an equation to describe your work.

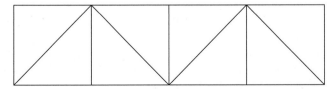

Guided Instruction

Connect: Fractions and mixed numbers

Jason has $\frac{9}{4}$ quarts of milk. Is that more or less than 2 quarts of milk?

To decide, write $\frac{9}{4}$ as a mixed number. Then compare the mixed number to 2. A mixed number shows the sum of a whole number and a fraction but does not have a + sign.

$\frac{9}{4} = \frac{4}{4} + \frac{4}{4} + \frac{1}{4}$ Write $\frac{9}{4}$ as a sum of fractions.

$\quad = 1 + 1 + \frac{1}{4}$ Write $\frac{4}{4}$ as 1.

$\quad = \quad 2 \quad + \frac{1}{4}$ Add the whole numbers.

$\quad = 2\frac{1}{4}$ Write the sum as a mixed number.

Remember!

$\frac{4}{4} = 1$

Compare. $2\frac{1}{4} > 2$, because $2 + \frac{1}{4}$ is more than 2.

➡️ Jason has more than 2 quarts of milk.

✏️ Try a different way to compare $\frac{9}{4}$ and 2. Write 2 as a fraction and compare it with $\frac{9}{4}$. Why is the answer the same?

Ms. Gordon has $4\frac{1}{2}$ dozen eggs to make scrambled eggs for breakfast at camp. She uses $\frac{1}{2}$ dozen for each batch. How many batches can she make?

To find out, write $4\frac{1}{2}$ as a fraction with a denominator of 2. The numerator will be the number of half-dozens of eggs.

$4\frac{1}{2} = 4 + \frac{1}{2}$ Write $4\frac{1}{2}$ as a sum of 4 plus $\frac{1}{2}$.

$\quad = 1 + 1 + 1 + 1 + \frac{1}{2}$ Write 4 as a sum of 1s.

$\quad = \frac{2}{2} + \frac{2}{2} + \frac{2}{2} + \frac{2}{2} + \frac{1}{2}$ Write 1 as a fraction with the denominator 2.

$\quad = \frac{2 + 2 + 2 + 2 + 1}{2}$ Add the numerators.

$\quad = \frac{9}{2}$; The numerator is 9. There are 9 half-dozens of eggs.

➡️ Ms. Gordon can make 9 batches of scrambled eggs.

Guided Practice

Complete each equation to write the fraction as a sum of other fractions. Use the model to help you.

1. $\frac{3}{5} = \frac{}{5} + \frac{}{5} + \frac{}{5}$

   $\frac{3}{5} = \frac{}{5} + \frac{}{5}$

2. $\frac{9}{8} = \frac{}{8} + \frac{}{8} + \frac{}{8} + \frac{2}{8} + \frac{1}{8}$

   $\frac{9}{8} = \frac{}{8} + \frac{}{8} + \frac{}{8} + \frac{}{8}$

   $\frac{9}{8} = \frac{}{8} + \frac{}{8} + \frac{}{8}$

| $\frac{1}{8}$ | $\frac{1}{8}$ | $\frac{1}{8}$ | $\frac{1}{8}$ | $\frac{1}{8}$ | $\frac{1}{8}$ | $\frac{1}{8}$ | $\frac{1}{8}$ |

| $\frac{1}{8}$ | | | | | | | |

Write each mixed number as a fraction. Show your work.

3. $2\frac{2}{3} = \frac{}{3}$

4. $1\frac{5}{8} = \frac{}{8}$

5. $4\frac{3}{5} = \frac{}{5}$

Write each fraction as a mixed number.

6. $\frac{9}{4} = $ _____

7. $\frac{7}{2} = $ _____

8. $\frac{10}{3} = $ _____

 **Think • Pair • Share**

MP6 9. Michael writes $\frac{10}{12}$ as $\frac{10}{10} + \frac{2}{12}$. Draw a model to show Michael's sum. Is his sum correct? If not, what mistakes did he make?

Independent Practice

Complete each equation to write the number as a sum of other fractions in different ways. Use the model to help you.

1. $\dfrac{3}{4} = \dfrac{}{4} + \dfrac{}{4} + \dfrac{}{4}$

$\dfrac{3}{4} = \underline{\quad} + \underline{\quad}$

2. $1\dfrac{4}{5} = \underline{\quad} + \dfrac{}{5}$

$1\dfrac{4}{5} = \dfrac{}{5} + \dfrac{}{5}$

$1\dfrac{4}{5} = \underline{\hspace{4cm}}$

Write the fraction as a sum of other fractions in four different ways. Draw a model if it helps.

3. $\dfrac{9}{12}$

$\dfrac{9}{12} = \underline{\hspace{8cm}}$

$\dfrac{9}{12} = \underline{\hspace{8cm}}$

$\dfrac{9}{12} = \underline{\hspace{8cm}}$

$\dfrac{9}{12} = \underline{\hspace{8cm}}$

4. $\dfrac{10}{10}$

$\dfrac{10}{10} = \underline{\hspace{8cm}}$

$\dfrac{10}{10} = \underline{\hspace{8cm}}$

$\dfrac{10}{10} = \underline{\hspace{8cm}}$

$\dfrac{10}{10} = \underline{\hspace{8cm}}$

5. $\dfrac{12}{5}$

$\dfrac{12}{5} = \underline{\hspace{8cm}}$

$\dfrac{12}{5} = \underline{\hspace{8cm}}$

$\dfrac{12}{5} = \underline{\hspace{8cm}}$

$\dfrac{12}{5} = \underline{\hspace{8cm}}$

Independent Practice

Circle the correct answer.

6. Which sum is not equivalent to $\frac{5}{6}$?

    a. $\frac{1}{6} + \frac{2}{6} + \frac{2}{6}$ **b.** $\frac{3}{6} + \frac{2}{6}$

    c. $\frac{1}{6} + \frac{1}{6} + \frac{1}{6}$ **d.** $\frac{4}{6} + \frac{1}{6}$

7. Which sum is equivalent to $\frac{10}{3}$?

    a. $3 + \frac{1}{3}$ **b.** $\frac{3}{3} + \frac{6}{3}$

    c. $2 + \frac{3}{3}$ **d.** $10 + \frac{1}{3}$

8. Look at the red point on the number line. It represents a fraction. Jessica wants to write the fraction as a sum of three addends.

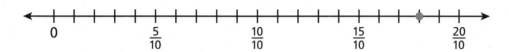

So far, she has two addends, $\frac{4}{10}$ and $\frac{6}{10}$. Which of the following can Jessica use as the third addend?

    a. $\frac{10}{10}$ **b.** $\frac{18}{10}$

    c. $1\frac{8}{10}$ **d.** $\frac{8}{10}$

Write each number as a sum in three different ways. You can use a model to help. Then answer the question below.

9. $2\frac{2}{12}$

    = _____

    = _____

    = _____

10. $\frac{22}{12}$

    = _____

    = _____

    = _____

11. Compare $2\frac{2}{12}$ and $\frac{22}{12}$. Write $<$, $=$, or $>$.

    $2\frac{2}{12}$ _____ $\frac{22}{12}$

Independent Practice

MP3 **12.** To write $\frac{35}{10}$ as a sum, Matt says you can find addends by subtracting fractions from $\frac{35}{10}$ until there is nothing left. Does Matt's method work? Explain.

MP2 **13.** Brianna is making a patchwork quilt with different size patches. She has a strip of fabric that is $1\frac{4}{8}$ yards long. How can writing $1\frac{4}{8}$ as a sum help Brianna to cut up the strip of fabric?

Solve the problems.

MP4 **14.** For each scoop of ice cream that you buy, the ice-cream shop crosses out 1 of the 8 boxes on a card. After 4 visits, $\frac{7}{8}$ of Juan's card is crossed out. Write an addition equation to show how Juan's card could have been crossed out in 4 visits.

➤ **Show your work.**

Answer _____

MP7 **15.** Bella serves pizza at her birthday party. Each pizza is cut into 6 equal slices. There are $\frac{13}{6}$ pizzas left after the party is over. The slices are in 3 different pizza boxes, and none of the boxes are full. What fraction of a whole pizza can be in each box?

➤ **Show your work.**

Answer _____

Independent Practice

MP2 **16.** Travis's family uses an automatic cat feeder when they are not home. The feeder has 8 sections that can each hold 1 cup of food. Travis has $\frac{26}{4}$ cups of cat food. Does he have enough to fill each section in the feeder with a full cup?

✏️ **Show your work.**

Answer _____

MP1 **17.** A piece of wood is $4\frac{2}{6}$ yards long. If $\frac{3}{6}$ yard is needed to make 1 shelf, how many shelves can you make from the piece of wood?

Answer _____

✏️ **Justify your answer using words, drawings, or numbers.**

MP8 **18.** To find the whole amounts in $\frac{27}{5}$, Molly divides the numerator by the denominator. Then she writes the remainder as the fraction part of a mixed number. Does Molly's method work? Draw a model and write $\frac{27}{5}$ as a sum to help support your answer.

Answer _____

✏️ **Justify your answer using words, drawings, or numbers.**

Add and Subtract Mixed Numbers with Like Denominators

Essential Question:
What methods can you use for adding and subtracting mixed numbers?
4.NF.3c

Guided Instruction

In this lesson you will learn different methods for adding and subtracting mixed numbers with like denominators.

Understand: Adding mixed numbers

> Max is training his puppy to walk with a leash. He spends $1\frac{3}{4}$ hours at dog school. He also practices with his dog at the park for $1\frac{2}{4}$ hours. How much time does Max spend training his puppy altogether?

You can use models of equivalent fractions or properties of addition to find the sum of $1\frac{3}{4} + 1\frac{2}{4}$.

One way is to use models of equivalent fractions.

Model each mixed number.

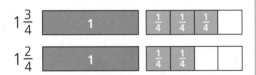

Rename each mixed number as an equivalent fraction.

$1\frac{3}{4} = \frac{7}{4}$

$1\frac{2}{4} = \frac{6}{4}$

Add. Write the sum as a mixed number.

$$\frac{7}{4} + \frac{6}{4} = \frac{13}{4} = \frac{12}{4} + \frac{1}{4}$$

$$= 3 + \frac{1}{4} = 3\frac{1}{4}$$

Another way is to use properties of addition. Using the properties of addition, you can add mixed numbers by first breaking them apart and then adding the whole numbers and the fractions separately.

$1\frac{3}{4} + 1\frac{2}{4}$	Write the sum you want to find.
$(1 + \frac{3}{4}) + (1 + \frac{2}{4})$	Write the mixed numbers as sums.
$1 + (\frac{3}{4} + 1) + \frac{2}{4}$	Use the Associative Property.
$1 + (1 + \frac{3}{4}) + \frac{2}{4}$	Use the Commutative Property.
$(1 + 1) + (\frac{3}{4} + \frac{2}{4})$	Use the Associative Property.
$2 \quad + \quad \frac{5}{4}$	Add the whole numbers. Add the fractions.
$2 \quad + 1 + \frac{1}{4}$	Rename $\frac{5}{4}$.
$3 \quad + \frac{1}{4}$	Add the whole numbers.
$3\frac{1}{4}$	Write the mixed number.

➡ Max spends $3\frac{1}{4}$ hours training his puppy.

Guided Instruction

Understand: Subtracting mixed numbers

Sofia is hanging a poster in her bedroom on the wall space between her windows. That space is $2\frac{1}{6}$ feet wide. Her poster is $1\frac{4}{6}$ feet wide. How much space is left after Sofia hangs her poster?

One way to subtract mixed numbers is to use equivalent fractions.

The models show that you need to regroup sixths to subtract $1\frac{4}{6}$ from $2\frac{1}{6}$.

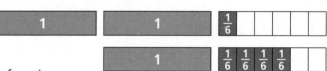

Rename each mixed number as an equivalent fraction greater than 1, with 6 as the denominator.

$$2\frac{1}{6} = 1 + 1 + \frac{1}{6}$$
$$= \frac{6}{6} + \frac{6}{6} + \frac{1}{6}$$
$$= \frac{13}{6}$$

$$1\frac{4}{6} = 1 + \frac{4}{6}$$
$$= \frac{6}{6} + \frac{4}{6}$$
$$= \frac{10}{6}$$

Now subtract the fractions to find the difference.

$$2\frac{1}{6} - 1\frac{4}{6} = \frac{13}{6} - \frac{10}{6}$$
$$= \frac{13 - 10}{6}$$
$$= \frac{3}{6}$$

Remember!
To add or subtract fractions with like denominators, add or subtract the numerators.

▶ Sofia has $\frac{3}{6}$ foot of space left after she hangs the poster.

Another way to subtract is to use the relationship between addition and subtraction.

Change the subtraction problem to an addition problem with an unknown addend.

$$2\frac{1}{6} - 1\frac{4}{6} = ? \qquad 1\frac{4}{6} + ? = 2\frac{1}{6}$$

Use a number line to find the unknown addend. Locate $1\frac{4}{6}$, or $\frac{10}{6}$, and $2\frac{1}{6}$, or $\frac{13}{6}$.

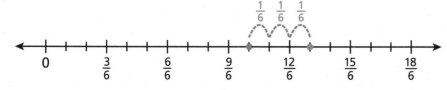

The distance between them is the unknown addend: $\frac{3}{6}$.

Guided Instruction

Connect: Using methods for adding and subtracting mixed numbers

Mitch, Ruby, and Tony are in a relay race. Mitch finishes the first part of the race in $3\frac{5}{10}$ minutes. Ruby does the second part in $2\frac{7}{10}$ minutes. If the team's total race time is 9 minutes, how long does Tony take to finish the last part?

To solve, add Mitch and Ruby's times, then subtract the sum from the team's total finishing time.

Step 1

Add $3\frac{5}{10}$ and $2\frac{7}{10}$ to find Mitch and Ruby's total time.

First, rename each mixed number as an equivalent fraction.

Since $1 = \frac{10}{10}$, you can find the total number of tenths in the whole number parts of the mixed numbers.

$$3\frac{5}{10} = \frac{10 \times 3}{10 \times 1} + \frac{5}{10} \qquad 2\frac{7}{10} = \frac{10 \times 2}{10 \times 1} + \frac{7}{10}$$
$$= \frac{30}{10} + \frac{5}{10} \qquad\qquad = \frac{20}{10} + \frac{7}{10}$$
$$= \frac{35}{10} \qquad\qquad\qquad = \frac{27}{10}$$

> **Remember!**
> You can write any whole number as a fraction with a denominator of 1.

Add the fractions. $\frac{35}{10} + \frac{27}{10} = \frac{35 + 27}{10} = \frac{62}{10}$

Step 2

Subtract $\frac{62}{10}$ from 9, the team's total time, to find Tony's time.

First, rename 9 as a fraction. $9 = \frac{10 \times 9}{10 \times 1} = \frac{90}{10}$

Subtract $\frac{62}{10}$ from $\frac{90}{10}$: $\frac{90}{10} - \frac{62}{10} = \frac{90 - 62}{10} = \frac{28}{10}$

Step 3

Rename the difference $\frac{28}{10}$ as a mixed number.

$$\frac{28}{10} = \frac{10}{10} + \frac{10}{10} + \frac{8}{10}$$
$$= 1 + 1 + \frac{8}{10}$$
$$= 2\frac{8}{10}$$

> **Remember!**
> Make sure the fraction in the mixed number is less than 1.

➡ Tony takes $2\frac{8}{10}$ minutes to finish the last part of the race.

Guided Practice

Rename each mixed number as an equivalent fraction greater than 1. Then add or subtract.

1. Add $2\frac{1}{5}$ and $1\frac{3}{5}$.

$\overbrace{}^{\text{2 wholes}}$

   a. Rename $2\frac{1}{5}$ as a fraction. $\qquad 2\frac{1}{5} = \frac{}{5} + \frac{}{5} + \frac{1}{5} = \frac{}{5}$

   b. Rename $1\frac{3}{5}$ as a fraction. $\qquad 1\frac{3}{5} = \frac{}{5} + \frac{3}{5} = \frac{}{5}$

   c. Add the renamed fractions. $\qquad \frac{}{5} + \frac{}{5} = \frac{}{5}$

   d. Write the sum as a mixed number. $\qquad \frac{19}{5} = \frac{}{5} + \frac{}{5} + \frac{}{5} + \frac{4}{5} = 3\frac{}{5}$

   e. Complete the addition equation. $\qquad 2\frac{1}{5} + 1\frac{3}{5} = \underline{\quad} -$

2. Subtract $1\frac{4}{8}$ from $3\frac{1}{8}$.

   a. To subtract $1\frac{4}{8}$ do you need to regroup $3\frac{1}{8}$? $\underline{\qquad}$

   Why? Because $\frac{1}{8} \underline{\quad} \frac{4}{8}$

   b. Rename $1\frac{4}{8}$ as a fraction. $\qquad 1\frac{4}{8} = \frac{}{8} + \frac{}{8} = \frac{}{8}$

   c. Rename $3\frac{1}{8}$ as a fraction. $\qquad 3\frac{1}{8} = \frac{8 \times}{8 \times} + \frac{}{8} = \frac{}{8} + \frac{1}{8} = \frac{}{8}$

   d. Subtract the renamed fractions. $\qquad \frac{}{} - \frac{}{} = \frac{}{}$

   e. Write the difference as a mixed number. $\qquad \frac{}{8} = \frac{}{8} + \frac{}{8} = \underline{\quad} -$

   f. Complete the subtraction equation. $\qquad 3\frac{1}{8} - 1\frac{4}{8} = \underline{\quad} -$

3. Find the sum $5\frac{2}{12} + 2\frac{11}{12}$. Use the properties of addition to break apart the numbers to add. Show your work.

⛄ Think • Pair • Share

MP7 4. Compare the methods you used to add in exercises 1 and 3. Which method is easier for you? Why?

Independent Practice

For exercises 1 and 2, use the model below.

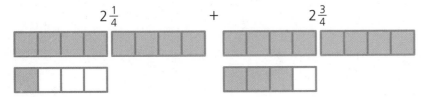

$2\frac{1}{4}$ + $2\frac{3}{4}$

1. Break apart $2\frac{1}{4}$ and $2\frac{3}{4}$. Then use properties to add.

$$2\frac{1}{4} + 2\frac{3}{4} = \underline{\quad} + \frac{}{4} + \underline{\quad} + -$$

$$= (\underline{\quad} + \underline{\quad}) + \frac{}{4} + \frac{}{4}$$

$$= \underline{\quad} + \frac{}{4}$$

$$= \underline{\quad} + \underline{\quad}$$

$$= \underline{\quad}$$

$$2\frac{1}{4} + 2\frac{3}{4} = \underline{\quad}$$

2. Rename $2\frac{1}{4}$ and $2\frac{3}{4}$ as equivalent fractions greater than 1.

$$2\frac{1}{4} = \frac{4 \times}{4 \times} + \frac{}{4} = \frac{}{4} + \frac{}{4} = \frac{}{4}$$

$$2\frac{3}{4} = \frac{4 \times}{4 \times} + \frac{}{4} + \frac{}{4} + \frac{}{4}$$

$$= \frac{}{4} + \frac{}{4} + \frac{}{4} + \frac{}{4} = \frac{}{4}$$

Add the fractions.

$$\frac{}{4} + \frac{}{4} = \underline{\hspace{3cm}}$$

$$2\frac{1}{4} + 2\frac{3}{4} = \underline{\quad}$$

Add with the method of your choice. Show your work.

3. $6\frac{1}{2} + 3\frac{1}{2} = \underline{\quad}$

4. $4\frac{2}{6} + 2\frac{3}{6} = \underline{\quad}$

Find the difference. Use the model if it helps.

5. $3\frac{2}{3} - 2\frac{1}{3}$

Do you need to regroup? _____

Subtract the whole numbers.

_____

$3\frac{2}{3} - 2\frac{1}{3} = \underline{\quad}$

Subtract the fractions.

$$\frac{2}{3} - \frac{1}{3} = -$$

Independent Practice

6. $3\frac{3}{5} - 2\frac{4}{5}$ Do you need to regroup? _____

Rename each number as an equivalent fraction greater than 1.

$3\frac{3}{5} = \frac{5 \times}{5 \times} + \frac{}{5} = \frac{}{5} + \frac{}{5} = \frac{}{5}$ $2\frac{4}{5} = \frac{5 \times}{5 \times} + \frac{}{5} = \frac{}{5} + \frac{}{5} = \frac{}{5}$

Subtract the fractions: $\frac{}{5} - \frac{}{5} = $ _____.
Use the model to show your work.

$3\frac{3}{5} - 2\frac{4}{5} = $ _____

Subtract with the method of your choice. Show your work.

7. $8\frac{7}{10} - 5\frac{2}{10} = $ _____

8. $3\frac{2}{5} - 1\frac{4}{5} = $ _____

Circle the correct answer or answers.

9. For which of the following subtraction problems do you need to regroup?

   a. $5 - 2\frac{1}{2}$

   b. $4\frac{6}{8} - 3\frac{5}{8}$

   c. $10\frac{1}{5} - 8\frac{3}{5}$

   d. $2\frac{50}{100} - 1\frac{9}{100}$

10. Penny is mailing two packages. To find their total weight, she is adding $8\frac{5}{12}$ pounds and $3\frac{7}{12}$ pounds. Which of the following is the best way to group the addends to add mentally?

   a. $8 + \frac{5}{12} + 3 + \frac{7}{12}$

   b. $3 + \frac{7}{12} + 8 + \frac{5}{12}$

   c. $8 + 3 + (\frac{5}{12} + \frac{7}{12})$

   d. $8 + 3 + (\frac{5}{12} + \frac{5}{12}) + \frac{2}{12}$

Unit 3 ■ Focus on Number and Operations—Fractions   **171**

Independent Practice

MP2 **11.** How is adding and subtracting mixed numbers different from adding and subtracting fractions less than 1?

MP7 **12.** When you break apart a mixed number to add, does it matter if you add the whole numbers first or the fractions first? Explain.

Solve the problems.

MP6 **13.** Greg is making homemade pizzas. For the crust, he uses $2\frac{2}{4}$ cups of whole wheat flour and $4\frac{2}{4}$ cups of regular flour. How much flour does Greg use altogether?

▸ **Show your work.**

Answer _____

MP1 **14.** A sports club is having a beginner's triathlon race. To finish the race, each athlete must swim $1\frac{5}{10}$ miles, run $3\frac{1}{10}$ miles, and ride a bicycle for $5\frac{8}{10}$ miles. What is the total length of the race in miles?

▸ **Show your work.**

Answer _____

Independent Practice

MP2 **15.** There are 12 eggs in 1 carton. In the delivery truck, $4\frac{5}{12}$ cartons of eggs break. In the store, a total of $2\frac{9}{12}$ cartons break. How many more cartons of eggs break in the truck than in the store?

➤ **Show your work.**

Answer _____

MP6 **16.** Justin subtracts $5\frac{1}{3}$ from $10\frac{2}{3}$ using the method shown at the right. Is Justin's difference correct?

$$10\frac{2}{3}$$
$$-\ 5\frac{1}{3}$$
$$\overline{5\frac{1}{3}}$$

Answer _____

➤ **Justify your answer using words, drawings, or numbers.**

MP8 **17.** Mariah needs to add $4\frac{10}{100}$ and $3\frac{20}{100}$. She starts by using a denominator of 10 to write equivalent fractions for $\frac{10}{100}$ and $\frac{20}{100}$. Then she adds the mixed numbers. Can Mariah find the correct sum with this method?

Answer _____

➤ **Justify your answer using words, drawings, or numbers.**

Problem Solving: Add and Subtract Fractions

Guided Instruction

In this lesson you will learn how to solve addition and subtraction problems involving fractions and mixed numbers with like denominators.

Understand: Using fraction models to represent and solve problems

Sarah has a watercolor paint set with 8 colors. First she uses up her favorite $\frac{1}{8}$ of the colors. When she uses up another $\frac{5}{8}$ of the colors, she buys a new paint set. How much of the paint set is left when Sarah buys a new one?

To solve the problem, you can make a model to represent the problem.

First read for information.

Sarah uses up $\frac{1}{8}$ and $\frac{5}{8}$ of the set. The denominator 8 in $\frac{1}{8}$ and $\frac{5}{8}$ shows the whole is divided into eighths.

Draw a model to represent the whole as $\frac{8}{8}$.

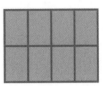

1 paint set $= \frac{8}{8}$

Use different color Xs to show the $\frac{1}{8}$ and $\frac{5}{8}$ that Sarah uses.

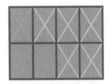

Then read again to find the question.
The problem asks how much of the paint set is left, not how much Sarah uses altogether.
So you need to subtract the sum of $\frac{1}{8} + \frac{5}{8}$ from the whole.

$$\frac{8}{8} - \left(\frac{1}{8} + \frac{5}{8}\right) = \frac{2}{8}$$

$\frac{2}{8}$ left

➡ When Sarah buys a new one, $\frac{2}{8}$ of the paint set is left.
Notice that the model shows the same answer.

✏ What if the problem asks how many of the 8 colors are left? Explain how to use your model to find this number.

Guided Instruction

Understand: Using equations to represent and solve problems

> The library is $2\frac{5}{6}$ miles from the school. David's father picks him up from school to go to the library. On the way, they stop at a store. Then they walk $1\frac{4}{6}$ miles to the library. How far is the store from the school?

You can use a model to help write an equation.

Identify what you know.
- The distance between the school and the library is $2\frac{5}{6}$ miles.
- The store is between the school and library.
- The distance between the store and library is $1\frac{4}{6}$ miles.

Identify what you need to find.
- the distance from the store to the school

Draw a model to represent the problem. The store is $1\frac{4}{6}$ miles away from the library. This location on the number line is the distance from the store to the school.

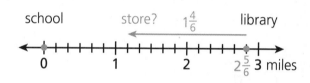

Write an equation for the problem.
You can use d to represent the unknown distance.

$$d + 1\frac{4}{6} = 2\frac{5}{6}$$

$$d = 2\frac{5}{6} - 1\frac{4}{6}$$

Subtract $1\frac{4}{6}$ from $2\frac{5}{6}$ to find d.

Since $\frac{4}{6} < \frac{5}{6}$, you can subtract without regrouping the 2 wholes.

school to library − store to library = school to store

$$2\frac{5}{6} \quad - \quad 1\frac{4}{6} \quad = \quad 1\frac{1}{6}$$

$$d = 1\frac{1}{6}$$

➡ The store is $1\frac{1}{6}$ miles from the school.

Remember!
Check whether you can subtract the whole numbers and the fractions separately.

Guided Instruction

Connect: What you know about writing equivalent fractions and using models.

Ava has $2\frac{4}{10}$ pounds of frozen strawberries. She needs $\frac{2}{10}$ pound of strawberries to make 1 shake. How many strawberry shakes can Ava make with all $2\frac{4}{10}$ pounds?

To solve the problem, use what you know about equivalent fractions to write an equation.

Step 1

Identify and model what you know.
- The total amount is $2\frac{4}{10}$ pounds.
- The amount for 1 shake is $\frac{2}{10}$ pounds.

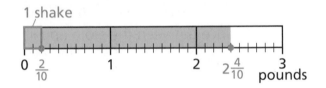

Identify what you need to find.
- how many shakes Ava can make

Step 2

Using a unit fraction makes it easier to find the number of shakes Ava can make. Find the unit fraction that is equivalent to $\frac{2}{10}$.

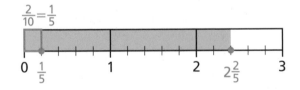

$$\frac{2}{10} = \frac{2 \div 2}{10 \div 2} = \frac{1}{5}$$

Ava needs $\frac{1}{5}$ pound of strawberries to make each shake.

Step 3

Plan how you will find the number of fifths in $2\frac{2}{5}$.
You can count the unit fractions of $\frac{1}{5}$ on the model, or you can write $2\frac{2}{5}$ as a sum of unit fractions, or you can write $2\frac{2}{5}$ as a fraction to find the total number of fifths.

Remember!

The numerator in a fraction shows the number of equal parts in a fraction.

Step 4

$$2\frac{2}{5} = 1 + 1 + \frac{2}{5} = \frac{5}{5} + \frac{5}{5} + \frac{2}{5} = \frac{12}{5}$$

There are 12 fifths in $2\frac{2}{5}$.

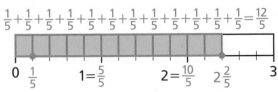

Ava can make 12 strawberry shakes with $2\frac{4}{10}$ pounds of strawberries.

Guided Practice

Use the model to answer the questions.

1. A town gets $2\frac{3}{4}$ inches of rain on Monday and $\frac{2}{4}$ inches of rain on Friday. How much rain does the town get on those two days?

   Rain on Monday

   Rain on Friday

   a. Color the model to show the given information.

   b. Circle the equation you can use to solve the problem.

   $$2\frac{3}{4} - \frac{2}{4} = r \qquad 2\frac{3}{4} + \frac{2}{4} = r \qquad 2\frac{3}{4} + r = \frac{2}{4}$$

   c. Solve the problem. Show your work.

   $$2\frac{3}{4} + \frac{2}{4} = \text{_____}$$

   Answer _____

Write an addition or subtraction equation to represent the problem. You can use the model to help. Then solve.

2. Vincent has a bag of apples. Green apples fill $\frac{3}{5}$ of the bag. Yellow apples fill the rest of the bag. What fraction of the bag has yellow apples?

   a. Equation _____

   b. Solve the problem. Show your work.

   Answer _____

 **Think • Pair • Share**

MP1   3. What are the whole amounts in exercises 1 and 2? How do you know that the mixed numbers and the fractions in each exercise are for the same whole? Explain.

Independent Practice

Use the model to represent the problem. Write and solve an equation to find the answer.

1. Brad has $1\frac{1}{3}$ boxes of birthday candles. He uses $\frac{2}{3}$ of the birthday candles on a birthday cake. What fraction of the candles is left?

    a. Equation _____

    b. Solve the problem. Show your work.

    Answer _____

2. Kate's favorite song is $3\frac{5}{8}$ minutes long. Ty's favorite song is $2\frac{7}{8}$ minutes long. How much longer is Kate's favorite song than Ty's?

    a. Equation

    _____

    b. Solve the problem. Show your work.

    Answer _____

Circle the correct answer.

3. Ayden works on his homework for $1\frac{1}{6}$ hours before dinner. It takes him another $1\frac{3}{6}$ hours to finish his homework after dinner. How much time does Ayden spend on homework?

    a. $\frac{2}{6}$ hour

    b. $1\frac{2}{6}$ hours

    c. $1\frac{4}{6}$ hours

    d. $2\frac{4}{6}$ hours

4. Talia is $\frac{1}{4}$ of her mother's age. Carl is $\frac{1}{4}$ of his mother's age. Who is older, Talia or Carl? Which statement about the problem is true?

    a. Subtract $\frac{1}{4} - \frac{1}{4}$ to solve.

    b. Add $\frac{1}{4} + \frac{1}{4}$ to solve.

    c. Carl and Talia must be the same age, since they are the same fraction of their mothers' ages.

    d. The problem cannot be solved without the ages of Carl and Talia's mothers.

Independent Practice

For exercises 5–8, use the number line. For exercises 6–9, write and solve an equation.

A car gets on the highway at the starting point, 0 miles. The next five highway exits are shown on the number line below.

Distances Between Highway Exits

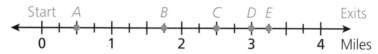

5. Label Exits *A*, *B*, *C*, and *E* with the fraction or mixed number for that location.

6. What is the distance between Exits *A* and *B*?

   Equation _____

   Answer _____

7. A driver misses Exit *B* and has to get off at Exit *C*. How far is Exit *C* from Exit *B*?

   Equation _____

   Answer _____

8. Mauricio and his mother get on the highway at Exit *A* and stay on it until Exit *E*. For how many miles do Mauricio and his mother stay on the highway?

   Equation _____

   Answer _____

9. Lauren's family is going to an amusement park. The drive usually takes $2\frac{2}{5}$ hours. Today it takes an extra $\frac{4}{5}$ hour. How long does it take Lauren's family today to drive to the amusement park?

   Equation _____

   Answer _____

Independent Practice

MP6 **10.** Dennis has a jigsaw puzzle that is missing $\frac{2}{100}$ of the edge pieces and $\frac{4}{100}$ of the inside pieces. Does this mean that the puzzle is only missing 6 pieces altogether?

MP3 **11.** Tracy says that the sum of the fractions modeled at the right could be either 1 or $\frac{2}{4}$. Do you agree? Explain.

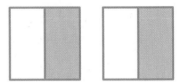

Solve the problems.

MP2 **12.** Two of the 10 players on Ryan's lacrosse team are sick. Another player has to miss practice to go to the dentist. What fraction of Ryan's team is missing from practice?

✎▸ **Show your work.**

Answer _____

MP1 **13.** An acre is an area that is a little smaller than a football field. Jeremy says that the size of the school playground is about $\frac{5}{12}$ of an acre. Susan says that the playground is at least $1\frac{6}{12}$ acres bigger than Jeremy thinks it is. About what does Susan think the area of the playground is?

✎▸ **Show your work.**

Answer _____

Independent Practice

MP6 **14.** The southern elephant seal at the zoo weighs $3\frac{1}{8}$ tons. The biggest hippopotamus at the zoo weighs $1\frac{4}{8}$ tons. How much more does the elephant seal weigh than the hippopotamus?

✏️ **Show your work.**

Answer _____

MP1 **15.** Jessica's bookcase is $4\frac{9}{12}$ feet tall. She wants to replace it with a taller bookcase that is $6\frac{1}{12}$ feet tall. Jessica says the new bookcase is about 1 foot taller. Is this a reasonable estimate?

✏️ **Show your work.**

Answer _____

MP2 **16.** Billy is estimating the combined amount of milk in two jugs. He says that $\frac{1}{2}$ gallon plus $\frac{4}{6}$ gallon must be greater than 1 whole gallon. Do you agree?

Answer _____

✏️ **Justify your answer using words, drawings, or numbers.**

MP7 **17.** Damon says that to write $1\frac{63}{100}$ as a sum of unit fractions, you need 163 addends. Kenya says that you need 64 addends. Who is correct?

Answer _____

✏️ **Justify your answer using words, drawings, or numbers.**

Essential Question:
How is multiplying a unit fraction by a whole number like multiplying a whole number by a whole number?
4.NF.4a

Guided Instruction

In this lesson you will learn how to multiply a unit fraction by a whole number and how to write any fraction as a product of a whole number and a unit fraction.

Understand: Multiplying a unit fraction by a whole number

There are 8 school photos on a whole sheet. So, each photo is $\frac{1}{8}$ of the sheet. Gary gives 6 of his school photos to friends. What fraction of a whole sheet does Gary give to his friends?

To find the fraction of a whole sheet made up of 6 photos that Gary gives to his friends you can use addition or multiplication.

$\frac{1}{8}$	$\frac{1}{8}$	$\frac{1}{8}$	$\frac{1}{8}$
$\frac{1}{8}$	$\frac{1}{8}$	$\frac{1}{8}$	$\frac{1}{8}$

The model shows that 6 photos are $\frac{6}{8}$ of a whole sheet.

Each photo is $\frac{1}{8}$ of a sheet. There are 6 photos.

$$\frac{1}{8} + \frac{1}{8} + \frac{1}{8} + \frac{1}{8} + \frac{1}{8} + \frac{1}{8} = \frac{1+1+1+1+1+1}{8} = \frac{6}{8}$$

Since all the addends are the same, you can think of them as equal groups.

Remember!
To find the total of equal groups, multiply the number in each group by the number of groups.

$$\overbrace{\frac{1}{8} + \frac{1}{8} + \frac{1}{8} + \frac{1}{8} + \frac{1}{8} + \frac{1}{8}}^{\text{6 addends}} = 6 \times \frac{1}{8}$$

So, $6 \times \frac{1}{8} = \frac{6}{8}$

and $\frac{6}{8} = 6 \times \frac{1}{8}$.

➡ Gary gives $\frac{6}{8}$ of a whole sheet of photos to his friends.

Remember!
A multiple of a number is a product of that number and a whole number.

Since $\frac{6}{8}$ is the product $6 \times \frac{1}{8}$, $\frac{6}{8}$ is a multiple of $\frac{1}{8}$.

✏ Count by eighths to write the first five multiples of $\frac{1}{8}$.

Guided Instruction

Connect: Writing a mixed number or a fraction greater than 1 as a product of a whole number and a unit fraction

Luz runs $1\frac{2}{5}$ miles around the park on Saturday. If one lap around the park is a distance of $\frac{1}{5}$ mile, how many laps around the park does Luz run in $1\frac{2}{5}$ miles?

To find the number of laps, write $1\frac{2}{5}$ as a product of a whole number and $\frac{1}{5}$.

$$1\frac{2}{5} = \overset{\text{number of laps}}{\overbrace{n}} \times \frac{1}{5}$$

Step 1

Rewrite $1\frac{2}{5}$ as a fraction greater than 1.

$$1\frac{2}{5} = 1 + \frac{2}{5} = \frac{5}{5} + \frac{2}{5} = \frac{7}{5}$$

Step 2

Rewrite the equation $1\frac{2}{5} = n \times \frac{1}{5}$ as $\frac{7}{5} = n \times \frac{1}{5}$.

Step 3

Find n, the number of laps. You can use a number line as a model.
The number line shows the first ten multiples of $\frac{1}{5}$.
Label $\frac{7}{5}$ on the number line.

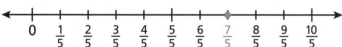

Now, use the number line to find the number of fifths in $\frac{7}{5}$.

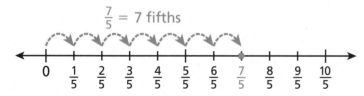

There are 7 fifths in $\frac{7}{5}$.
So, $\frac{7}{5} = 7 \times \frac{1}{5}$.
$n = 7$.

▶ Luz runs 7 laps around the park in $1\frac{2}{5}$ miles.

✏️ • Write $\frac{7}{5}$ as a sum of unit fractions. How many addends are there?

Guided Practice

Complete the equation to find each product. Color the model to show the product.

1. $2 \times \frac{1}{4} = \frac{1}{4} + \frac{1}{4} = \frac{}{4}$

2. $3 \times \frac{1}{4} = \frac{1}{4} + \frac{1}{4} + \frac{1}{4} = \frac{}{4}$

3. $4 \times \frac{1}{8} = \frac{}{8}$

4. $5 \times \frac{1}{8} = -$

For exercises 5–10, write the multiple of $\frac{1}{3}$ that names each point on the number line.

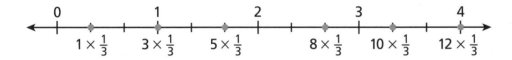

5. $1 \times \frac{1}{3} =$ _____

6. $3 \times \frac{1}{3} =$ _____

7. $5 \times \frac{1}{3} =$ _____

8. $8 \times \frac{1}{3} =$ _____

9. $10 \times \frac{1}{3} =$ _____

10. $12 \times \frac{1}{3} =$ _____

11. Write the missing fractions to count by thirds.

$\frac{1}{3},$ _____ $, \frac{3}{3},$ _____ $, \frac{5}{3},$ _____ $,$ _____ $, \frac{8}{3},$ _____ $, \frac{10}{3},$ _____ $, \frac{12}{3}$

Guided Practice

Solve the problems.

12. Complete the number pattern of multiples.
    Rule: Start with $\frac{1}{2}$ and add $\frac{1}{2}$.

    $\frac{1}{2}$, ———, $\frac{3}{2}$, ———, ———, ———, ———, ———, . . .

13. Sam has 2 pounds of peanuts. He is going to make snack bags with $\frac{1}{4}$ pound of peanuts each. How many snack bags can Sam make? Explain your answer.

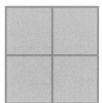 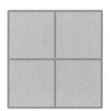

Write each fraction or mixed number as the product of a whole number and a unit fraction.

14. $\frac{2}{5} = 2 \times$ ——————

15. $\frac{4}{6} =$ ——————

16. $\frac{10}{8} =$ ——————

17. $\frac{7}{10} =$ ——————

18. $1\frac{2}{3} =$ ——————

19. $2\frac{2}{5} =$ ——————

Think • Pair • Share

MP3 20. Explain why the denominator stays the same when you multiply a unit fraction by a whole number.

Independent Practice

Complete the equation to find each product. Color the model to support your answer.

1. $4 \times \frac{1}{5} = \frac{}{5}$

2. $1 \times \frac{1}{6} = -$

3. $10 \times \frac{1}{10} = —$

Complete the equation to find each product. Use the number line model to support your answer.

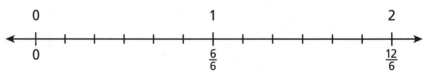

4. $3 \times \frac{1}{6} = \frac{}{6}$

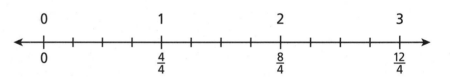

5. $5 \times \frac{1}{4} = -$

Draw lines to match.

6. $2 \times \frac{1}{6}$

7. $2 \times \frac{1}{10}$

8. $10 \times \frac{1}{2}$

9. $12 \times \frac{1}{10}$

10. $12 \times \frac{1}{2}$

a. $\frac{12}{10}$

b. $\frac{10}{2}$

c. $\frac{2}{10}$

d. $\frac{6}{2}$

e. $\frac{12}{2}$

f. $\frac{2}{6}$

Independent Practice

Write each fraction or mixed number as the product of a whole number and a unit fraction.

11. $\frac{5}{6} = 5 \times$ _____

12. $\frac{4}{4} =$ _____

13. $\frac{7}{12} =$ _____

14. $\frac{20}{3} =$ _____

15. $1\frac{5}{10} =$ _____

16. $3\frac{1}{3} =$ _____

Solve.

17. Circle all the multiples of $\frac{1}{5}$.

$\frac{2}{5}$ $\frac{1}{10}$ $\frac{3}{5}$ $\frac{3}{4}$ $\frac{7}{6}$ $\frac{11}{5}$

  a. Write each multiple of $\frac{1}{5}$ as a product of a whole number and $\frac{1}{5}$.

  b. Write each multiple of $\frac{1}{5}$ as a sum.

Circle the correct answer or answers.

18. Which of the sums are also multiples of $\frac{1}{3}$?

  a. $\frac{1}{1} + \frac{1}{2} + \frac{1}{3}$ **b.** $1 + \frac{1}{3}$

  c. $\frac{1}{2} + \frac{1}{1}$ **d.** $\frac{1}{3} + \frac{1}{3} + \frac{1}{3} + \frac{1}{3}$

19. Which fraction is a multiple of $\frac{1}{8}$ that equals 1?

  a. $\frac{1}{8}$ **b.** $\frac{8}{8}$

  c. $\frac{8}{1}$ **d.** $\frac{80}{10}$

Independent Practice

MP3 **20.** Carrie says that fractions can only have other fractions as multiples. Eva says that this is not true, because 2 is a multiple of $\frac{1}{2}$. Who is correct? Explain.

MP3 **21.** Nicolas and Jun Ho are making up riddles for multiples of fractions. Nicolas says his number is a multiple of $\frac{1}{3}$ that has an even number as a denominator. Jun Ho says this is impossible. Can you guess Nicolas's number? Explain.

Solve the problems.

MP1 **22.** A restaurant makes big hamburgers with $\frac{1}{4}$ pound of beef in each. If the restaurant makes 12 hamburgers in one hour, how many pounds of beef does the restaurant use?

◖▭▷ **Show your work.**

Answer _____

MP4 **23.** Reagan's town has a clock tower with bells that ring once every $\frac{1}{2}$ hour. If the bells ring 6 times, how many hours have gone by?

◖▭▷ **Show your work.**

Answer _____

Independent Practice

MP5 **24.** The picture shows a ruler marked with some fractions of an inch. The markings are multiples of $\frac{1}{4}$ and $\frac{1}{2}$.

For each of these fractions, what is the greatest multiple less than 5 inches? To help you identify each multiple, write it as a product of the fraction and a whole number.

✏ **Show your work.**

Answer _____

MP4 **25.** Victoria says that $\frac{17}{6}$ is not a multiple of $\frac{1}{6}$. As proof, she says that $\frac{17}{6}$ equals $2\frac{5}{6}$ instead of a whole number. Is Victoria correct? Draw a model to justify your answer.

Answer _____

✏ **Justify your answer using words, drawings, or numbers.**

MP8 **26.** Samir says that you can write any fraction as a product of a whole number and a unit fraction. Do you agree? Give an example to support your answer.

Answer _____

✏ **Justify your answer using words, drawings, or numbers.**

Essential Question:
How can you multiply a fraction that is not a unit fraction by a whole number?
4.NF.4b

Guided Instruction

In this lesson you will learn how to multiply any fraction by a whole number.

Understand: Multiplication as repeated addition

Sabrina is making carrot muffins. Her muffin pan has 6 baking cups. Sabrina will put $\frac{2}{3}$ cup of batter in each baking cup. How much batter does she need for all 6 baking cups?

To find the total cups of batter, multiply $6 \times \frac{2}{3}$.

Draw a model for the 6 groups of $\frac{2}{3}$.
The model shows that $6 \times \frac{2}{3}$ is the same as $\frac{2}{3} + \frac{2}{3} + \frac{2}{3} + \frac{2}{3} + \frac{2}{3} + \frac{2}{3}$.

$\frac{2}{3}$ cup

6 addends

$$6 \times \frac{2}{3} = \frac{2}{3} + \frac{2}{3} + \frac{2}{3} + \frac{2}{3} + \frac{2}{3} + \frac{2}{3}$$

$$= \frac{2 + 2 + 2 + 2 + 2 + 2}{3}$$

$$= \frac{6 \times 2}{3}$$

$$= \frac{12}{3}$$

Write the product $\frac{12}{3}$ as a whole number. You can use the fact $12 = 4 \times 3$ to help you find the whole number.

$$\frac{12}{3} = \frac{4 \times 3}{3} = \frac{3}{3} + \frac{3}{3} + \frac{3}{3} + \frac{3}{3} = 4$$

➡ Sabrina needs 4 cups of batter for all 6 baking cups.

Remember!
You can break apart the numerator of a fraction in the same way as a whole number.

✏ Write the first six multiples of $\frac{2}{3}$.

Understand: Writing the fraction as a multiple of a unit fraction before multiplying

> How can you multiply a fraction by a whole number without using repeated addition?

You can solve Sabrina's muffin problem in a different way. To multiply $6 \times \frac{2}{3}$, you can think of $\frac{2}{3}$ as $2 \times \frac{1}{3}$ and then use the Associative Property of Multiplication.

$6 \times 2 = 12$ $\frac{2}{3}$ cup

$2 \times \frac{1}{3}$

$2 \times \frac{1}{3}$

$2 \times \frac{1}{3}$

$2 \times \frac{1}{3}$

$2 \times \frac{1}{3}$

$2 \times \frac{1}{3}$

2 thirds

$$6 \times \frac{2}{3} = 6 \times \left(2 \times \frac{1}{3}\right)$$

$$= (6 \times 2) \times \frac{1}{3}$$

$$= 12 \times \frac{1}{3}$$

$$= \frac{12}{3}$$

$$= 4$$

Remember!
The Associative Property of Multiplication states that you can change the grouping of the factors without changing the product.

The product is the same as with the repeated addition method.

➡ To multiply any fraction by a whole number, you can multiply the numerator of the fraction by the whole number. Then write the product over the denominator.

$$6 \times \frac{2}{3} = \frac{6 \times 2}{3} = \frac{12}{3} = 4$$

✏️ Find the total cups of batter Sabrina will need for a pan with 9 baking cups instead of 6.

Guided Instruction

Connect: Multiplying a mixed number by a whole number

> Damian is teaching himself to play the guitar. This week, he plays his guitar for $1\frac{3}{4}$ hours on each of 4 days. For how many hours does Damian play his guitar this week?

To find how many hours Damian plays his guitar, multiply $4 \times 1\frac{3}{4}$.
You can use an equivalent fraction for the mixed number.

Step 1

Rewrite $1\frac{3}{4}$ as a fraction greater than 1.

$$1\frac{3}{4} = 1 + \frac{3}{4}$$
$$= \frac{4}{4} + \frac{3}{4}$$
$$= \frac{7}{4}$$

So, rewrite the multiplication as $4 \times \frac{7}{4}$.

Step 2

Multiply 4 times the numerator in the fraction $\frac{7}{4}$.
Write the total number of fourths over the denominator.
$$4 \times \frac{7}{4} = \frac{4 \times 7}{4} = \frac{28}{4} = 7$$

To check, you can mark off 4 groups of $\frac{7}{4}$ on a number line.

The fourth multiple of $\frac{7}{4}$ is the product, $\frac{28}{4} = 7$.

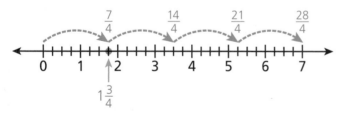

Damian plays his guitar for 7 hours this week.

Sarah says that you can also multiply $4 \times 1\frac{3}{4}$ by writing $4 \times (1 + \frac{3}{4})$ and then adding 4×1 and $4 \times \frac{3}{4}$. Do you agree?

Guided Practice

Use the model or the number line to show that your product is correct.

1. $2 \times \frac{3}{5} = \frac{3}{5} + \frac{3}{5} = \frac{\times 3}{5} = \frac{-}{-} = 1\frac{-}{-}$

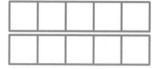

2. $3 \times \frac{4}{6} = \frac{4}{6} + \frac{4}{6} + \frac{4}{6} = \frac{\times}{} = \frac{}{} = \underline{}$

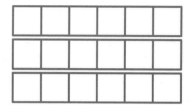

3. $3 \times \frac{5}{8} = \frac{\times}{8} = \frac{}{8} = \underline{}\frac{-}{-}$

Complete the equation to multiply. If the product is greater than 1, write it as a whole or mixed number.

4. $7 \times \frac{3}{10} = \frac{\times}{10} = \frac{}{10} = \underline{}\frac{-}{-}$

5. $4 \times 2\frac{1}{2} = 4 \times \frac{}{2} = \frac{\times}{} = \frac{-}{-} = \underline{}$

⭐ **Think • Pair • Share**

MP4 6. Compare the problem in exercise 2 to multiplying the whole numbers 3 × 4. How are the problems alike? How are they different?

Independent Practice

Use the model or the number line to show that your product is correct.

1. $2 \times \dfrac{7}{10} = \dfrac{ \times }{10} = \dfrac{}{} = 1\dfrac{}{}$

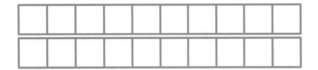

2. $3 \times \dfrac{4}{5} = \dfrac{ \times }{} = \dfrac{}{} = \underline{}\dfrac{}{}$

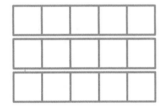

3. $5 \times \dfrac{3}{6} = \dfrac{ \times }{} = \dfrac{}{} = \underline{}\dfrac{}{}$

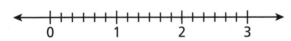

List the first five multiples of $\dfrac{3}{6}$. Use the model to help you.

_____

4. $4 \times 1\dfrac{3}{8} = 4 \times \dfrac{}{8} =$

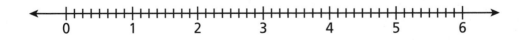

Independent Practice

For exercises 5–9, use the number line. The number line shows multiples of $\frac{3}{4}$. Write each multiple as a product of a whole number and a fraction.

5. $\frac{3}{4}$ = _____

6. $\frac{6}{4}$ = _____

7. $\frac{9}{4}$ = _____

8. What are the next three multiples?

_____

9. Are there any multiples of $\frac{3}{4}$ between $\frac{6}{4}$ and $\frac{9}{4}$? Explain.

Multiply. If the product is greater than 1, write it as a whole or mixed number. You can use a model to help.

10. $5 \times \frac{2}{5}$ = _____

11. $4 \times \frac{5}{6}$ = _____

12. $3 \times \frac{9}{12}$ = _____

13. $6 \times 2\frac{2}{10}$ = _____

Independent Practice

MP2 **14.** Brenda wants to write the product $\frac{14}{3}$ as a mixed number. How can Brenda use multiplication to help her rename the product?

MP1 **15.** How does drawing a model help you multiply a fraction by a whole number? Explain your opinion.

Solve the problems.

MP1 **16.** Kristin is making soup. The recipe calls for $\frac{6}{8}$ pound of beef. Kristin wants to make 4 times the amount of soup in the recipe. How many pounds of beef does Kristin need?

✏ · **Show your work.**

Answer _____

MP6 **17.** Levi watched his favorite movie 9 times on DVD. The movie is $1\frac{6}{10}$ hours long. How many hours did it take Levi to watch the movie 9 times?

✏ · **Show your work.**

Answer _____

Independent Practice

MP1 **18.** A gardener is moving some houseplants into bigger pots. She has 3 plastic pots that hold $4\frac{1}{12}$ quarts of soil each. She also has 4 clay pots that hold $3\frac{2}{5}$ quarts of soil each. Does the gardener need more soil for the plastic pots or the clay pots?

▸ **Show your work.**

Answer _____

MP1 **19.** Darius reads $\frac{2}{10}$ of his book in 3 days. He says that if he reads the rest of the book at the same speed, it should take him 15 more days to finish the book. Is Darius correct?

Answer _____

▸ **Justify your answer using words, drawings, or numbers.**

MP7 **20.** Jenny is helping to pack supplies for a school picnic. Each of three boxes of drinking straws are filled with only 50 out of 100 straws. Jenny says that she can multiply $3 \times \frac{1}{2}$ instead of $3 \times \frac{50}{100}$ to find the total number of full boxes. Is Jenny correct?

Answer _____

▸ **Justify your answer using words, drawings, or numbers.**

23 Problem Solving: Multiply Fractions by Whole Numbers

Essential Question: How can multiplying fractions by whole numbers help you to solve real-world problems?

4.NF.4c

Guided Instruction

In this lesson you will learn how to multiply a fraction or a mixed number by a whole number to solve word problems.

Understand: Multiplying a fraction by a whole number and comparing two amounts

> Jordan is buying modeling clay to use for a project. He can buy six $\frac{3}{5}$-pound sticks of different colors. The store also sells a 5-pound pack of colors for the same price. Which should Jordan buy to get more clay?

To solve the problem, find the total weight of the 6 sticks and then compare it to 5 pounds.

Remember!

$$6 \times \frac{3}{5} = \frac{3}{5} + \frac{3}{5} + \frac{3}{5} + \frac{3}{5} + \frac{3}{5} + \frac{3}{5}$$

You can use a model to show 6 groups of $\frac{3}{5}$ pound.

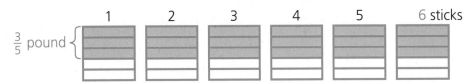

$\frac{3}{5}$ pound

1   2   3   4   5   6 sticks

Find the total number of pounds in 6 sticks. You can count the shaded fifths in the model or you can write and solve an equation. Use w to represent the number of pounds of clay in 6 sticks.

$$w = 6 \times \frac{3}{5}$$
$$6 \times \frac{3}{5} = \frac{6 \times 3}{5} = \frac{18}{5} \text{ and } \frac{18}{5} = \frac{15}{5} + \frac{3}{5} = 3 + \frac{3}{5} = 3\frac{3}{5}$$
$$w = 3\frac{3}{5}$$

The total weight of the 6 sticks is $3\frac{3}{5}$ pounds.

Compare $3\frac{3}{5}$ to 5. Since $3 < 5$, the 5-pound pack has more clay. $3\frac{3}{5} < 5$

➤ Jordan should buy the 5-pound pack instead of six $\frac{3}{5}$-pound sticks to get more clay.

✎ How many fifths of a pound are in the 5-pound pack? How many more pounds are in the 5-pound pack than in six $\frac{3}{5}$-pound sticks?

Understand: Multiplying a fraction or mixed number greater than 1 by a whole number

> Jordan buys 3 different colors of paint. He needs $1\frac{1}{2}$ gallons of each color. How much paint does he buy?

Method 1

Solve the problem using visual models. Show 3 groups of $1\frac{1}{2}$.

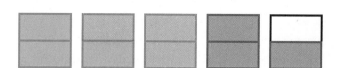

The model shows that Jordan buys $\frac{9}{2}$ or $4\frac{1}{2}$ gallons of paint.

➡ Jordan buys $4\frac{1}{2}$ gallons of paint.

Method 2

Solve the problem using an equation. Let g represent the total number of gallons of paint Jordan buys.　　$g = 3 \times 1\frac{1}{2}$

One Way to Solve the Equation

$g = 3 \times 1\frac{1}{2}$

$g = 3 \times (1 + \frac{1}{2})$

$g = 3 \times (\frac{2}{2} + \frac{1}{2})$

$g = 3 \times (\frac{3}{2})$

$g = \frac{3 \times 3}{2}$

$g = \frac{9}{2}$

$g = \frac{8}{2} + \frac{1}{2}$

$g = 4 + \frac{1}{2}$

$g = 4\frac{1}{2}$

Another Way to Solve the Equation

$g = 3 \times 1\frac{1}{2}$

$g = 3 \times (1 + \frac{1}{2})$

$g = (3 \times 1) + (3 \times \frac{1}{2})$

$g = 3 + \frac{3}{2}$

$g = 3 + (\frac{2}{2} + \frac{1}{2})$

$g = 3 + (1 + \frac{1}{2})$

$g = 3 + 1\frac{1}{2}$

$g = 4\frac{1}{2}$

Remember!

Multiplying a number by a sum is the same as multiplying the number by each addend of the sum and then adding the products.

➡ Jordan buys $4\frac{1}{2}$ gallons of paint.

✏ If Jordan can only buy gallon cans of paint, how many gallon cans must Jordan buy? Explain your reasoning.

Guided Instruction

Connect: Solving a multi-step problem using equations and models

Natalie and Rachel are hiking with their families. Natalie's family hikes a $3\frac{1}{4}$-mile trail to the end, and then hikes back on the same trail. Rachel's family hikes around a $\frac{3}{4}$-mile loop 8 times. Which family hikes more miles?

You can use equations and models to solve.

Step 1

Find the total distance Natalie's family hikes.

Use n for the number of miles Natalie's family hikes.

Solve $n = 2 \times 3\frac{1}{4}$.

> **Remember!**
> Estimate: $2 \times 3 = 6$

$n = 2 \times 3\frac{1}{4} = 2 \times (3 + \frac{1}{4})$

$= (2 \times 3) + (2 \times \frac{1}{4})$ ← Distributive Property

$= 6 + \frac{2 \times 1}{4}$

$= 6\frac{2}{4}$

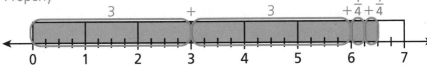

So, $n = 6\frac{2}{4}$. Natalie's family hikes $6\frac{2}{4}$ miles.

Step 2

Find the total distance Rachel's family hikes.

Use r for the number of miles Rachel's family hikes.

Solve $r = 8 \times \frac{3}{4}$.

$r = 8 \times \frac{3}{4} = \frac{8 \times 3}{4}$

$= \frac{24}{4}$

$= 6$

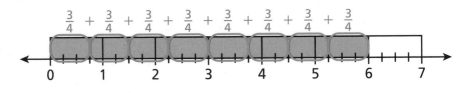

So, $r = 6$. Rachel's family hikes 6 miles.

Step 3

Compare the distances: $6\frac{2}{4} > 6$.

➡ Natalie's family hikes more miles than Rachel's family.

Guided Practice

Use the model to represent the word problem. Answer the questions below.

1. The class learns about 3 different subjects for $\frac{5}{6}$ hour each. What is the total amount of time the class spends on these 3 subjects?

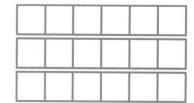

a. What do you need to find? _____

b. Color the model to show the given information.

c. Write an equation you can use to solve the problem. Use h to represent the unknown number of hours.   _____

d. Multiply to solve the equation. $h = 3 \times \frac{5}{6} = \frac{\times}{6} = $ ——

Answer _____

2. Lee needs 4 pieces of ribbon, each $1\frac{1}{3}$ yards long. How many yards of ribbon does she need in all?

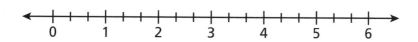

a. What do you need to find? _____

b. Draw and label ____ loops on the number line to represent the problem.

c. Write an equation that you can use to solve the problem. Use r to represent the unknown.   _____

d. Solve the equation. If the solution is equal to or greater than 1, write it as a whole or mixed number.

$r = $ _____

Answer _____

 **Think•Pair•Share**

MP2 3. Show a different way to multiply $4 \times 1\frac{1}{3}$. Which way do you prefer?

Independent Practice

For problems 1–3, identify what you need to find. Then use the model and an equation to solve the problem.

1. Alyssa has 4 snack bags of raisins. Each bag has $\frac{2}{3}$ cup of raisins. How many cups of raisins does Alyssa have altogether?

   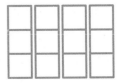

   Find _____

   Equation _____

   Answer _____

2. Luis mixes equal amounts of orange, cranberry, and grape juice to make a fruit punch. He uses $1\frac{1}{4}$ cups of each kind of juice. How many cups of punch does Luis make?

   Find _____

   Equation _____

   Answer _____

MP5 3. In Diana's class, $\frac{2}{5}$ of the students ride the Blue Bus to school. In Troy's class, 2 times as many students ride the Blue Bus as in Diana's class. If both classes have the same number of students, what fraction of Troy's class rides the Blue Bus?

   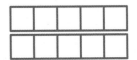

   Find _____

   Equation _____

   Answer _____

MP1 4. If 12 students in Diana's class ride the Blue Bus, how many students in Troy's class ride the Blue Bus? Use exercise 3 to solve.

   ✏ **Show your work.**

   Answer _____

Independent Practice

**Circle the correct answer or answers to solve the problems.
You can use a model to help.**

MP6 **5.** Carrie uses fishing wire to make beaded necklaces. She uses $1\frac{3}{4}$ feet of wire to make one necklace. How much wire does Carrie need to make 5 necklaces?

    a. $3\frac{3}{4}$ feet   **b.** $6\frac{3}{4}$ feet

    c. $8\frac{3}{4}$ feet   **d.** 9 feet

MP4 **6.** About $\frac{6}{100}$ of the people in the United States are less than 5 years old. Four times as many people are less than 18 years old. What fraction of the people in the U.S. are less than 18 years old?

    a. $\frac{13}{100}$ **b.** $\frac{18}{100}$

    c. $\frac{20}{100}$ **d.** $\frac{24}{100}$

MP1 **7.** Andrew runs around a $\frac{1}{4}$-mile track 6 times. Which of the following do NOT describe the total number of miles Andrew runs?

    a. $1\frac{1}{4}$ miles   **b.** $1\frac{1}{2}$ miles

    c. between 1 and 2 miles   **d.** more than 2 miles

MP2 **8.** There are 4 quarts in 1 gallon. Marlon is trying to find out how many quarts of milk are in six $\frac{1}{2}$-gallon cartons. Which of the following does NOT represent the total number of quarts of milk?

    a. $6 \times \frac{1}{2}$ **b.** 4×3

    c. $4 \times (6 \times \frac{1}{2})$ **d.** $24 \times \frac{1}{2}$

    Explain your answer.

Independent Practice

MP2   **9.** Why is the product of 6 and $\frac{11}{12}$ less than 6? Is the product of a whole number and a fraction always less than the whole number?

MP4   **10.** What multiplication example does the model show? Write and solve a word problem that the model could represent.

Solve the problems.

MP5   **11.** Daniella is using the length of her hand to measure the width of her desk. Her hand is $\frac{5}{12}$ feet long. The width of her desk is 7 lengths of her hand. How many feet wide is Daniella's desk?

🖉 **Show your work.**

Answer _____

MP6   **12.** Brad is making popcorn in the microwave. It takes $3\frac{3}{4}$ minutes to pop one bag of popcorn. How long will Brad take to pop 4 bags, one at a time?

🖉 **Show your work.**

Answer _____

Independent Practice

MP1 **13.** Chelsea buys 3 bags of cherries that each weighs $\frac{3}{4}$ of a pound. Her sister buys 4 bags of cherries that each weighs $\frac{1}{2}$ of a pound. Who buys more pounds of cherries?

➤ **Show your work.**

Answer _____

MP4 **14.** Angela needs $\frac{3}{4}$ cup of milk for each batch of pancakes she makes. She draws the model below to find the amount of milk she needs to make 5 batches.

Is Angela's model correct?

Answer _____

➤ **Justify your answer using words, drawings, or numbers.**

MP8 **15.** Kenny knows that it takes him 13 minutes to walk 1 mile. His friend lives $2\frac{7}{8}$ miles away. Kenny writes the equation below to find out how long it will take to walk to his friend's house.

$$13 \times 2\frac{7}{8} = 13 \times (2 + \frac{7}{8}) = (13 \times 2) + \frac{13 \times 7}{8}$$

Can Kenny find the correct number of minutes with this method? Use Kenny's or a different method to solve the problem.

Answer _____

➤ **Justify your answer using words, drawings, or numbers.**

Essential Question:
How can you use the relationship between 10 and 100 to add tenths and hundredths?

4.NF.5

Words to Know:
tenth
hundredth

Guided Instruction

In this lesson you will learn how to write equivalent fractions so that you can add fractions with denominators of 10 and 100.

Understand: Tenths and hundredths of a whole

> One dollar equals 10 dimes or 100 pennies. If Carla has 6 dimes, how many tenths of a dollar does she have? If she has 6 pennies, how many hundredths of a dollar does she have?

To represent dimes and pennies as fractions of a dollar, you can use 10 and 100 as denominators.

First, model the 10 dimes in 1 dollar.
Use 1 whole partitioned into 10 equal parts.
Each part is 1 tenth, or $\frac{1}{10}$, of the whole.

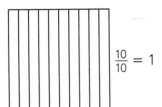

$\frac{10}{10} = 1$

Six dimes is $\frac{6}{10}$ of a dollar.

To show 6 dimes, shade 6 tenths in the model.
Write the fraction for the shaded part.

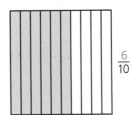

$\frac{6}{10}$

Now model the 100 pennies in 1 dollar.
Use 1 whole partitioned into 100 equal parts.
Each part is 1 hundredth, or $\frac{1}{100}$, of the whole.

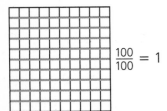

$\frac{100}{100} = 1$

Six pennies is $\frac{6}{100}$ of a dollar.

To show 6 pennies, shade 6 hundredths in the model.
Write the fraction for the shaded part.

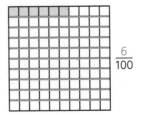

$\frac{6}{100}$

➡ If Carla has 6 dimes, she has 6 tenths of a dollar. If Carla has 6 pennies, she has 6 hundredths of a dollar.

Guided Instruction

Understand: Equivalent tenths and hundredths of dollars

> Carla wants to exchange her 6 dimes for pennies. How many pennies will Carla get that equal 6 dimes?

You can rename tenths as hundredths the same way you write other equivalent fractions.

Look at the 6 tenths model below. Shade the same area of the hundredths model. How many hundredths did you shade? 60 hundredths

You can partition each tenth into 10 equal parts to make hundredths.
1 tenth equals 10 hundredths.

$$\frac{1}{10} = \frac{10 \times 1}{10 \times 10} = \frac{10}{100}$$

6 tenths equals 60 hundredths.

$$\frac{6}{10} = \frac{10 \times 6}{10 \times 10} = \frac{60}{100}$$

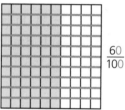

Since 1 hundredth dollar is 1 penny, 60 hundredths dollar is 60 pennies.
So, 6 dimes equal 60 pennies.

➡ Carla will get 60 pennies for 6 dimes.

Understand: Addition of tenths and hundredths when the whole is a dollar

> One dollar equals 100 cents. Jason has $\frac{8}{10}$ dollar in dimes and $\frac{15}{100}$ dollar in pennies. How many cents does Jason have altogether?

To find the total number of cents, rename the tenths as hundredths and then add.
Model the 8 tenths of a dollar.
Write an equivalent fraction for $\frac{8}{10}$ using 100 as the denominator.

$$\frac{8}{10} = \frac{10 \times 8}{10 \times 10} = \frac{80}{100}$$

8 tenths equals 80 hundredths.

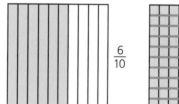

$\frac{80}{100}$ and $\frac{15}{100}$ have like denominators, so you can add the hundredths.

8 dimes 15 pennies
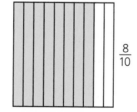
$$\frac{80}{100} + \frac{15}{100} = \frac{95}{100}$$

Remember!
To add fractions with like denominators, add the numerators.

One hundredth of a dollar is 1 cent, so 95 hundredths of a dollar is 95 cents.

➡ Jason has 95 cents altogether.

Guided Instruction

Connect: Adding tenths and hundredths when the whole is not a dollar

Every school day, Maria walks to school in the morning and walks back home in the afternoon. When she walks to school in the morning, she takes a direct route which is $\frac{2}{10}$ mile. When she walks home, she takes a different route that goes along a jogging trail. That route is $\frac{34}{100}$ mile. How far does Maria walk each day during her trip to and from school?

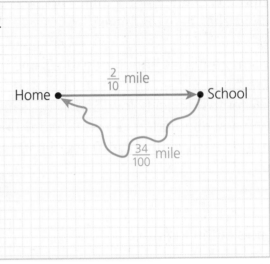

In this problem, the whole is 1 mile. You can add fractions of a mile just like you added fractions of a dollar.

Step 1

Rename $\frac{2}{10}$ as hundredths.
Write an equivalent fraction using 100 as the denominator.

$$\frac{2}{10} = \frac{10 \times 2}{10 \times 10} = \frac{20}{100}$$

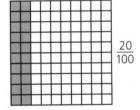

$\frac{20}{100}$

Step 2

Now add $\frac{20}{100}$ and $\frac{34}{100}$.

$$\frac{20}{100} + \frac{34}{100} = \frac{20 + 34}{100} = \frac{54}{100}$$

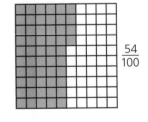

$\frac{54}{100}$

➡ Maria walks $\frac{54}{100}$ mile during her trip to and from school.

✏ Does Maria walk more or less than $\frac{1}{2}$ mile during her trip to and from school? How did you decide?

Color the model to show the tenths. Then rename the tenths as an equivalent number of hundredths.

1. 1 tenth

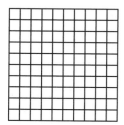

$$\frac{1}{10} = \frac{10 \times}{10 \times} = \frac{}{100}$$

2. 5 tenths

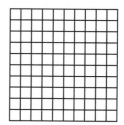

$$\frac{5}{10} = \frac{10 \times}{10 \times} = \frac{}{100}$$

Rename the tenths as an equivalent fraction with a denominator of 100. Add. Use the model to show the addition.

3. 3 tenths + 42 hundredths

$$\frac{3}{10} = \underline{\hspace{2cm}}$$

$$\frac{}{100} + \frac{}{100} = \frac{}{100}$$

4. 20 hundredths + 11 tenths

$$\frac{11}{10} = \underline{\hspace{2cm}}$$

$$\frac{}{100} + \frac{}{100} = \frac{}{100}$$

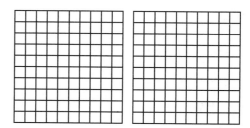

★ Think • Pair • Share

MP7 **5.** Look at exercise 4 above. What is another way to write 11 tenths? What is another way to write 20 hundredths? Use your model to help you.

Independent Practice

Look at the model. Name the fraction shown. Rename using equivalent fractions.

1.

$$\frac{}{10} = \frac{10 \times}{10 \times} = \frac{}{100}$$

2.

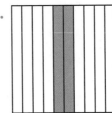

$$\frac{}{10} = \frac{10 \times}{10 \times} = \frac{}{100}$$

3.

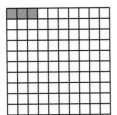

$$\frac{}{100} = \frac{}{10}$$

4.

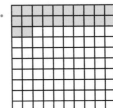

$$\frac{}{100} = \frac{20}{100} + \frac{}{100} = \frac{}{10} + \frac{2}{100}$$

Rename the tenths as hundredths.

5. 7 tenths = _____ hundredths

$$\frac{7}{10} = \underline{\quad}$$

6. 9 tenths = _____ hundredths

$$\underline{\quad} = \underline{\quad}$$

Circle the correct answer.

7. Which fraction is modeled below?

   a. $\frac{3}{100}$ b. $\frac{30}{100}$

   c. $\frac{3}{10}$ d. $\frac{30}{10}$

8. Which of the following is NOT equivalent to the fraction in the model?

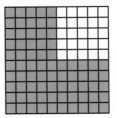

   a. $\frac{75}{100}$ b. $\frac{75}{10}$

   c. $\frac{5}{10} + \frac{25}{100}$ d. $\frac{50}{100} + \frac{25}{100}$

Independent Practice

Use equivalent fractions to find each sum. Show your work.

9. $\frac{1}{10} + \frac{1}{100}$

10. $\frac{4}{10} + \frac{14}{100}$

Answer _____

Answer _____

11. $\frac{50}{100} + \frac{8}{10}$

12. $\frac{5}{10} + \frac{85}{100} + \frac{6}{10}$

Answer _____

Answer _____

13. In exercises 9–12, which sums are greater than 1?

_____

Draw lines to match each addition exercise with the correct sum.

14. 7 hundredths + 7 tenths   a. $\frac{177}{100}$

15. 7 tenths + 70 hundredths   b. $\frac{91}{100}$

16. 1 tenth + 17 hundredths   c. $\frac{140}{100}$

17. 10 tenths + 4 hundredths   d. $\frac{77}{100}$

18. 7 hundredths + 17 tenths   e. $\frac{27}{100}$

19. 11 hundredths + 8 tenths   f. $\frac{104}{100}$

Independent Practice

MP7 20. What is the relationship between tenths and hundredths? Discuss both the number of parts in 1 whole and the size of each part.

MP4 21. Lily says that the amount modeled below can only be broken apart and written as a sum of hundredths. Do you agree with Lily? Write this amount as a sum of two addends.

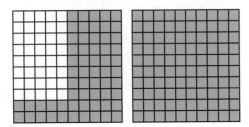

For problems 22 and 23, use the table at the right.

MP1 22. Curtis buys a book and gets pennies back in change. The pennies have the same value as 5 dimes. How many pennies does Curtis get?

✏️ **Show your work.**

Money Amounts	
Coin	**Fraction of 1 Dollar**
Dime	$\frac{1}{10}$
Penny	$\frac{1}{100}$

Answer _____

MP6 23. A cashier at a store counts the change in the register drawer. She has 3 dimes and 12 pennies. What is the total fraction of a dollar for these coins?

✏️ **Show your work.**

Answer _____

Independent Practice

For problems 24–26, use the diagram at the right.

MP5 **24.** Tara is using wood to make a picture frame. The diagram shows the lengths of the pieces of wood she needs to make each side. She wants to know how much longer the bottom side of the picture frame is than the right side. She writes this equation to find the difference between the two lengths. $\frac{2}{10} + x = \frac{38}{100}$

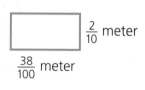
$\frac{2}{10}$ meter
$\frac{38}{100}$ meter

What is the difference between the two lengths?

✏️ **Show your work.**

Answer _____

MP1 **25.** Tara bought 1 meter of wood to make the picture frame. Does Tara have enough wood for all four sides of the picture frame?

Answer _____

✏️ **Justify your answer using words, drawings, or numbers.**

MP3 **26.** Geoffrey says that Tara should rename the lengths of the bottom and top of the picture frame as tenths instead of hundredths. He thinks this will make it easier to measure the correct lengths. Do you agree with Geoffrey? You can use the hundredths model below to explain.

Answer _____

✏️ **Justify your answer using words, drawings, or numbers.**

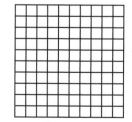

Write and Compare Decimal Fractions

Essential Question:
How can you use place value to write and compare tenths and hundredths?

4.NF.6; 4.NF.7

Words to Know:
decimal
decimal point

Guided Instruction

In this lesson you will learn how to write and compare decimal numbers for tenths and hundredths.

Understand: Equivalent decimals and fractions for tenths

> Matt is making a cage for his hamster. The directions say to make the cage 0.7 meter long. Matt says this is the same as $\frac{7}{10}$ meter. Is Matt correct? Do 0.7 and $\frac{7}{10}$ name the same number?

A decimal fraction, or decimal, is a number that uses place value and a decimal point. You can also write a decimal as a fraction with a denominator of 10 or 100. The decimal point separates the whole-number part (which may be 0) and the part less than 1.

0.7
↑
decimal point

You can use a fraction or a decimal to name the same number of tenths. Compare the model and the place-value chart.

The fraction $\frac{7}{10}$ names 7 tenths of the whole.

7 of the $\frac{1}{10}$-size parts are shaded.

tens	ones	.	tenths	hundredths
	0	.	7	

The decimal 0.7 also names 7 tenths, with the digit 7 in the tenths place. The tenths place is to the right of the ones and the decimal point.

You can use the same point on a number line diagram to represent $\frac{7}{10}$ and 0.7.

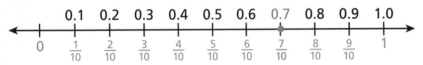

You can also read the numbers the same way.
seven tenths = 7 tenths = $\frac{7}{10}$ = 0.7

➡ Yes, Matt is correct. 0.7 and $\frac{7}{10}$ name the same number, seven tenths.

▬▬▶ What do you think the number 1.7 means?

Guided Instruction

Understand: Equivalent decimals and fractions for hundredths

One side of Matt's hamster cage is too long. It measures 0.79 meter instead of 0.7 meter. What equivalent fraction represents the length 0.79 meter?

To understand the decimal 0.79, use place value to write an equivalent fraction and model the amount.

Look at 0.79 in a place-value chart.

Remember!
The value of each place is $\frac{1}{10}$ the value of the place to the left.

tens	ones	.	tenths	hundredths
	0	.	7	9

The 7 in the tenths place names 7 tenths, or 0.7.
The 9 in the hundredths place names 9 hundredths, or 0.09.

As with fractions, you can rename the decimal 7 tenths as 70 hundredths.

$$0.7 = \frac{7}{10} = \frac{10 \times 7}{10 \times 10} = \frac{70}{100} = 0.70$$

Now add 9 hundredths.
$$0.70 + 0.09 = 0.79$$

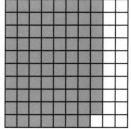

$\frac{70}{100} + \frac{9}{100}$
or
$0.70 + 0.09$

So altogether, 0.79 is equivalent to 79 hundredths, or *seventy-nine hundredths*. The equivalent fraction is $\frac{79}{100}$.

➡ The equivalent fraction that represents 0.79 meter is $\frac{79}{100}$ meter.

Look at the number line below. The decimal 0.79, or $\frac{79}{100}$, is just 1 hundredth less than $\frac{80}{100}$. This means it is a little to the left of $\frac{80}{100}$ on the number line.

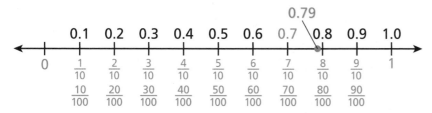

✏ ➡ Write both $\frac{79}{100}$ and 0.79 as sums of tenths and hundredths.

Guided Instruction

Connect: Comparing decimal tenths and hundredths

Carmen wants to find the shortest way to the museum. She calls for directions and someone at the museum says one route is about four and three tenths miles long. A map website shows a different route that is 4.05 miles long. Which route is shorter?

First write both numbers as decimals. Then make models and use equivalent fractions to help you compare the two decimals.

Step 1

Write "four and three tenths" as a decimal. The "and" tells you where to place the decimal point.

$$4.3 = 4\frac{3}{10}$$
four and three tenths
4.3

Step 2

Make sure the decimals name parts of the same unit or whole amount. In this problem, the unit, or whole amount, is 1 mile. 4.3 and 4.05 are both numbers of miles, so you can compare them.

Remember!

Tenths and *hundredths* are parts of a whole.

Step 3

Now compare the numbers. Both decimals have 4 as a whole number amount, so you can model just the tenths and hundredths.

$0.3 = \frac{3}{10} = \frac{30}{100}$; $0.05 = \frac{5}{100}$

$\frac{30}{100} > \frac{5}{100}$ and $0.3 > 0.05$

$4.3 > 4.05$

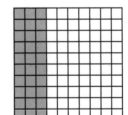

4.3 > 4.05
4.30 > 4.05

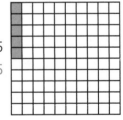

➡ The route from the map website is shorter.

You can also line up 4.3 and 4.05 by their decimal points and compare them as you compare whole numbers. Compare the values of the digits in the first place where they are different.

tens	ones	.	tenths	hundredths
	4	.	3	
	4	.	0	5

3 tenths > 0 tenths, so 4.3 > 4.05.

✏ How much shorter is the website's route?

Color the model to show each amount. Then write the amount as both a fraction and a decimal.

1. 6 tenths

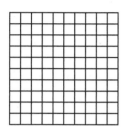

$\dfrac{6}{} = 0.\underline{}$

2. 8 hundredths

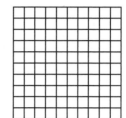

$\dfrac{8}{} = 0.\underline{}$

**Color the models to show the decimals. Then write <, =, or >
to compare.**

3. 0.52

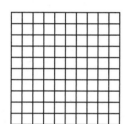

0.9

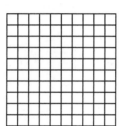

0.52 ____ 0.9

What is the first place where the digits are different?

_____

**Label points on the number line diagram to show the decimals.
Then write <, =, or > to compare.**

4. 0.21 and 0.29

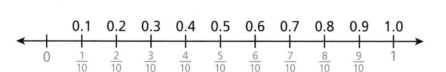

0.21 ____ 0.29

What is the first place where the digits are different?

_____

Think • Pair • Share

MP5   **5.** Look at exercise 3 above. Explain how the place values of the digits in 0.52 and 0.9 relate to the models, and show which decimal is greater. Discuss the number and values of the digits.

Independent Practice

Identify the amount as a number of tenths or hundredths. Then write an equivalent fraction and decimal.

1.
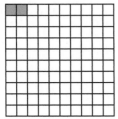

2 _____

$\dfrac{2}{}$ = 0._____

2.
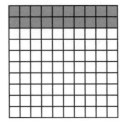

_____ tenths

$\dfrac{}{}$ = 0._____

3.
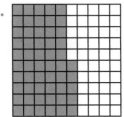

_____

$\dfrac{}{}$ = _____

4.
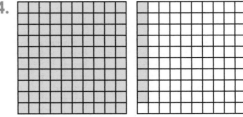

1 and _____

$1\dfrac{}{}$ = _____

Draw points on the number line diagram to represent the numbers. Label each point as a fraction and decimal.

5. 5 hundredths

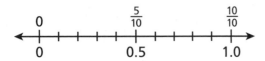

6. 68 hundredths

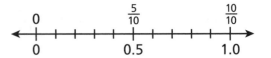

7. Compare the numbers in exercises 5 and 6 above. Which is the greater decimal? Explain.

8. 8 tenths, 91 hundredths, 1 and 38 hundredths

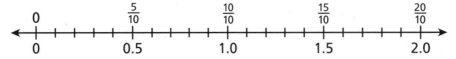

Independent Practice

Write each money amount as a sum of fractions. Then write the expanded decimal form. Use the table at the right to help.

Money Amounts	
Coin	Fraction of 1 Dollar
Dime	$\frac{1}{10}$
Penny	$\frac{1}{100}$

9. 5 dimes and 3 pennies

fraction: _____ = _____ + _____

decimal: $0.53 = _____ + _____

10. 13 pennies and 2 dimes

fraction: _____ = _____ + _____

decimal: $0.33 = _____ + _____

11. 1 dollar and 7 pennies

fraction: _____ = _____ + _____

decimal: $1.07 = _____ + _____

12. 4 dollars and 9 dimes

fraction: _____ = _____ + _____

decimal: $4.90 = _____ + _____

All of the fractions are for the same-size whole. Write the fractions as decimals. Use <, =, or > to compare. Use the place-value chart to help.

tens	ones	.	tenths	hundredths
		.		

13. $\frac{1}{10}$ and $\frac{8}{10}$

_____ _____

14. $\frac{15}{100}$ and $\frac{7}{100}$

_____ _____

15. $\frac{32}{100}$ and $\frac{9}{10}$

_____ _____

16. $\frac{6}{10}$ and $\frac{40}{100}$

_____ _____

17. $1\frac{18}{100}$ and $1\frac{2}{10}$

_____ _____

18. $2\frac{5}{10}$ and $2\frac{50}{100}$

_____ _____

Independent Practice

MP1 **19.** Use the patterns in the table to help you write decimals for fractions with a denominator of 100. What decimals are equivalent to $\frac{4}{100}$, $\frac{14}{100}$, and $1\frac{14}{100}$?

Fraction	Decimal
$\frac{3}{10}$	0.3
$\frac{3}{100}$	0.03
$1\frac{3}{100}$	1.03

Answer _____

✏️ **Justify your answer using words, drawings, or numbers.**

MP7 **20.** Annika says that you can use this pattern to write a fraction or mixed number for a decimal: if a decimal has two places to the right of the decimal point, the denominator will be 100, so there will be two zeros in the denominator; if a decimal has one place to the right of the decimal point, the denominator will be 10, so there will be one zero in the denominator. Do you agree? Give examples.

MP3 **21.** Steven says that decimals are easier to compare than fractions. Do you agree? Use the amounts modeled below as an example.

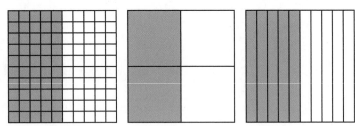

MP6 **22.** Priya needs to measure a length of exactly 0.45 meter for science class. Where does 0.45 belong on a number line?

✏️ **Show your work.**

Answer _____

Independent Practice

MP1 23. One bottle has 1.25 pints of water. The other bottle has 1.4 pints of water. Which bottle has more water?

➤ **Show your work.**

Answer _____

MP7 24. Dennis thinks he may have a fever. In the morning, his temperature is 99.45 degrees. In the afternoon, the school nurse says his temperature is ninety-nine and 6 hundredths. Does Dennis's temperature go up or down by the afternoon?

➤ **Show your work.**

Answer _____

MP2 25. Jacob says that 1.5 is not the same as 1.50 because 1 dollar and 5 dimes equal $1.50, not $1.5. Do you agree that 1.5 and 1.50 are not equivalent? You can use hundredths models to help support your answer.

Answer _____

➤ **Justify your answer using words, drawings, or numbers.**

Add or subtract.

1. $\frac{1}{5} + \frac{1}{5} =$ _____

2. $\frac{8}{6} - \frac{3}{6} =$ _____

3. $4\frac{1}{8} + \frac{7}{8} =$ _____

4. $3\frac{1}{4} - 1\frac{3}{4} =$ _____

Compare. Write <, =, or >.

5. $\frac{3}{4} \bigcirc \frac{9}{12}$

6. $\frac{3}{3} \bigcirc \frac{9}{10}$

7. $\frac{2}{5} \bigcirc \frac{2}{3}$

Circle the correct answer.

8. Which fraction is equivalent to $\frac{1}{2}$?

  a. $\frac{10}{24}$

  b. $\frac{6}{12}$

  c. $\frac{2}{3}$

  d. $\frac{3}{4}$

9. Which fraction is equivalent to $\frac{40}{100}$?

  a. $\frac{10}{4}$

  b. $\frac{5}{10}$

  c. $\frac{2}{5}$

  d. $\frac{1}{5}$

10. Jaxon is writing a fraction as a sum of three addends. The fraction is represented by the point on the number line.

So far, Jaxon has two addends, $\frac{3}{8}$ and $\frac{7}{8}$. Which of the following can Jaxon use as the third addend?

  a. $\frac{4}{8}$

  b. $\frac{6}{8}$

  c. $\frac{10}{8}$

  d. $\frac{14}{8}$

11. Shade the model to show $7 \times \frac{1}{5}$. Then multiply.

$7 \times \frac{1}{5} =$ _____

Write an equation to multiply. Write the product as a whole number or mixed number.

12. $2 \times \frac{4}{5}$

13. $9 \times \frac{5}{9}$

14. Draw a model to show that $0.6 > 0.52$.

15. Draw and label the point 0.67 on the number line.

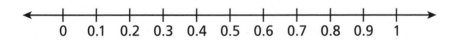

Solve the problems.

16. Peyton surveyed 100 students about their transportation to school. Forty-three hundredths students reported riding bicycles to school and $\frac{3}{10}$ students said they walked. What fraction of the students surveyed rode bicycles or walked to school?

▱▭▸ **Show your work.**

Answer _____

17. A pancake recipe calls for $\frac{2}{4}$ cup whole wheat flour, $\frac{2}{4}$ cup white flour, and $\frac{1}{4}$ cup corn flour. How many cups of flour does the recipe call for in all?

▱▭▸ **Show your work.**

Answer _____

MP8 **18.** Liko used a 10 × 10 grid and Yuri used an 8 × 8 grid to represent the same whole unit. Each boy shaded grid squares to show $\frac{1}{4}$. How many grid squares did Liko shade? How many grid squares did Yuri shade?

Answer _____

✏️ **Use fraction models. Show why Liko and Yuri had to shade a different number of squares to show $\frac{1}{4}$.**

MP3 **19.** Samantha says that $\frac{3}{6} = \frac{2}{3} + \frac{1}{3}$. Describe Samantha's error and tell how to correct it.

✏️ **Justify your answer using words, drawings, or numbers.**

MP2 **20.** For a class party Ms. Vega estimates each student will eat $\frac{1}{6}$ pizza. There are 22 students. How many pizzas should Ms. Vega order? How much pizza will be left over?

Answer _____

✏️ **Justify your answer using words, drawings, or numbers.**

4.OA.1, 4.OA.2, 4.OA.3, 4.NBT.1, 4.NBT.2, 4.NF.3a, 4.NF.3d, 4.NF.4a, 4.NF.4c, 4.NF.6, 4.NF.7

Performance Tasks

Performance Tasks show your understanding of the Math that you have learned. You will be doing various Performance Tasks as you complete your work in this text.

Beginning This Task

The next five pages provide you with the beginning of a Performance Task. You will be given 5 items to complete, and each item will have two or more parts. As you complete these items you will:

I   Demonstrate that you have mastered mathematical skills and concepts

II Reason through a problem to a solution, and explain your reasoning

III Use models and apply them to real-world situations.

Extending This Task

Your teacher may extend this Performance Task with additional items provided in our online resources at sadlierconnect.com.

Scoring This Task

Your response to each item will be assessed against a rubric, or scoring guide. Some items will be worth 1 or 2 points, and others will be worth more. In each item you will show your work or explain your reasoning.

Performance Task 1

A Visit to the Natural History Museum

1. The fourth-grade students go on a field trip to the Natural History Museum. They vote to decide where they will start their visit in the museum.

   a. Seven children vote to start at the Whale Exhibit. Three times as many children vote to start at the Minerals Hall. Draw a diagram to show the comparison.

   Whale Exhibit

   Minerals Hall

   b. Explain how your diagram shows the comparison.

   c. Write an equation to show the comparison.
      w = number of votes for the Whale Exhibit
      m = number of votes for the Minerals Hall

   d. Use your equation and the information given in the problem to find the number of students who vote to start at the Minerals Hall.

Deep-Sea Minerals

2. A scientist will talk about deep-sea minerals. Many students will listen to the scientists. Fifty-four students are already seated. The remaining 32 students are standing in line. The seats are arranged in rows. Each row has 9 seats.

   a. Describe the steps you will take to find how many rows of seats are needed for all the students.

   b. Write an equation that shows how you can find the number of rows of seats the students will need. Use *r* to represent the unknown number of rows.

   c. Find the number of rows the students will need. Explain how you decided on the final answer.

   d. Check that your answer is reasonable. Use reasoning or mental math. Justify your reasoning.

Ocean Giants

3. At the Whale Exhibit, the class sees whale fossils, whale skeletons, and whale models. The table shows the masses of different species of whales.

Whales	
Species	Mass (kg)
Orca	five thousand, seven hundred sixty-four
Blue	100,000 + 60,000 + 3000 + 70 + 2
Humpback	30,000 + 4000 + 200 + 90
Gray	thirty-three thousand, three hundred eight
Beluga	6000 + 100 + 70 + 8

a. Write the mass of each whale in standard form.

b. Which whale has the greatest mass? Which whale has the least mass?

c. Explain how you found the whale with the greatest mass and the whale with the least mass.

d. Write the names of the whales in order from least mass to greatest mass.

Dinosaur Tracks

4. A museum guide shows the fourth-grade class a model of dinosaur tracks found in Utah. Each step is $\frac{1}{3}$ meter long. The dinosaur took 7 steps.

   a. Draw a model to show the total length of the 7 steps.

   b. Write an addition equation that represents the length of the 7 steps. Use *m* to represent the total length.

   c. Write a multiplication expression that represents the length of the 7 steps. Use *m* to represent the total length.

   d. Find the total length of the 7 steps. Explain your method and why you chose that method.

Fossil Footprints

5. The children see a display of five fossil dinosaur footprints. The data below shows the lengths of the footprints in meters.

Footprint Lengths (meter)

$\frac{2}{10}$	0.15	$\frac{6}{100}$	$\frac{42}{100}$	0.1

a. Each large square represents 1 whole. Color the models to show each fraction and decimal from the data.

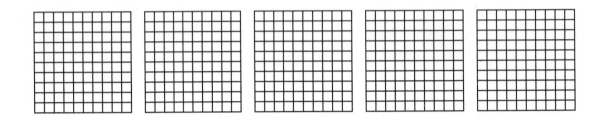

b. Label points on the number line to show each fraction and decimal from the data.

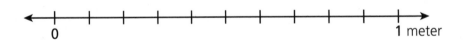

0   1 meter

c. Order the lengths of the footprints from least to greatest. Explain the method you used and why you chose that method.

Progress Check

Look at how the Common Core standards you have learned and will learn connect.

It is very important for you to understand the standards from the prior grade level so that you will be able to develop an understanding of measurement and data in this unit and be prepared for next year. To practice your skills, go to sadlierconnect.com.

UNIT 4

GRADE 3 — I Can...	Before Unit 4	GRADE 4 — Can I ?	After Unit 4	GRADE 5 — I Will...
	☐	**4.MD.1** Express measurements in a larger unit in terms of a smaller unit within the same system	☐	**5.MD.1** Convert among different-sized measurement units within the same measurement system while solving problems
3.MD.2 Measure and estimate liquid volumes and masses Solve one-step problems involving masses or volumes	☐	**4.MD.2** Solve word problems involving distance, time, liquid volumes, masses, and money	☐	
3.MD.7 Find the area of a rectangle **3.MD.8** Solve real-world and mathematical problems involving perimeter	☐	**4.MD.3** Solve real-world and mathematical problems using the area and perimeter formulas for rectangles	☐	**5.MD.5** Apply the volume formulas for rectangular prisms in real-world and mathematical problems
3.MD.4 Display a set of measurements in inches, half inches, and quarter inches on a line plot	☐	**4.MD.4** Make a line plot and use the data to solve problems	☐	**5.MD.2** Make a line plot and use the data to solve problems
	☐	**4.MD.5** Understand angles and angle measurement	☐	
	☐	**4.MD.6** Measure angles using a protractor or sketch angles with a given number of degrees	☐	
	☐	**4.MD.7** Solve problems by using addition and subtraction to find unknown angle measures	☐	

HOME◆CONNECT...

In this unit your child will:

- Convert customary and metric measurement units.

- Solve problems involving measurement, area and perimeter formulas, and line plots.

- Use a protractor to measure angles.

- Find unknown angle measures.

NOTE: All of these learning goals for your child are based on the Grade 4 Common Core State Standards for Mathematics.

Ways to Help Your Child

Writing neatly and showing math work clearly is important. Your child's teacher will analyze math homework to better understand your child's progress and thought processes. During homework time, encourage neat drawing and writing.

The customary system of measurement is most commonly used in the United States of America. In other parts of the world, the metric system of measurement, which is based on 10, is more common. Units of measurement can be converted as equivalent measurements in smaller or larger units.

The meter is a basic metric unit of length. The table below shows the relationship between the sizes of units shorter than and greater than 1 meter.

Metric Unit of Length	Equivalent Lengths	
kilometer	1000 meters	10 hectometers
meter	1 meter	10 decimeters
centimeter	$\frac{1}{100}$ meter	10 millimeters
millimeter	$\frac{1}{1000}$ meter	

Conversation Starter: Make a game of naming units of metric or customary measurement that would most likely be used when measuring distances, liquid volumes, or weights. For example:

- The length of a caterpillar
- The weight of a dog
- The volume of a water bottle
- The volume of a swimming pool

ONLINE

For more Home Connect activities, continue online at sadlierconnect.com

Focus on Measurement and Data

Essential Question:
How can measurement data be used to solve problems?

Convert Customary Measurement Units

Essential Question:
How are larger and smaller customary units of measurement related?
4.MD.1

Words to Know:
customary units

Guided Instruction

In this lesson you will learn about customary units of measurement and how to convert measurements expressed in larger units as measurements in equivalent smaller units.

Understand: **Relative sizes of customary units of weight**

> A restaurant serves 1 ounce of butter with each basket of bread. Will 4 pounds of butter be enough for 50 baskets of bread?

Customary units are the measurement units used in the United States customary system of measurement. A pound and an ounce are customary units of weight. 1 pound is heavier than 1 ounce, so 1 pound is a larger unit.

The model shows the relationship between 1 pound and 1 ounce of butter. The long bar represents 1 pound and the short bar represents 1 ounce.

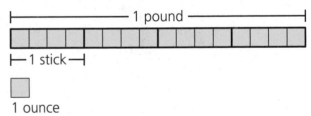

Customary Units of Weight
1 pound (lb) = 16 ounces (oz)

Complete this conversion table to express pounds as ounces.

Pounds	Ounces	
1	16	
2	32	← 2 × 16
3	48	← 3 × 16
4	64	← 4 × 16

Four pounds of butter is equivalent to 64 ounces. 64 > 50

➡ Four pounds of butter will be enough for 50 bread baskets.

Guided Instruction

Understand: Relative sizes of customary units of liquid volume

Lisa's mother goes to the corner store to buy 3 gallons of milk. When she gets there, she sees that there are only quart containers of milk left. How many quarts of milk should she buy?

A gallon, a quart, a pint, and a cup are customary units of liquid volume. The picture shows how the units are related.

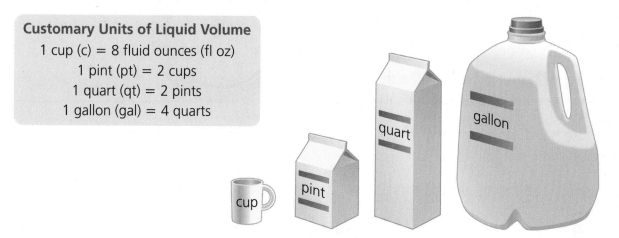

Customary Units of Liquid Volume
1 cup (c) = 8 fluid ounces (fl oz)
1 pint (pt) = 2 cups
1 quart (qt) = 2 pints
1 gallon (gal) = 4 quarts

Use the information above to complete the conversion table.

Gallons	Quarts
1	4
2	8	← 2 × 4
3	12	← 3 × 4

Three gallons of milk is the same amount as 12 quarts.

➡ Lisa's mother should buy 12 quarts of milk.

✏ How many cups of milk can Lisa's mother pour from 3 gallons of milk? Explain.

Guided Instruction

Connect: Relating units and converting time measurements

> Kevin is helping his mother fold and put letters in envelopes. If it takes him 9 seconds for each envelope, how many envelopes can Kevin complete in 3 minutes?

An hour, a minute, and a second are units of time.

Units of Time

1 minute (min) = 60 seconds (s)

1 hour (h) = 60 minutes

The clock shows that there are 60 minutes in 1 hour. There are also 60 seconds in each minute.

The minute hand moves around the clock one complete turn (60 minutes) each hour.

The second hand moves around the clock one complete turn (60 seconds) each minute.

To solve the problem, first find how many seconds are in 3 minutes. Then find how many groups of 9 seconds are on that number of seconds.

Step 1

Complete the conversion table to find the number of seconds in 3 minutes.

Minutes	Seconds	
1	60	
2	120	← 2 × 60
3	180	← 3 × 60

Step 2

Find the number of envelopes Kevin can complete in 180 seconds.

To find how many groups of 9 seconds there are in 180 seconds, divide 180 by 9.

180 ÷ 9 = 20

➡ Kevin can complete 20 envelopes in 3 minutes.

✏ How many seconds are there in 1 hour? Explain.

Guided Practice

Customary Units of Measurement	
Length	**Weight**
1 foot = 12 inches 1 yard = 3 feet	1 pound = 16 ounces 1 ton = 2,000 pounds
Liquid Volume	**Time**
1 cup = 8 fluid ounces 1 pint = 2 cups 1 quart = 2 pints 1 gallon = 4 quarts	1 minute = 60 seconds 1 hour = 60 minutes 1 day = 24 hours 1 week = 7 days

Complete the sentence to compare the sizes of the units.

1. The smallest customary unit of time is 1 _____.

2. 1 yard is _____ times as long as 1 foot.

3. 1 quart is 2 times as much as 1 _____.

4. 1 ton is _____ times as heavy as 1 _____.

5. 1 quart is 4 times as much as 1 _____.

6. 1 yard is _____ times as long as 1 inch.

Complete the conversion tables. Then use the pattern to complete the equations below.

7.

Cups	Fluid Ounces
1	8
2	
3	

4 cups = ___ ounces

8.

Pounds	Ounces
1	
2	
3	

6 pounds = ___ ounces

Think • Pair • Share

MP7　9. What equation can you use to convert 3 pounds to ounces directly, without a conversion table?

Independent Practice

Customary Units of Measurement	
Length	**Weight**
1 foot = 12 inches 1 yard = 3 feet	1 pound = 16 ounces 1 ton = 2,000 pounds
Liquid Volume	**Time**
1 cup = 8 fluid ounces 1 pint = 2 cups 1 quart = 2 pints 1 gallon = 4 quarts	1 minute = 60 seconds 1 hour = 60 minutes 1 day = 24 hours 1 week = 7 days

Write < or > to compare the sizes of the units. Then write a comparison using multiplication.

1. foot _____ inch

   1 foot is _____

   _____ .

2. second _____ minute

   1 minute is _____

   _____ .

3. fluid ounce _____ cup

   1 cup is _____

   _____ .

4. pint _____ fluid ounce

   1 pint is _____

   _____ .

Complete the conversion tables. Then use the pattern to complete the equations below.

5.

Feet	Inches
1	12
2	
3	
4	

5 feet = _____ inches

6.

Pints	Cups
1	
2	
3	
4	

10 pints = _____ cups

Write the equivalent measurement.

7. 5 yards = _____ feet

8. 3 pounds = _____ ounces

9. 6 quarts = _____ pints

10. 1 day = _____ minutes

Independent Practice

Convert the measurements. You can use the Customary Units of Measurement chart on page 238.

11. 3 yards = _____ feet

12. 2 pounds = _____ ounces

13. 4 gallons = _____ quarts

14. 4 days = _____ hours

15. 2 yards = _____ inches

16. 5 quarts = _____ cups

For exercises 17–22, circle the correct answer.

17. Claudia uses eye drops to help with her contact lenses. The bottle of eye drops is about the size of a thumb. Which unit is probably printed on the bottle?

    a. pint
    b. fluid ounces
    c. quart
    d. cup

18. Jerry is mailing 4 boxes of books. Which unit should Jerry use to measure the total weight of the 4 boxes?

    a. ounces
    b. pounds
    c. tons
    d. quarts

19. Each student has 5 minutes to explain his or her project to the class. How many seconds does each student have?

    a. 50 seconds
    b. 60 seconds
    c. 300 seconds
    d. 360 seconds

20. A restaurant offers a large order of chicken soup. If the large order is 3 pints of soup, how many fluid ounces (fl oz) do you get?

    a. 6 fl oz
    b. 8 fl oz
    c. 12 fl oz
    d. 48 fl oz

21. The tallest living man in the world is 8 feet and 3 inches tall. What is his height in inches?

    a. 27 inches
    b. 96 inches
    c. 99 inches
    d. 128 inches

22. One mile is 5,280 feet. How many yards equal 1 mile?

    a. 440 yards
    b. 1,760 yards
    c. 15,840 yards
    d. 63,360 yards

Independent Practice

MP6 **23.** Michael says that if you convert a whole number of feet to inches, the number of inches must be a multiple of 12. Is Michael correct?

MP7 **24.** Charlotte's baby brother weighs 9 pounds 12 ounces when he is born. Charlotte says that this weight is already in the smallest units possible, because it includes ounces. Is Charlotte correct, or can you convert the weight to smaller units?

Solve the problems.

MP5 **25.** A clothing designer needs 4 yards of fabric to make a sample outfit. If the designer has 16 feet of the fabric, is there enough fabric to make one outfit?

▯▭▶ **Show your work.**

Answer _____

MP6 **26.** Tammy drinks 2 pints of milk every day. Her doctor says that girls her age should drink 3 cups of milk every day to be healthy. How many extra cups of milk does Tammy drink in 1 week?

▯▭▶ **Show your work.**

Answer _____

Independent Practice

MP1 **27.** Steve wants to paint his room light blue. He picks up 3 gallons of white paint at the store. He also buys 2 quarts of blue to mix with the white paint. How many quarts of paint does Steve buy altogether?

✏️▶ **Show your work.**

Answer _____

MP3 **28.** Molly says that to convert 100 fluid ounces to cups, you can divide 100 by 8. Then any remainder will be a whole number of fluid ounces. Is Molly correct?

Answer _____

✏️▶ **Justify your answer using words, drawings, or numbers.**

MP8 **29.** William makes the table below to convert fractions of an hour to minutes.

Hour	Minutes
$\frac{1}{4}$	25
$\frac{1}{2}$	50
$\frac{3}{4}$	75
1	100

Did William convert the measurements correctly?

Answer _____

✏️▶ **Justify your answer using words, drawings, or numbers.**

Convert Metric Measurement Units

Essential Question:
How are larger and smaller metric units of measurement related?
4.MD.1

Words to Know:
metric units

Guided Instruction

In this lesson you will learn about metric units of measurement and how to convert measurements expressed in larger units as equivalent measurements in smaller units.

Understand: Relative sizes of metric measurements of length

> What are the metric units of length and which units are used most often?

Metric units are the measurement units used in the metric system of measurement.
A meter is the basic unit of length in the metric system.

The chart shows how each metric unit of length compares to 1 meter. The units used most often are kilometer, meter, centimeter, and millimeter. These units are highlighted in the chart.

Like the base-ten number system, the metric system is also based on 10. Each unit is 10 times the length of the next smaller unit.

Metric Unit of Length	Equivalent Lengths	
kilometer	10 hectometers	1000 meters
hectometer	10 dekameters	100 meters
dekameter	10 meters	10 meters
meter	10 decimeters	1 meter
decimeter	10 centimeters	$\frac{1}{10}$ meter
centimeter	10 millimeters	$\frac{1}{100}$ meter
millimeter		$\frac{1}{1000}$ meter

Remember!
Each place value in whole and decimal numbers is 10 times the next place to the right.

➡ The chart above shows the metric units of length. The highlighted rows show the units used most often.

✏ Which units in the chart are longer than 1 meter? Which units are shorter than 1 meter? What is the longest unit in the chart? What is the shortest unit?

Guided Instruction

Understand: Converting metric units of length

Lucy is running a 5K race. A 5K race is 5 kilometers long. She stops for a few seconds at the halfway point. How many meters does Lucy have left to run?

The chart shows how the most often used metric units of length are related.

Metric Units of Length
1 kilometer (km) = 1000 meters (m)
1 meter = 100 cm (cm)
1 centimeter = 10 millimeters (mm)

- **1 kilometer** is about the distance you walk if you walk around a football field 3 times.

- **1 meter** is about the distance from a door knob to the floor.

- **1 centimeter** is about the width of your finger.

- **1 millimeter** is about the thickness of a dime.

To solve the problem, find the number of meters in a 5K race.

The chart shows that 1 kilometer = 1000 meters.
Complete this conversion table.

Kilometers	Meters	
1	1000	
2	2000	← 2 × 1000
3	3000	← 3 × 1000
4	4000	← 4 × 1000
5	5000	← 5 × 1000

The race is 5000 meters long.

2500 is exactly between 0 and 5000 on the number line.

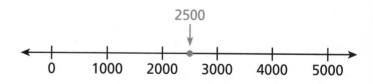

The halfway point is at 2500 meters. Lucy has run 2500 meters and has 2500 meters left to run.

➡ Lucy has 2500 meters left to run.

✏ Which is longer: a kilometer or a meter? A millimeter or a meter? Explain.

Guided Instruction

Connect: Converting metric units of liquid volume and mass

> Andrew buys 6 bottles of orange juice. Each has 355 milliliters of juice. Does Andrew buy more or less than 2 liters of juice?

The chart shows how the metric units of liquid volume are related.

Metric Units of Liquid Volume
1 liter (L) = 1000 milliliters (mL)

- **1 liter** is about the amount of 8 small juice boxes.
- **1 milliliter** is about 20 drops.

To solve the problem, first find the number of milliliters in 2 liters.

Liters	Milliliters
1	1000
2	2000

←— 2 × 1000   2 liters of juice is equivalent to 2000 milliliters.

Compare 2000 milliliters to the number of milliliters in the 6 bottles of juice.

6 × 355 = 2130   The 6 bottles have _____ milliliters.   2130 > 2000

➡ Andrew buys more than 2 liters of juice.

> A nickel has a mass of 5 grams. How many nickels are in a pile of nickels that has a mass of 3 kilograms?

Metric Units of Mass
1 kilogram (kg) = 1000 grams (g)

- **1 kilogram** is about the mass of 10 apples.
- **1 gram** is about the mass of 1 paperclip.

To solve the problem, first find the number of grams in 3 kilograms.

Kilograms	Grams
1	1000
2	2000
3	3000

←— 2 × 1000
←— 3 × 1000   3 kg is equivalent to 3000 g.

Find the number of groups of 5 in 3000 grams. 3000 ÷ 5 = _____

➡ There are 600 nickels in the pile.

Guided Practice

Metric Units of Measurement		
Length	**Liquid Volume**	
1 kilometer = 1000 meters 1 meter = 100 cm 1 centimeter = 10 millimeters	1 liter = 1000 milliliters	
	Mass	
	1 kilogram = 1000 grams	

Complete the sentences to compare the sizes of the units.

1. A _____ is 1000 times as heavy as a gram.

2. There are 1000 _____ in 1 liter.

3. A _____ is 10 times as long as 1 millimeter.

4. A meter is _____ times as long as 1 centimeter.

5. A meter is _____ times as long as 1 millimeter.

Complete the conversion tables. Then use the pattern to complete the equations below.

6.

Liters	Milliliters
1	1000
2	
3	
4	

5 liters = _____ milliliters

7.

Kilograms	Grams
1	
2	
3	

6 kilograms = _____ grams

Think · Pair · Share

MP2　8. Discuss these metric units—meter, gram, and liter. Which of these units has a very small size? Can you think of a reason why this unit is the one that is sometimes used as the basic unit?

Independent Practice

Metric Units of Measurement		
Length	Liquid Volume	Mass
1 kilometer = 1000 meters 1 meter = 100 cm 1 centimeter = 10 millimeters	1 liter = 1000 milliliters	1 kilogram = 1000 grams

Draw lines to match each metric unit with what it measures.

1. meter

gram

liter

a. mass

b. length or distance

c. liquid volume

Write an example of something that could be measured with each metric unit.

2. meter   **3.** gram   **4.** liter

_____   _____   _____

Write < or > to compare the sizes of the units. Then write a comparison using multiplication.

5. meter ____ centimeter

1 meter is _____ as long as
1 centimeter.

6. milliliter ____ liter

1 liter is

_____.

7. meter ____ kilometer

1 kilometer is

_____.

8. gram ____ kilogram

1 kilogram is

_____.

Complete the conversion tables. Then use the pattern to complete the equations below.

9.

Meters	Centimeters
1	
2	
3	
4	

5 meters = _____ centimeters

10.

Liters	Milliliters
1	
2	
3	
4	

8 liters = _____ milliliters

Independent Practice

Convert the measurements. You can use the Metric Units of Measurement chart on page 246.

11. 4 centimeters = _____ millimeters

12. 6 kilometers = _____ meters

13. 5 meters = _____ centimeters

14. 2 kilograms = _____ grams

15. 8 grams = _____ milligrams

16. 3 meters = _____ millimeters

For exercises 17–20, circle the correct answer.

17. Several rolls of yarn are needed to knit a pair of mittens. Which unit is best used to measure lengths of yarn?

    a. meter   b. kilometer

    c. milliliter   d. liter

18. Which of these units is most likely to be used to measure the mass of a comic book?

    a. kilograms   b. grams

    c. centimeters   d. liters

19. Josh uses a dropper to give medicine to his cat. Which is the best estimate for the total amount of medicine Josh gives his cat?

    a. 2 milliliters   b. 2 millimeters

    c. 2 liters   d. 2 meters

20. Amy jogs every day. Which of the following might be the distance she jogs each day?

    a. 6 millimeters   b. 6 kilograms

    c. 6 kilometers   d. 6 liters

Independent Practice

MP5 **21.** In science class, the students are growing beans and measuring the roots. A meter stick is 1 meter long, and a metric ruler is about 30 centimeters long. Which tool is better for measuring the bean roots? Explain.

MP7 **22.** Allison says that 5 centimeters can also be written as 50 millimeters. Dave says that 50 millimeters is incorrect, since 50 millimeters can be written as a whole number of centimeters. Who do you agree with? Explain.

Solve the problems.

MP1 **23.** A school textbook has a mass of about 1 kilogram. Joel is taking 3 textbooks home from school. In grams, what is the combined mass of the books that Joel is taking?

➤ **Show your work.**

Answer _____

MP6 **24.** One milliliter of water has a mass of 1 gram. Trisha buys 5 liters of water. What is the mass of the water in kilograms?

➤ **Show your work.**

Answer _____

Independent Practice

MP3 **25.** Toni has a bottle of grape juice that is labeled 1893 milliliters. Oliver has a bottle of grape juice that is labeled 2 liters. Toni says that her bottle has more grape juice than Oliver's. Is Toni correct?

✏️ **Show your work.**

Answer _____

MP7 **26.** The produce section of a grocery store has a digital scale that customers can use. The scale shows that a bunch of bananas has a mass of 1.2 kilograms. If the bunch has 6 bananas that are about the same size, what could be the mass in grams of 1 banana?

Answer _____

✏️ **Justify your answer using words, drawings, or numbers.**

MP8 **27.** A very small unit of mass is the milligram (mg). One gram is equivalent to 1000 milligrams. Raul learns that he should have at least 1 gram of calcium each day. A glass of milk has about 300 milligrams of calcium. If Raul drinks 4 glasses of milk, will that give him enough calcium for the day?

Answer _____

✏️ **Justify your answer using words, pictures, or numbers.**

Essential Question:
How can you use what you know about whole numbers, fractions, and decimals to solve measurement problems?
4.MD.2

Guided Instruction

In this lesson you will learn how to use diagrams and what you know about measurement to solve real-world problems.

Understand: Using a diagram with a measurement scale to solve a problem

> Mrs. Norton buys 30 liters of fruit punch for the fourth grade end-of-year party. Does she buy enough punch so that each of the 114 students can have 250 milliliters of punch?

To find out if Mrs. Norton buys enough punch, find the number of 250-ml servings in 30 liters and compare that number to the number of students.

Draw a diagram to show 1 liter as milliliters.

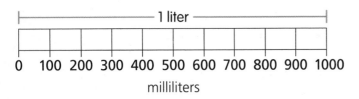

Remember!
1 liter = 1000 milliliters

Color the diagram to find the number of servings in 1000 milliliters. Each serving is 250 milliliters.

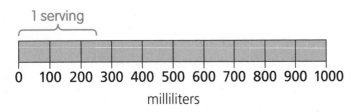

There are 4 servings in 1000 milliliters, or 1 liter.

So, there are 30 × 4, or 120 servings in 30 liters.

120 > 114

➡ Yes, Mrs. Norton buys enough punch.

✏️ How could you use a calculator to solve the problem in a different way?

Guided Instruction

Understand: Using models for units of time

> Cindy goes to see a movie. The movie starts at 2:30 P.M. and ends 2 hours and 45 minutes later. What time does the movie end?

To solve the problem, you can use a number line to model the time and the number of hours and minutes.

The clock at the right shows:

1 hour = 60 minutes

$\frac{1}{4}$ hour = 15 minutes

$\frac{1}{2}$ hour = 30 minutes

$\frac{3}{4}$ hour = 45 minutes

The number line shows the time in quarter hours starting at 2:30 P.M.

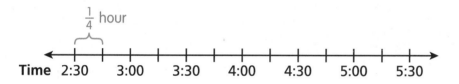

Remember!

A quarter hour is $\frac{1}{4}$ hour or 15 minutes.

Use the number line to count 2 hours 45 minutes ahead.
Move 2 hours to the right. Then add $\frac{3}{4}$ hour.

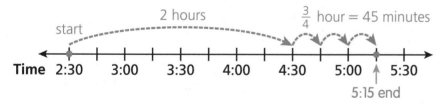

➡ The movie ends at 5:15 P.M.

✏ Cindy's mother picks her up $\frac{1}{2}$ hour after the movie ends. What time does Cindy's mother pick her up? Explain.

Guided Instruction

Connect: Modeling and converting customary units

> Zach is helping his parents plan their vegetable garden. The garden is 6 yards wide. Zach's family wants 4 sections of equal width to plant 4 different kinds of vegetables. How many feet wide should Zach's family make each section?

To solve the problem, you can work with yards and then convert your answer to feet.

Step 1

The model shows the width of the garden as 6 yards. Partition the model into 4 equal sections. First, mark half the area. Then split each half in half to make 4 equal sections, or fourths.

Each section will be $1\frac{1}{2}$ yards wide.

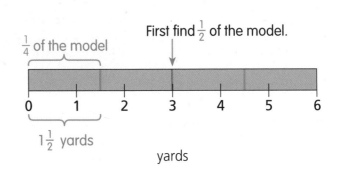

$\frac{1}{4}$ of the model

First find $\frac{1}{2}$ of the model.

$1\frac{1}{2}$ yards

yards

Step 2

Now convert $1\frac{1}{2}$ yards to feet.

$$1 \text{ yard} = 3 \text{ feet}$$

$$\frac{1}{2} \text{ yard} = 1\frac{1}{2} \text{ feet}$$

So, $1\frac{1}{2}$ yards = 3 feet + $1\frac{1}{2}$ feet

$$= 4\frac{1}{2} \text{ feet}$$

➡ Zach's family should make each section $4\frac{1}{2}$ feet wide.

✏ Explain how you could use the model in Step 1 to explain that $\frac{1}{2}$ yard is $1\frac{1}{2}$ feet.

Guided Practice

Read the problem and answer the questions. Use the model to help you solve. Show your work.

1. Vicky buys 6 kilograms of potatoes. Each potato is about the same size and has a mass of 500 grams. How many potatoes does Vicky buy?

   a. What do you need to find?

   _____

   b. What units will you use?

   _____

   Answer _____

2. The directions on a bottle of plant food say to mix $\frac{2}{3}$ cup of plant food with 1 gallon of water. If there are $2\frac{1}{2}$ gallons of water in a watering can, how much plant food should you use?

   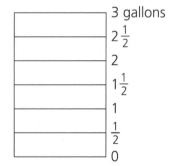

   a. What do you need to find?

   _____

   _____

   b. What units will you use?

   _____

   Answer _____

🏅 Think ∙ Pair ∙ Share

MP2 **3.** Why is it important to pay attention to the units of measurement in a word problem? Use the problems above to explain your answer.

Independent Practice

Read the problem and answer the questions. Use the model to help you solve. Show your work.

1. The third showing of a movie starts at 3 P.M. The movie is $1\frac{1}{2}$ hours long. The theater workers spend 15 minutes cleaning the theater in between showings. At what time is the first showing of the movie?

   a. What do you need to find?

   b. What units will you use?

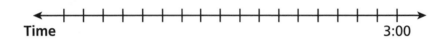

Time   3:00

   Answer _____

2. Three friends rent a car and take turns driving. Julia drives 75 kilometers, Imani drives 68 kilometers, and Kate drives 47 kilometers. They only used the car radio for 0.1 of the ride. How many meters did they travel with the radio on?

   a. What do you need to find?

   b. What units will you use?

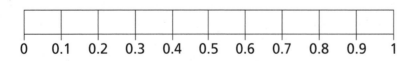

   0   0.1   0.2   0.3   0.4   0.5   0.6   0.7   0.8   0.9   1

   Answer _____

Independent Practice

For exercises 3–5, circle the correct answer. You may use
a model to help.

3. Marisa is decorating a room with streamers for a party. She uses 15 feet
of red streamers and three times that length of blue streamers. How
many yards of streamers does Marisa use altogether?

   a. 15 yards   b. 20 yards

   c. 45 yards   d. 60 yards

4. A worker at the grocery story cuts a 2-kilogram melon into 5 equal-sized
pieces. What is the mass of each piece?

   a. 40 grams   b. 400 grams

   c. 40 kilograms   d. 400 kilograms

MP1 5. A DVD of a cartoon show has five 25-minute cartoons and one special
cartoon that is longer. If the total length of the DVD is 3 hours, how long
is the special cartoon?

   a. 55 minutes   b. 65 minutes

   c. 80 minutes   d. 125 minutes

MP5 6. Sunita and three friends share some frozen yogurt with extra topping.
The yogurt costs $6.25 and the topping costs $3.75. If they split the
cost equally, how much will each person pay?

   ✏️ **Show your work.**

   Answer _____

Independent Practice

For problems 7 and 8, use the chart at the right.

MP7 **7.** Billy's school serves half-pint cartons of milk. Billy wants the school to let students pour their own milk from half-gallon containers. He says that this way, the school will recycle $\frac{1}{8}$ the number of milk cartons that it recycles now. Is Billy correct? Explain.

Customary Units of Liquid Volume
1 cup (c) = 8 fluid ounces
1 pint (pt) = 2 cups
1 quart (qt) = 2 pints
1 gallon (gal) = 4 quarts

MP6 **8.** Mandy says that it is more difficult to convert customary units of weight than it is to convert metric units of mass. Do you agree? Why might Mandy think this is true? Explain.

Solve the problems.

MP4 **9.** James takes swimming lessons at a large pool that is divided into lanes. Today, $\frac{1}{5}$ of the lanes are saved for slower swimmers to use. The combined width of the saved lanes is 5 meters. How wide is the whole pool? You can use the model below.

✏️ **Show your work.**

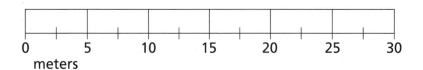

Answer _____

Independent Practice

Solve the problems.

MP6 **10.** Curtis is shopping for a new fish tank. One is labeled as having a volume of 21 liters. He also likes two smaller tanks that have 9500 milliliter and 11,900 milliliter volumes. Which has a greater volume, the 21-liter tank or the two smaller tanks combined?

✏️ **Show your work.**

Answer _____

MP6 **11.** A baker is making loaves of cinnamon bread. He has 2 kilograms of flour. His recipe uses 385 grams of flour for each loaf. Does he have more or less flour than he needs to make 4 loaves? Tell how much more flour he needs or how much more he has than he needs.

✏️ **Show your work.**

Answer _____

MP1 **12.** Felix mixes cashews and pecans together to make a nut mixture. The weight of the pecans is three times the weight of the cashews. The mixture weighs 1 pound altogether. How many ounces do the cashews weigh?

Answer _____

✏️ **Justify your answer using words, drawings, or numbers.**

Problem Solving: Apply Area and Perimeter Formulas

Essential Question:
How can you use area and perimeter formulas for rectangles to solve problems?

4.MD.3

Words to Know:
length
width
formula

Guided Instruction

In this lesson you will learn how to apply area and perimeter formulas to different problem situations.

Understand: Perimeter formulas for rectangles

The model at the right shows the distances of the park where Tate rides his scooter every Saturday. This Saturday Tate forgets to charge the battery for his electric scooter. He rides the scooter all the way around the park only once before the battery dies. How many meters is Tate able to ride the scooter?

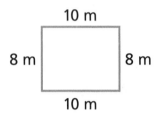

10 m

8 m　　8 m

10 m

To find out how far Tate rides, find the perimeter of the rectangular park. Perimeter is the total distance around a figure or shape.

One way to find the perimeter is to add the measures of all the sides. The measure of each side in one pair of opposite sides is called the length of the rectangle. The measure of each side in the other pair is called the width. Write an addition equation:

Remember!
Opposite sides of a rectangle are sides that do not intersect.

$$\text{Perimeter} = \underset{\text{length}}{10m} + \underset{\text{length}}{10m} + \underset{\text{width}}{8m} + \underset{\text{width}}{8m} = 36 \text{ meters}$$

➡ Tate rides his scooter 36 meters.

Since the opposite sides of a rectangle are the same length, you add the same length and width twice. This means you can also multiply to find the perimeter of a rectangle. You can:

Double the length and double the width. Then add.

or Use the Distributive Property. Add the length and width, and multiply the sum by 2.

$$\text{Perimeter} = (2 \times \underset{\text{length}}{10}) + (2 \times \underset{\text{width}}{8})$$
$$= 20 + 16$$
$$= 36 \text{ meters}$$

$$\text{Perimeter} = 2 \times (\underset{\text{length}}{10} + \underset{\text{width}}{8})$$
$$= 2 \times 18$$
$$= 36 \text{ meters}$$

These methods work for all rectangles, so we describe each method with a formula. A formula is a rule that is written with symbols, such as ℓ for length and w for width. To find the perimeter you can use these formulas.

$$P = \ell + \ell + w + w \qquad P = (2 \times \ell) + (2 \times w) \qquad P = 2 \times (\ell + w)$$

Guided Instruction

Understand: Area formula for rectangles

Nicole is using a favorite photograph to cover a magnet she is making. The length and width of her photograph are shown at the right. Nicole glues the photo onto a magnetic sheet that is the same size as the photograph. How many square inches of a magnetic sheet does Nicole use to cover the whole back of the photo?

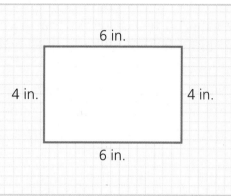

Since the photo is a rectangle, you can multiply its length and width to find its area.

$$\begin{aligned} \text{Area} &= \overset{\text{length}}{6\text{in.}} \times \overset{\text{width}}{4\text{in.}} \\ &= 24 \text{ square inches} \end{aligned}$$

It takes 24 inch squares (1 inch on each side) to cover the rectangle. The area is 24 square inches.

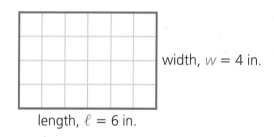

width, w = 4 in.

length, ℓ = 6 in.

▶ Nicole uses 24 square inches of a magnetic sheet.

The formula for the area of a rectangle is
$$A = \ell \times w.$$
You can use this formula to find the area of any rectangle, including squares.

If you know the area of a rectangle, you can also use the formula to find an unknown side length.
$$15 \text{ square inches} = 3 \times \,?$$
$$15 \div 3 = 5$$

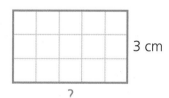

3 cm

?

Write another factor pair for each area that you found above.

Guided Instruction

Connect: Using formulas for perimeter and area

A gardener has 30 feet of bricks that he can use to make the border of a rectangular garden. He will place bricks along each edge and place lights in the corners. The gardener wants to make the garden 5 feet wide. What is the greatest possible length for the garden? What will the area of a garden be with these measurements?

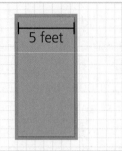

5 feet

You can use the formula for the perimeter of a rectangle to find the length of the garden, and then find its area.

Perimeter formulas
$$P = \ell + \ell + w + w$$
$$P = (2 \times \ell) + (2 \times w)$$
$$P = 2 \times (\ell + w)$$

Step 1

Identify the information given and what you need to find in the problem. The perimeter of the rectangle is 30 feet. The width of the rectangle is 5 feet.

Area formula
$$A = \ell \times w$$

You need to find the length of the largest rectangle that the gardener can make with 30 feet of bricks.

Step 2

Write an equation to represent the problem. You know that the perimeter is 2 times the sum of the length and the width. So, half of the perimeter equals the sum of the length and width. Half of the perimeter is 15.

Perimeter
$30 = 2 \times (\ell + 5),$
so $15 = \ell + 5.$

Step 3

Solve the equation $15 = \ell + 5$ to find the unknown length.

$\ell = 10$

Check that the length ℓ of 10 feet will give you a perimeter of 30 feet.

$2 \times (10 + 5) = 2 \times 15 = 30,$
so 10 feet is correct.

Step 4

Now use the length of 10 feet to find the area of the garden.

$$\text{Area} = \overset{\text{length}}{10} \times \overset{\text{width}}{5}$$
$$= 50 \text{ square feet}$$

➡ The greatest possible length for the garden is 10 feet. The garden will have an area of 50 square feet.

Guided Practice

Write an equation to find the area or perimeter of the rectangle. Outline the border or color the inside of the rectangle to represent your answer.

10 in.

1. Find the distance around all four sides of the rectangle.

   Equation _____   **Perimeter** _____

   10 in.

2. Find how many inch squares will cover the entire rectangle.

   Equation _____   **Area** _____

   10 in.

   10 in.

For exercises 3 and 4, use the figure at the right. Write an equation to represent each. Then solve.

12 in.

2 in.

3. Peter is making bumper stickers for his baseball team. How much sticky paper does Peter need to make each sticker?

   Find the _____ of the rectangle.

   Equation _____

   Answer _____

4. Peter decides to glue plastic string along the edge of each sticker. How much string will Peter need for all four sides?

   Find the _____ of the rectangle.

   Equation _____

   Answer _____

 **Think • Pair • Share**

MP1 5. The area of a storage room floor is 36 square feet. Nancy knows that the length of the room is 9 feet long. She wants to buy shelves to fit all the way across the width of the room. What is the width of the room?

   36 square feet   ? ft

   9 ft

   Find the _____ of the rectangle.

   Equation _____

   Answer _____

Independent Practice

For exercises 1–3, find the area and perimeter of the rectangle at the right.

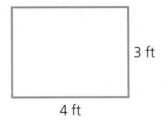

3 ft

4 ft

1. *Area = length × width*

   = _____ × _____

   = _____

   The area of the rectangle is _____ _____ feet.

2. *Perimeter = (2 × length) + (2 × width)*

   = (2 × _____) + (2 × 3)

   = _____ + _____

   = _____

   The perimeter of the rectangle is _____ feet.

3. Use a different method to find the perimeter of the rectangle. Add the lengths of all four sides.

   _____

Draw and label a model and then write an equation to represent the problem. Use *P* or *A* to represent what you need to find. Then solve the equation and answer the question.

Perimeter formulas
$P = \ell + \ell + w + w$
$P = (2 × \ell) + (2 × w)$
$P = 2 × (\ell + w)$

Area formula
$A = \ell × w$

4. An architect is designing a wall of square windows. The wall is 20 feet wide and 10 feet high. How many squares of glass will fill the window if each square is 1 foot square?

   Equation _____

   Answer _____

5. Shelby wants to wrap a string of small lights around the border of her bedroom window. Her window is 2 feet wide and 4 feet tall. How many feet of stringed lights does Shelby need to go around the whole window?

   Equation _____

   Answer _____

Independent Practice

Find the perimeter of the rectangle or square. Write an equation and show your work.

6.

12 cm

12 cm

Perimeter _____

7.

3 m

18 m

Perimeter _____

8. a rectangle 17 inches long and 11 inches wide

Perimeter _____

9. a square with side length 25 feet

Perimeter _____

Find the area of the rectangle or square. Write an equation and show your work.

10.

7 in.

2 in.

Area _____ square inches

11.

9 km + 10 km

6 km

Area _____

12. a square with side length 15 miles

Area _____

15 miles

15 miles

13. a rectangle 16 inches long and 5 inches wide

Area _____

Independent Practice

MP2 **14.** Ralph draws a square and writes the equations $P = 16$ inches and $A = 16$ square inches. George says that Ralph has made a mistake because the perimeter and the area can never have the same number. Do you agree or disagree with George?

MP7 **15.** What is the least amount of information that you need to find an unknown length of a side in a given rectangle, such as the one shown at the right?

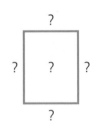

Solve the problems.

MP5 **16.** The fourth graders are having a class party at school. To make one big rectangular table for everyone to sit at, they push two tables together. One table is 8 feet long and 5 feet wide and the other table is a square, 5 feet on each side. What is the perimeter of the combined table that the students make?

    ▱▭▶ **Show your work.**

    Answer _____

MP1 **17.** Lisa is choosing new carpet for her bedroom floor. Her bedroom is 12 feet long and 10 feet wide. If the carpet costs $5 per square foot, how much will a carpet to cover Lisa's whole bedroom floor cost?

    ▱▭▶ **Show your work.**

    Answer _____

Independent Practice

MP5 **18.** The fabric store sells scrap pieces of fabric that are all 1 yard wide. A rectangular piece is labeled "9 square yards." How long is this piece of fabric? Sketch the rectangle to help you find the unknown side length.

✏️ **Show your work.**

Answer _____

MP4 **19.** A town is placing a wire fence around a rectangular field. The town orders 100 yards of fencing, which is the exact amount needed to surround the entire field. One end of the field is 30 yards long. What are the lengths of the other three sides of the field?

✏️ **Show your work.**

Answer _____

MP7 **20.** Gary's mother is replacing the tiles in a rectangular section of the bathroom floor. Each tile is square with an area of 4 square inches. Gary's mother uses 32 tiles (without cutting any tiles). Gary says that there is only one possible length and width for the rectangular section of the floor. His friend Angela says that there is more than one possible rectangular shape. Who is correct?

Answer _____

✏️ **Justify your answer using words, drawings, or numbers.**

MP7 **21.** Tabitha is drawing models of rectangles that have a perimeter of 4 yards. Each side length is a whole number of feet. How many different models can Tabitha draw?

Answer _____

✏️ **Justify your answer using words, drawings, or numbers.**

Problem Solving: Use Line Plots

Essential Question:
How can representing data on a line plot help you to better understand and interpret a set of measurements?

4.MD.4

Words to Know:
line plot
data

Guided Instruction

In this lesson you will learn how to display measurements on a line plot and make observations about the data.

Understand: Using number lines to display data

Debbie collects some red leaves from a maple tree. She is surprised to see that the leaves are different lengths, even though they are from the same tree. Debbie measures the leaves to the nearest eighth of an inch. How can you display her data in a more organized way?

Maple Leaf Lengths
(to nearest $\frac{1}{8}$ inch)

$2\frac{5}{8}$	$2\frac{2}{8}$	$2\frac{6}{8}$	$2\frac{4}{8}$
$2\frac{4}{8}$	$2\frac{4}{8}$	$2\frac{6}{8}$	2
3	$2\frac{1}{8}$	3	$2\frac{3}{8}$

You can organize and display data with a line plot. A line plot uses symbols or marks to show how many times each number, or measurement, appears in a set of data. The numbers or measurements are shown along a number line.

The least and greatest measurements in Debbie's data are 2 inches and 3 inches. Draw and label a number line to show these numbers. Use tick marks and labels to show all the $\frac{1}{8}$-units in between.

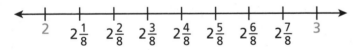

Now display the data. Draw an X above the location on the number line for each piece of data. If a piece of data appears more than once, draw an X above the previous X for each.

Maple Leaf Lengths

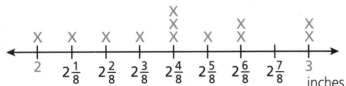

inches

Title the line plot and label the number line with the units used.

➡ The line plot shows the data in a more organized way.

Guided Instruction

Understand: Reading and using line plots

What information can you learn from the line plot of Debbie's leaf data?

The line plot shows all 12 of Debbie's measurement data in order from least to greatest number of inches.

Maple Leaf Lengths (to nearest $\frac{1}{8}$ inch)

$2\frac{5}{8}$	$2\frac{2}{8}$	$2\frac{6}{8}$	$2\frac{4}{8}$
$2\frac{4}{8}$	$2\frac{4}{8}$	$2\frac{6}{8}$	2
3	$2\frac{1}{8}$	3	$2\frac{3}{8}$

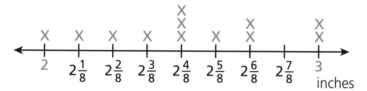

Maple Leaf Lengths

Looking at the line plot, some of the things you can learn are:

- There are 12 Xs so there are 12 measurements altogether.

- All of the leaves are between 2 and 3 inches long.

- There are 2 leaves that are $2\frac{6}{8}$ inches long and 2 leaves that are 3 inches long.

- Three leaves are $2\frac{4}{8}$ inches long.

- No leaves are $2\frac{7}{8}$ inches long.

Use the information in the line plot to answer these questions.

- Where would you draw the X for a leaf that measures $2\frac{1}{4}$ inches long? Explain.

- How many of Debbie's leaves are longer than $2\frac{1}{2}$ inches? How do you know?

- What is the difference between the longest leaf and the shortest leaf that Debbie measured?

Guided Instruction

Connect: Displaying and interpreting data

Devan asks some friends how much time they spend eating dinner. He asks them to give their answers to the nearest quarter hour. Devan records their answers in a line plot. What is the difference between the greatest amount of time and the least amount of time?

Time Eating Dinner
(to nearest $\frac{1}{4}$ hour)

$\frac{3}{4}$	$\frac{1}{2}$	$\frac{1}{4}$
$\frac{1}{2}$	1	$\frac{3}{4}$
$\frac{3}{4}$	$\frac{3}{4}$	$\frac{1}{2}$

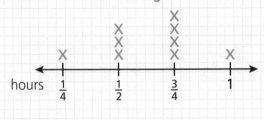

Time Eating Dinner

You can use the line plot to answer the question.

Step 1

Look at the number line used for the line plot.

The number with the least value is $\frac{1}{4}$, and the number 1 has the greatest value. All of the points on the line are the same distance apart, so, Devan used fourths as the scale.

Step 2

Use the number line on the line plot to find the difference between the greatest amount of time and the least amount of time.

$\frac{4}{4} - \frac{1}{4} = \frac{3}{4}$

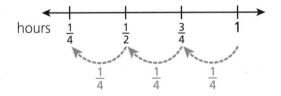

➡ The difference between the greatest amount of time spent eating and the least amount of time is $\frac{3}{4}$ hour.

Guided Practice

For exercises 1–4, use the data shown at the right.

1. Use the smallest unit to rename the amounts of rain as equivalent fractions.

   $\frac{1}{4}$ inch = $\frac{}{8}$ inch

   $\frac{1}{2}$ inch = $\frac{}{8}$ inch

   $\frac{3}{4}$ inch = $\frac{}{8}$ inch

Amount of Rain for Rainy Days in May (in inches)

$\frac{3}{4}$	$\frac{1}{8}$	$\frac{1}{4}$	$\frac{1}{2}$
$\frac{1}{8}$	$\frac{1}{4}$	$\frac{3}{4}$	$\frac{1}{8}$

2. Find the least and greatest amounts of rain in the data.

   Least amount: _____ inch   Greatest amount: _____ inch

3. Label the number line below to show the $\frac{1}{8}$-inch units.

   inches

4. Display the data. Then write a title for the line plot.

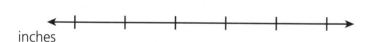

   inches

Use your line plot to solve the problems.

5. What is the total number of days that it rained in May?

   There are _____ Xs on the line plot.   It rained on _____ days.

6. What is the difference between the greatest and least amounts of rain?

   $\frac{6}{8}$ − _____ = _____ inch

☗ Think • Pair • Share

MP1   7. Use the line plot to find the total amount of rain for rainy days in May. Explain your method.

Independent Practice

1. Complete the line plot to display the given data.

**Weight of Packages
of Cheese (in pounds)**

$\frac{7}{8}$	$\frac{2}{8}$	$\frac{1}{8}$
$\frac{2}{8}$	$\frac{7}{8}$	

Weight of Packages of Cheese

pounds

2. Write the weights of the packages of cheese in order from least
to greatest.

_____

3. How many packages were weighed? ____ packages

4. What is the weight of the lightest package? ____ pound

5. What is the weight of the heaviest package? ____ pound

6. What is the difference in the weights of the heaviest and lightest
packages?

____ ____ ____

_____

Solve the problem.

MP5   **7.** Susie recorded the distances for her walks.
The numbers of miles are shown at the
right. To show this data on a line plot,
what numbers should Susie use on the
number line? Explain.

**Distance Walked in
One Week (in miles)**

$1\frac{1}{2}$	$1\frac{1}{4}$	$1\frac{3}{4}$	$1\frac{1}{2}$
$1\frac{1}{4}$	$1\frac{3}{4}$	$1\frac{1}{2}$	$1\frac{1}{4}$

Independent Practice

MP2 **8.** Adam measured the lengths of the pencils in his desk. Make a line plot to display his data.

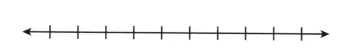

Pencil Lengths
(in inches)

$3\frac{1}{2}$	4	$5\frac{1}{2}$	4
4	$5\frac{1}{2}$	2	$6\frac{1}{2}$

For exercises 9–14, use the line plot from exercise 8 to answer the questions.

9. How many pencils does Adam have altogether?

_____

10. How many more 4-inch long pencils are there than 2-inch long pencils?

_____

11. How much longer is Adam's longest pencil than his shortest pencil?

_____

12. What is the total length of the pencils longer than 4 feet?

_____

13. What is the combined length of all of the pencils?

_____

14. Adam finds another pencil that is $2\frac{2}{4}$ inches long in his backpack. Which of these best describes how Adam should change his line plot to include this data?

a. He should add another tick mark for $2\frac{2}{4}$ on the number line.

b. He should add another tick mark for $\frac{10}{4}$ on the number line.

c. He should add 1 X above $2\frac{1}{2}$ inches.

d. He should extend the number line and draw 2 Xs above $\frac{1}{2}$.

Independent Practice

MP3 **15.** George is making a line plot to show the ages of children in a music group. He lists the ages in years: 13, $10\frac{1}{2}$, $13\frac{1}{2}$, 12, 14, 13, $10\frac{1}{2}$. He says that the number line on his line plot will have exactly 5 tick marks. Mandy says that the number line will show exactly 7 tick marks. Liz says that it must show at least 8 tick marks. Who is right? Explain. What numbers will the number line show?

MP6 **16.** Lisa is trying to choose a name for her new kitten. She writes her four top choices and then asks each of her 12 friends to choose one of the names. She places an X above the name that each friend chooses. Her friend Sandy says that Lisa is making a line plot. Lisa says that it is not really a line plot. Who is right?

For exercises 17 and 18, use the line plot.

Weight of Apples in 1 Bag

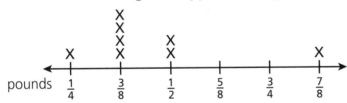

MP1 **17.** How much heavier is the heaviest apple in the bag than the lightest apple?

▉▶ **Show your work.**

Answer _____

MP1 **18.** How much does the whole bag of apples weigh?

▉▶ **Show your work.**

Answer _____

Independent Practice

For exercises 19–21, use the data below.

Michelle reads that 1 yard is about the distance from the tip of your nose to your fingertip, with your arm stretched out to your side. She measures this length for herself and some other people. The list below shows Michelle's data.

Distance from Nose to Fingertip (feet)

| $2\frac{4}{6}$ | $2\frac{1}{6}$ | $2\frac{4}{6}$ | $2\frac{2}{6}$ | $2\frac{2}{6}$ | 3 | $2\frac{3}{6}$ | $2\frac{4}{6}$ | 3 | $2\frac{2}{6}$ | 2 |

MP5 **19.** Make a line plot of Michelle's measurement data.

✏️ **Show your work.**

Answer

MP4 **20.** Michelle makes a line plot for her data that starts at 2 feet and ends at 3 feet. Does the number line for Michelle's plot still represent the size of each measurement as a distance from 0 feet?

Answer _____

✏️ **Justify your answer using words, drawings, or numbers.**

MP2 **21.** Based on Michelle's data, is the distance from your nose to your fingertip a good estimate of one yard?

Answer _____

✏️ **Justify your answer using words, drawings, or numbers.**

Essential Question:
How is the measure of an angle related to a circle?

4.MD.5a; 4.MD.5b

Words to Know:
- ray
- point
- endpoint
- angle
- vertex
- degree (°)
- one-degree angle
- right angle
- straight angle

Guided Instruction

In this lesson you will learn about angles and angle measures.

Understand: Angles and parts of angles

The positions of the hands of a clock show the time. What geometric figure do the two hands of a clock form?

To decide what geometric figure is formed by a clock's hand, you need to learn about rays and angles.

A ray starts at a point called an endpoint and goes on straight in one direction forever.

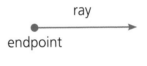

Two rays that share the same endpoint form an angle. The two rays of an angle are the sides of the angle. Their shared endpoint is the vertex of the angle.

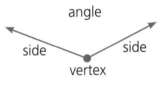

The hour and minute hands of the clock are like two rays that begin at the same point. That point in the center of the clock is like the vertex of an angle.

▶ The two hands of a clock form an angle.

Changing the length of the sides of an angle does not change the angle measure.
The angles below are all the same size as the clock angle.

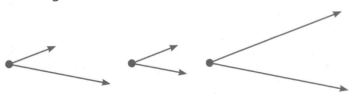

✏️▸ Trace one of the angles. Then move the traced angle to match the vertex and rays of another angle. What do you notice?

Guided Instruction

Understand: Angle measures and fractions of a circle

> Carrie opens her laptop computer to the angle shown at the right. What is the measure of the angle of Carrie's open laptop?

To answer this question, you need to find an angle measure. The unit of measure for angles is the degree and its symbol is °.

Think of the vertex of an angle as the center of a circle. An angle forms as it turns through the circle. A circle measures 360 degrees, so a one-degree angle is $\frac{1}{360}$ of a circle. The measure of an angle is the number of one-degree angles it turns through.

A one-degree angle turns through just $\frac{1}{360}$ of a circle.

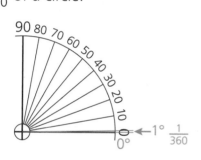

A 90° angle turns through $\frac{90}{360}$, or $\frac{1}{4}$, of a circle. This is a right angle.

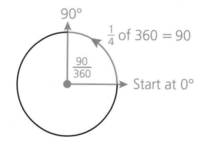

A 180° angle, or straight angle, turns through $\frac{1}{2}$ of a circle. The rays of a straight angle form a line.

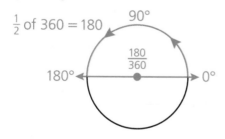

A 360° angle turns through a whole circle. One ray rests on top of the other.

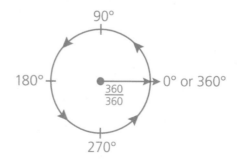

When Carrie opens her laptop, she turns the cover through 110 one-degree angles. The angle it forms measures 110°.

➤ The measure of the angle of Carrie's open laptop is 110°.

To name an angle, use the symbol ∠. Write the letter for a point on one ray and the letter for the vertex followed by the letter for a point on the other ray. This angle is ∠ABC or ∠CBA. A short form is ∠B.

Guided Instruction

Connect: Identify angles and angle measures in degrees

One of the angles in the figure at the right turns through $\frac{1}{6}$ of a circle. What is the size of this angle? What part of the figure shows this angle?

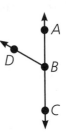

To identify the angle size and matching angle in the figure, use what you know about the degrees in a circle.

Step 1

Find the number of one-degree angles in $\frac{1}{6}$ of a circle. Think: One whole circle has 360 one-degree angles.

You can multiply to find $\frac{1}{6}$ of 360.

$$\frac{1}{6} \times 360 = \frac{1 \times 360}{6} = \frac{360}{6} = 60 \text{ one-degree angles}$$

Since each one-degree angle is 1°, 60 one-degree angles equal 60°.

➡ The angle that turns through $\frac{1}{6}$ of a circle is a 60° angle.

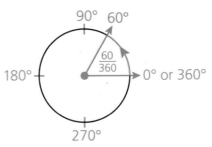

Step 2

Identify which angle in the figure is the 60° angle. Use the points on the rays to name the angles.

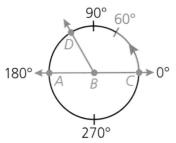
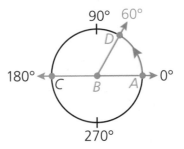

Angles *DBC* and *ABC* are both greater than 60°.

Angle *DBA* measures 60°.

➡ The part of the figure that shows the 60° angle is angle *DBA*.

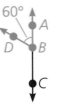

Guided Practice

Name the measure of the angle for the fraction of a circle.

1.

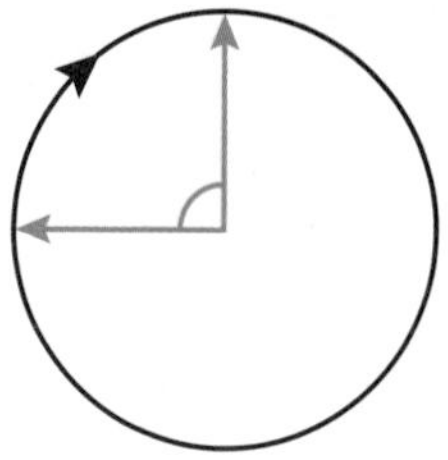

$\frac{1}{4} = \frac{___}{360}$

Angle measure ____°

2.

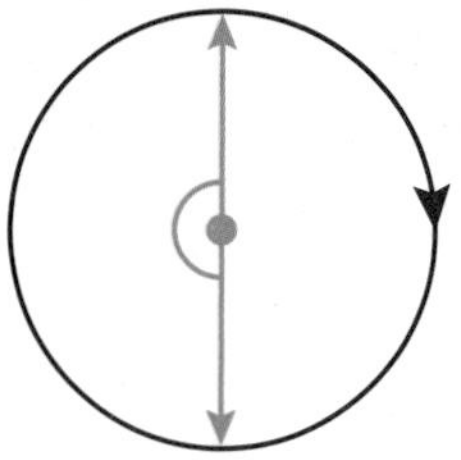

$\frac{1}{2} = \frac{___}{360}$

Angle measure ____°

3.

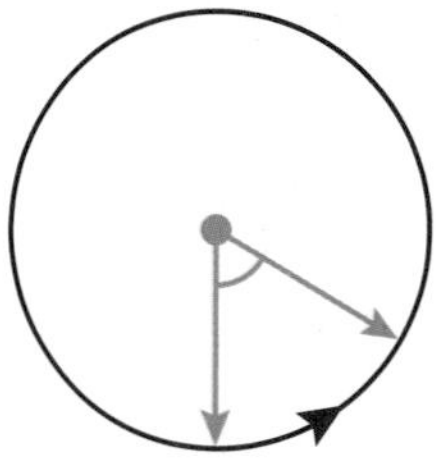

$\frac{1}{6} = \frac{___}{360}$

Angle measure ____°

Use the words at the right to complete the sentences. Then name an example in the figure at the right.

vertex
right angle
ray
straight angle

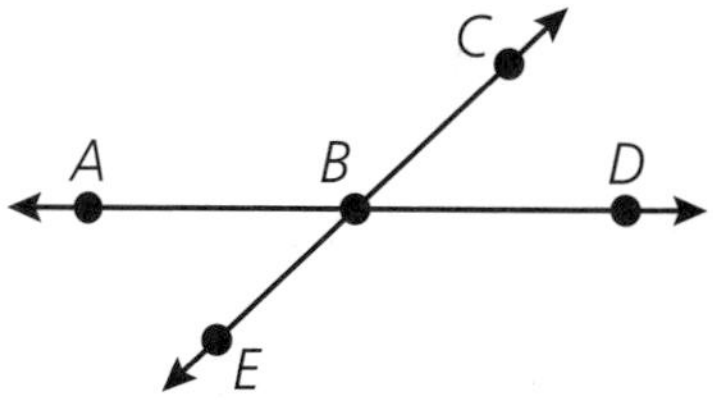

4. A ______________ measures 180°.

Example ______________________________

5. The point shared by two rays to form an angle is called the ______________.

Example ______________________________

6. A ______________ is a line with one endpoint that goes on forever in one direction.

Example ______________________________

7. Angle *ABC* has a greater measure than a ______________.
Name another angle that turns through more than 90 one-degree angles.

____

Think • Pair • Share

MP2 **8.** Shelly rides the Ferris wheel at the carnival. Her car moves $\frac{5}{8}$ of the way around the whole circle when the ride stops to let other people on. What is the measure of the angle between the starting and stopping point? Explain your solution.

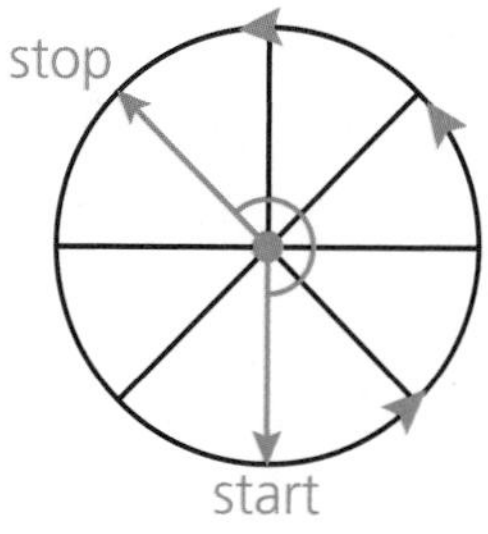

Independent Practice

Name the measure of the angle for the fraction of a circle.

1.
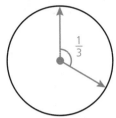

$$\frac{1}{3} = \frac{}{360}$$

Angle measure _____°

2.
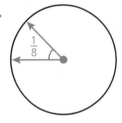

$$\frac{1}{8} = \text{——}$$

Angle measure _____°

3.
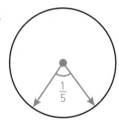

$$\frac{1}{5} = \text{——}$$

Angle measure _____°

4. Identify the parts of the angle below.

5. The table shows the angle between the hour and minute hand of a clock at different times of the day. Write the missing angle measures to complete the table.

Time	Angle
1:00	30°
2:00	
3:00	

6. Angles A and B represent a door opening into a room.

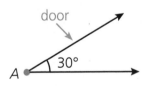

a. Compare the measures of the angles and the number of one-degree angles for each.

b. Describe the relationship between the sizes of the angles.

Independent Practice

For exercises 7–9, use the figure.

Street Intersection

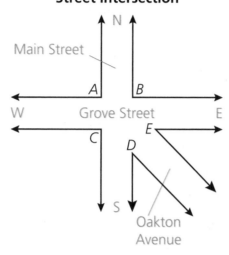

7. A car drives south along Main Street and makes a 90° turn onto Grove Street. Name two angles that can represent the corner where the car turns.

_____

8. Which angles represent sharp turns that measure less than a right angle?

_____

9. A car drives through the intersection along a straight angle. Which street or streets is the car driving on?

_____

Circle the correct answer.

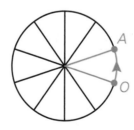

10. A fin on a windmill moves from point O to point A. As it moves, it turns through $\frac{1}{10}$ of a circle. What is the measure of the angle?

   a. 10°   **b.** 36°

   c. 90°   **d.** 100°

Independent Practice

11. What is the measure of ∠XYZ?

    a. between 0° and 90°

    b. exactly 90°

    c. between 90° and 180°

    d. exactly 180°

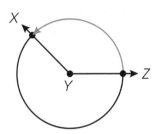

12. The circle is divided into 3 equal sections. For each section, name the fraction of the circle and the measure of the angle.

    a. $\frac{1}{3}$, 60°

    b. $\frac{1}{3}$, 120°

    c. $\frac{1}{9}$, 40°

    d. $\frac{1}{9}$, 90°

Solve the problems.

MP7 **13.** The table below shows the relationship between angle measures and sections of a circle. Complete the table.

Angle Measure	Circle Section
40°	
72°	$\frac{1}{5}$
	$\frac{1}{4}$
120°	
	$\frac{1}{2}$

    Show your work.

Independent Practice

MP7 **14.** What is the measure of angle *MNP*?

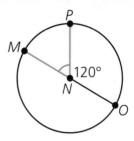

✏ **Show your work.**

Answer _____

MP3 **15.** Mark is taking leftover slices of pizza from different boxes and putting them into one box. The 5 leftover pizza slices are shown below in gold.

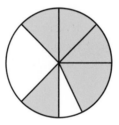

Are all the gold slices shown the same size?

Answer _____

✏ **Justify your answer using words, drawings, or numbers.**

MP1 **16.** Kendra's bicycle wheels cover a distance of about 6 feet with each full turn. She bikes two blocks and covers a distance of 420 feet. Kendra says that her wheels turned 2,520 times during her ride. Is Kendra right?

Answer _____

✏ **Justify your answer using words, drawings, or numbers.**

Essential Question:
How can classifying angles and using a protractor help you measure angles?
4.MD.6

Words to Know:
acute angle
perpendicular
obtuse angle
protractor

Guided Instruction

In this lesson you will learn how to measure and draw angles using a protractor.

Understand: Classifying angles by size

> Meg says that there are only three types of angles: right angles, straight angles, and 360° angles. Is Meg's information correct?

You learned that angle measure is the number of one-degree angles that an angle turns through in a circle. You can classify or group angles by their angle measure.

> **Remember!**
> Two rays that share the same endpoint form an angle.

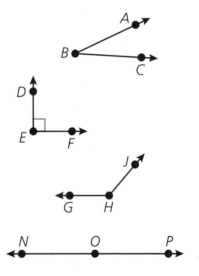

- An acute angle measures between 0° and 90°. Angle *ABC* is an acute angle.

- A right angle is exactly 90°. Angle *DEF* shows the right angle symbol: a square at the vertex. Two rays that meet at a right angle are perpendicular, like the sides of a square or rectangle.

- An obtuse angle measures between 90° and 180°. Angle *GHJ* is an obtuse angle.

- A straight angle measures exactly 180°. Straight angle *NOP* is also a line.

▶ There are more than 3 types of angles, so Meg's information is not correct.

You can use benchmark angles such as right angles and straight angles to help you visualize angles in the problems that you work on.

▸ Explain why there are acute angles with many different angle measures but there is only one angle measure for a right angle.

Guided Instruction

Understand: How to measure angles with a protractor

Tim says that the measure of ∠*ABC* is
50° and the measure of ∠*DEF* is 130°.
Is Tim correct?

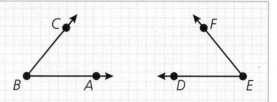

To find the exact measure of an angle, you can use a protractor.
A protractor is a tool for measuring the number of degrees in an angle.

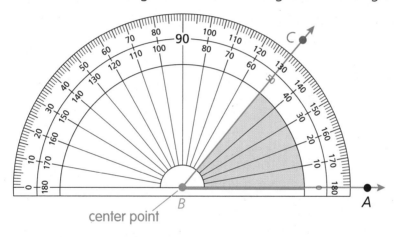

center point

On the protractor, find the center hole at the bottom. Place this directly over
the vertex of the angle you are measuring. For ∠*ABC*, this is point *B*.

Line up one ray of the angle, such as ray *BA*, with the 0 on the
inner number scale. On the inner scale, the degrees increase
counterclockwise. When a ray is too short to reach the number
scale, use the straight side of the protractor to extend the ray.

> A short way to write
> the measure of angle
> *ABC* is m∠*ABC*.

Look where the other ray of the angle crosses this scale.
Ray *BC* goes through the tick mark for 50, so m∠*ABC* is 50°.

Now measure ∠*DEF* in the figure at the right.
Place the center point of the protractor over vertex *E*
and line up ray *ED* with 0 on the outer number scale.
Ray *EF* goes through 50 on the outer number scale.
The degrees increase clockwise.
On the outer scale, m∠*DEF* is 50°, not 130°.

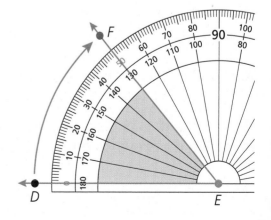

➡ Tim is correct about the measure of ∠*ABC* but
not about the measure of ∠*DEF*. The angles have the
same angle measure.

Guided Instruction

Connect: Use a protractor to draw an angle

Janna wants to put a peg on the wall to hang her jacket on. She starts to make a sketch of the peg's position. She wants the angle to be 135°. Help Janna draw an angle of 135°.

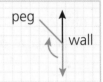

You can use a protractor to draw the angle.

Step 1

Put more information on Janna's sketch.
Name the angle *PEG*. Let line *WEG* represent the wall.

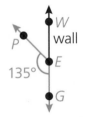

Step 2

Draw ray *EG*.
Use the straight edge of the protractor to draw ray *EG*.
Mark point *E* and draw a ray down from Point *E*. Label any point on the ray *G*.

Step 3

Draw ray *EP*.
Place the protractor over ray *EG*, with the center on *E* and ray *EG* lined up with 0.
Mark point *P* at 135° on the outer number scale.
Draw a ray connecting *P* and *E*.

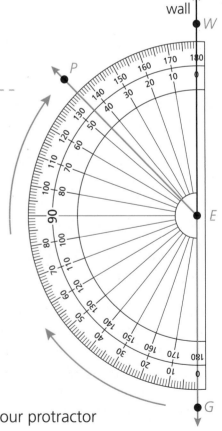

➡ The three steps show how Janna can draw an angle of 135°.

What is the measure of angle *PEW*?
Straight angle *WEG* measures 180°.
180 − 135° = 45°, so angle *PEW* measures 45°.
Look at the inner number scale to check.

✏ Choose an angle measure between 0° and 180°. Use your protractor to draw the angle on another sheet of paper.

Guided Practice

Match the angle with its description. Use angle benchmarks to help.

1. ∠AQC

2. ∠BQD

3. ∠AQB

a. acute angle

b. right angle

c. obtuse angle

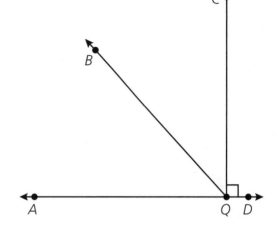

Use a protractor. Find the angle measure.

4. m∠AQC _____°

5. m∠BQD _____°

6. m∠AQB _____°

Sketch an example of each type of angle.

7. acute

8. straight

9. obtuse

Use a protractor to draw an angle with the given measure.

10. 90°

11. 60°

12. 120°

☆☆ Think ● Pair ● Share

MP5 **13.** On this drawing of angle *BEN*, draw two angles: a 45° angle and a 135° angle. Label your angles and explain your method. How are the angles related?

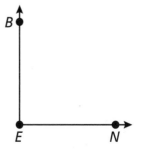

Independent Practice

Use a protractor. Find the angle measure of each. Then identify the type of angle.

1. measure _____

   type _____

2. measure _____

   type _____

3. measure _____

   type _____

4. measure _____

   type _____

Use a protractor to draw an angle with the given measure.

5. 55°

6. 138°

7. 175°

Independent Practice

For exercises 8–9, circle the correct answer.

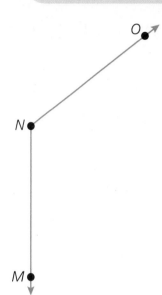

8. What is the measure of ∠MNO?
   Use a protractor.

   a. 53°   **b.** 120°

   c. 127°   **d.** 130°

9. What type of angle is ∠MNO?

   a. acute   **b.** obtuse

   c. right   **d.** straight

10. Use a protractor to measure angle *ACD* and angle *ECB*.

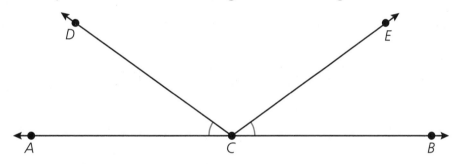

   a. Write the angle measures.

   $m\angle ACD$ _____ $m\angle ECB$ _____

   b. Complete the sentence. Use *acute*, *right*, *obtuse*, or *straight*.

   Angle *ACB* is a _____ angle.

   c. Use your protractor to find the measure of angle *DCE*.

   $m\angle DCE$ _____

   d. Draw angle *DCB*. $m\angle DCB = 145°$

Independent Practice

MP7 **11.** Classify the angle at the right. Use an angle benchmark to explain your reasoning.

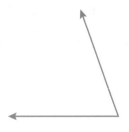

MP3 **12.** Carrie says that if you combine the measures of two acute angles, the new angle is always acute. Do you agree? Give an example to explain your answer.

Solve the problems.

MP5 **13.** On the line below, use a protractor to draw two angles. Use point *A* as the vertex for both angles. Write the measure of each angle below.

✏ **Show your work.**

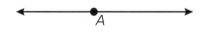

Angle measures _____

MP2 **14.** The figure at the right shows the angles formed by two lines, line *AC* and line *ED*. Angle *ABE* measures 70°. What is the sum of the measures of angles *DBC*, *CBE*, and *ABE*?

✏ **Show your work.**

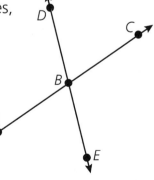

Answer _____

Independent Practice

MP5 **15.** Complete the table. Identify and then sketch each angle.

Angle Measure	Angle Type	Sketch
60° + 30°	right angle	
90° + 90°		
30° + 30°		
120° − 20°		

MP4 **16.** George says that if you subtract 185° from an angle that measures 360°, the new angle is an obtuse angle. Is George's thinking correct? Use a protractor to draw a figure supporting your answer.

Answer _____

✏ **Justify your answer using words, drawings, or numbers.**

MP2 **17.** A store has a ramp up to its back door for deliveries. The ramp is angled at 30° up from the ground, as shown below.

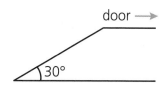

The delivery person says that the ramp is too steep.
How can you change the ramp to make it less steep?
Draw your new design onto the drawing above.

Answer _____

✏ **Justify your answer using words, drawings, or numbers.**

Essential Question:
How can you use known relationships between angle measures to solve problems?

4.MD.7

Words to Know:
supplementary angles
complementary angles

Guided Instruction

In this lesson you will learn how to use the relationships between angles to find angle measures and solve problems.

Understand: Supplementary and complementary angles

Tobey is making a photo collage. The bottom right corner of photo 1 is cut at a 70° angle. Tobey wants to fit photo 1 next to photo 2 so that the corners do not overlap or have a gap in between them. At what angle should Tobey cut the bottom left corner of photo 2?

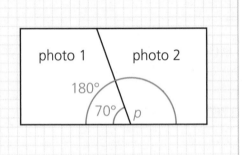

To find the angle measure Tobey needs for photo 2, you can use the relationship between supplementary angles.

Supplementary angles are two angles whose measures add to 180°. When supplementary angles have a side in common, they make a straight angle or line.

Remember!
A straight angle measures 180°.

For Tobey's two photos to fit together perfectly, the angles must be supplementary.

Write an equation that represents the relationship of the angle measures. Use p as the measure of the corner angle of photo 2.

sum of supplementary angles = sum of the two angle measures
$$180° = 70° + p$$
$$180° - 70° = p$$
$$110° = p$$

Tobey should cut the bottom left corner of photo 2 at a 110° angle.

Complementary angles are two angles whose measures add to 90°. When complementary angles have a side in common, they make a right angle.

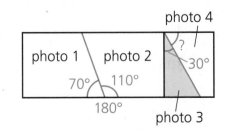

Find the measure of the upper left corner angle for photo 4 in the collage.

Guided Instruction

Understand: Breaking apart and combining angles

A flower pattern in a quilt is made with identical hexagons. All of the angles in the hexagons have the same measure. What is the measure of each angle in the hexagons?

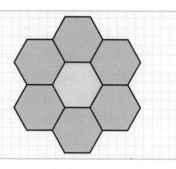

To find the measure of each angle, you can break apart, or decompose, a 360° angle about any point in the pattern. Then use the information given in the problem and what you know about angles to write and solve an equation.

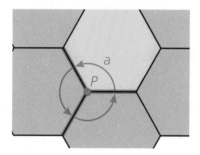

- The diagram shows that each point in the pattern is a vertex for three hexagons.

- The problem tells you that all of the angles in the hexagons have the same measure.

- A full circle is a 360° angle. At each point in the pattern, a circle is decomposed into 3 equal angles.

The three angles sharing a vertex at a point, P, have a combined measure of 360°. You can use a to represent the unknown measure of one angle.

Write and solve an equation that represents this problem.

$$360° = a + a + a$$
$$360° = 3 \times a$$
$$360° \div 3 = a$$
$$120° = a$$

➤ The measure of each angle in the hexagons is 120°.

Guided Instruction

Connect: Using a drawing and an equation to represent a problem

> A ladder is leaning against a wall that forms a 90° angle with the floor. The bottom of the ladder makes a 60° angle with the floor. The ladder, wall, and floor form the three sides of a triangle. The combined measure of the angles in a triangle is 180°. What is the measure of the angle between the top of the ladder and the wall?

To find the unknown measure of the third angle, sketch a drawing to represent the problem and write an equation.

Step 1

- Use the given information to represent the problem.

- Sketch the triangle formed by the ladder, wall, and floor.

- Label each of the known angles with the given measures. Use x to represent the unknown angle measure.

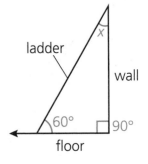

To represent a problem situation, you do not need to draw the angles with exact measures.

Step 2

The sum of the measures of the three angles in a triangle is 180°. Write an equation for the sum.

$$180° = 60° + 90° + x$$
$$180° = 150° + x$$
$$180° - 150° = x$$
$$30° = x$$

➡ The angle between the top of the ladder and the wall measures 30°.

✏️ What is the measure of the angle that is supplementary to the 60° angle from the floor?

Guided Practice

Complete the equation to show the relationship between the angles. Then find the measure of the unknown angle.

1.

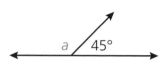

$a + 45° =$ _____

$a =$ _____ $- 45°$

$a =$ _____

2.

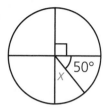

$x + 50° =$ _____

$x =$ _____ $-$ _____

$x =$ _____

Write an equation to represent the problem. Then solve.

3. Tanya is practicing her golf swing. Her first swing turns through 75° of a circle. For each of her next three tries, the angle of her swing increases by 10°. What is the angle of Tanya's last swing?

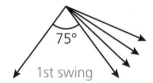

$75° + 3 \times$ ____° $= s$

Answer _____

4. Mallory has a triangular wedge of wood. The sum of the angles in the triangle equals 180°. What is the angle measure, x, of the third corner of the wedge?

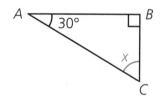

Answer _____

 **Think · Pair · Share**

MP2 5. Draw two angles that share a side and whose measures have a sum of 90°. Explain why both angles are acute.

Independent Practice

Solve the problems.

1. Write an equation to find the complementary angle of 57°.

   $x \underline{\quad} 57° = 90°$

   $x = \underline{\quad}$

2. The diagram shows three roads that meet at angles.

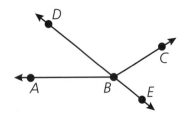

   Name two pairs of supplementary angles.

Write an equation to represent the problem. Then solve.

MP1 3. Jerome uses a telescope to look at stars at night. Each night, he increases the angle between the telescope and its stand by 5° to look at a different part of the sky. If this angle is 148° tonight, what was the angle 5 days ago?

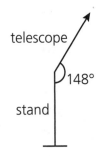

telescope

148°

stand

   $148° - \underline{\qquad\qquad}° = s$

   Answer _____

MP3 4. Two angles, $\angle ROE$ and $\angle JOE$, share a common side and form a straight angle. The measure of $\angle ROE$ is three times that of $\angle JOE$. Find the measure of $\angle ROE$ and of $\angle JOE$.

   Show your work.

   Answer _____

Independent Practice

For exercises 5–8, circle the correct answer.

5. Which angle measure is supplementary to a 25° angle?

   a. 25°

   b. 65°

   c. 90°

   d. 155°

6. Which of the following pairs of angle measures are not complementary?

   a. 45°, 45°

   b. 30°, 60°

   c. 20°, 90°

   d. 15°, 75°

7. The figure below shows two supplementary angles.

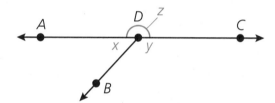

   Which of the following equations shows the relationship between the two angles?

   a. $x + z = 180°$

   b. $x + y = 180°$

   c. $z + y = 180°$

   d. $z - y = 180°$

8. Which of the following statements is true?

   a. Two angles whose measures add to 90° must share a side.

   b. Two angles whose measures add to 180° must share a side.

   c. Two angles formed by a straight angle always have measures that add to 180°.

   d. Two right angles always form complementary angles.

Independent Practice

MP2 **9.** A circle is divided into 4 equal parts. Any two angles formed in this circle are supplementary. Use this information to show that the circle has a total of 360 degrees.

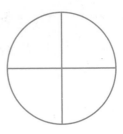

MP6 **10.** Jeremy says that finding an unknown angle measure in a geometric figure is like finding the unknown side length of a rectangle. What do you think Jeremy means by this statement? Do you agree?

Solve the problems.

MP2 **11.** If angle *B* below is a right angle, what is the value of *y*?

✏️ **Show your work.**

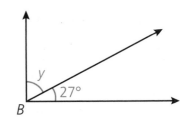

Answer _____

MP7 **12.** A circle is divided into eight equal parts and labeled as shown below. Find the missing angle measures for the figure.

✏️ **Show your work.**

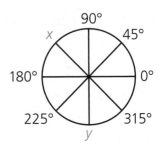

Answer _____

Independent Practice

MP2 **13.** The equation $\frac{110}{360} + \frac{70}{360} = x$ represents fractions of a circle. Solve the equation. Then rewrite it with degree measures instead of fractions of circles. Describe the relationship between the two angles.

> **Show your work.**

Answer _____

MP5 **14.** Draw two angles that are complementary and do not share a side.

> **Show your work.**

MP3 **15.** Tom builds an adjustable table with legs crossed, as shown at the right. Angles x and y are supplementary angles. As the height of the table is raised or lowered, angle x changes. As angle x changes, angle y changes too. Tom says that when the table is raised or lowered, the measures of angle y and angle x change in the same way. Is this true?

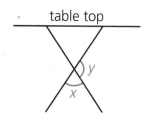
table top

Answer _____

> **Justify your answer using words, drawings, or numbers.**

MP4 **16.** The library has two identical entrance ramps that have an angle up from the ground of 9°. The diagram shows the two ramps set back-to-back. Sharon says that the sum $x + 9° = 90°$. Is that true?

9°   x

Answer _____

> **Justify your answer using words, drawings, or numbers.**

In exercises 1 and 2, ray *BA* and ray *BC* are perpendicular.
Find the missing angle.

1.

$m =$ _____

2.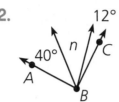

$n =$ _____

Kilograms	Grams
1	
2	
3	
4	
5	

3. Complete the conversion table.

4. How many kilograms is 10,000 grams?

_____

Ms. Kohl's gym class measured their standing long jumps to the nearest quarter foot. Their recorded data is shown at the right. Use the data for exercises 5–10.

Long Jumps (ft)

$5\frac{3}{4}$	$5\frac{2}{4}$	$6\frac{1}{4}$	$6\frac{1}{4}$	$6\frac{3}{4}$
7	$5\frac{3}{4}$	$6\frac{1}{4}$	$7\frac{1}{4}$	$6\frac{2}{4}$
$6\frac{2}{4}$	7	$7\frac{1}{4}$	$5\frac{3}{4}$	$6\frac{3}{4}$
$6\frac{3}{4}$	6	$6\frac{1}{4}$	$7\frac{1}{4}$	$7\frac{1}{4}$

MP6   5. Make a line plot of the long jump data. Give your line plot a title.

<———>

6. How many students had a long jump of $5\frac{3}{4}$ feet? _____

7. What distance did the most students jump? _____

8. What was the longest jump? _____

How many students jumped that far? _____

9. What was the shortest jump? _____

How many students jumped that far? _____

10. What was the difference between the longest and shortest jumps?

_____

Circle the correct answer.

11. How many inches are in 6 ft?

    a. $\frac{1}{2}$ in.   **b.** 12 in.

    c. 36 in.   **d.** 72 in.

12. How many ounces are in 2 pounds?

    a. 40 oz.   **b.** 32 oz.

    c. 20 oz.   **d.** 16 oz.

13. Use a protractor to draw a 60° angle on the line at the right. Write the measurement on the figure.

14. What is the length of the rectangle?

    ✏️ **Show your work.**

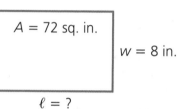

$A = 72$ sq. in.

$w = 8$ in.

$\ell = ?$

Answer _____

15. A water sprinkler rotates one-degree turn at each interval. If the sprinkler rotates a total of 110°, how many one-degree turns has the sprinkler made?

_____

For exercises 16 and 17 use the figure at the right. The two angles form a straight angle.

MP5 **16.** Use a protractor to measure each angle. Write the measurements on the figure.

MP7 **17.** Amilah says that once you find the measure of one of the angles, you can calculate the measure of the other angle without using a protractor. Is she correct? Explain.

Answer _____

Solve the problems.

MP4 **18.** The championship game is at 4:15 P.M. It takes the team bus 60 minutes to get to Central School where the game will be played. The coach wants the team to arrive at Central School 30 minutes before the game starts. What time should the team bus leave for the game?

Answer _____

▸ **Justify your answer using words, drawings, or numbers.**

MP5 **19.** Joel is making a small rectangular blanket. He has 360 centimeters of fringe, which is the exact amount he needs to go around the edge of the blanket. One end of the blanket is 80 cm long. What are the lengths of the other three sides?

Answer _____

▸ **Show your work.**

MP2 **20.** The supermarket sells 1 quart of milk for $1.89 or $\frac{1}{2}$ gallon for $3.00. Which is the better buy?

Answer _____

▸ **Justify your answer using words, drawings, or numbers.**

 **Progress Check**

 UNIT **5**

Look at how the Common Core standards you have learned and will learn connect.

It is very important for you to understand the standards from the prior grade level so that you will be able to develop an understanding of geometry in this unit and be prepared for next year. To practice your skills, go to sadlierconnect.com.

GRADE 3	GRADE 4	GRADE 5
I Can...	Before Unit 5 — **Can I ?** — After Unit 5	**I Will...**

GRADE 4 — Can I?

4.G.1
☐ Draw points, lines, line segments, and rays ☐

☐ Draw right angles, acute angles, and obtuse angles ☐

☐ Draw parallel and perpendicular lines ☐

☐ Identify lines and angles in two-dimensional figures. ☐

GRADE 5 — I Will...

5.G.1
Understand the concept and representation of the coordinate plane

GRADE 3 — I Can...

3.G.1
Explain that shapes in different categories may share attributes; for example, rectangles and squares both have four straight sides

Classify quadrilaterals by their attributes

GRADE 4 — Can I?

4.G.2
☐ Classify shapes by properties of their lines and angles ☐

☐ Recognize right triangles as a category ☐

GRADE 5 — I Will...

5.G.3
Understand relationships among categories of figures; for example, all rectangles have four right angles and squares are rectangles, so all squares have four right angles

5.G.4
Classify two-dimensional figures [in a hierarchy] based on properties

4.G.3
☐ Identify and draw lines of symmetry ☐

☐ Identify figures that have line symmetry ☐

HOME◆CONNECT...

In this unit your child will:

- Draw and identify points, lines, and angles.

- Classify two-dimensional figures.

- Identify lines of symmetry.

NOTE: All of these learning goals for your child are based on the Grade 4 Common Core State Standards for Mathematics.

Ways to Help Your Child

Encourage your child to share math vocabulary words and their meanings with your family. Using the mathematical vocabulary will help your child to make connections, as well as to avoid misconceptions.

Your child will use the language of geometry to analyze and classify angles and geometric figures. Support your child by using the following Math vocabulary:

- An **angle** is formed when two **rays** share the same endpoint, called the **vertex**.

- A **straight angle** forms a straight line. It measures 180°.

- A **right angle** measures 90° and is formed by the intersection of two perpendicular lines.

- An **acute angle** is less than a right angle, or measures between 0° and 90°.

- An **obtuse angle** is more than a right angle, or measures between 90° and 180°.

Activity: Plan a shape scavenger hunt for your child and some friends or siblings. Make a list of two-dimensional figures (such as right triangle, parallelogram, rectangle, pentagon), and ask the children to safely search around your home or other safe locale to find examples of each figure.

ONLINE

For more Home Connect activities, continue online at sadlierconnect.com

Focus on Geometry

Essential Question:
How does understanding lines and angles help you identify geometric shapes?

34 Draw and Identify Points, Lines, and Angles

Essential Question:
How do you draw and identify points, lines, and angles in geometric figures?

4.G.1

Words to Know:
line
line segment
parallel lines
perpendicular lines

Guided Instruction

In this lesson you will learn how to use the language of geometry to analyze and classify geometric figures.

Understand: Using and applying geometric terms

Using this geometric figure, what geometric terms can you define?

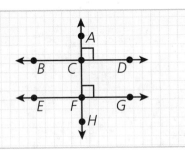

You learned that a point is an exact location in space. Points are named using capital letters. On this figure, points *A* through *H* identify locations.

A line is an endless collection of points along a straight path. To name a line, use any two points on the line. Look at lines *AH*, *BD*, and *EG*. Each line can also be named by any other two points on the line, for example, *CF* or *FH* also name line *AH*.

A line segment is part of a line that has two endpoints. Using the endpoints you can name line segments *AH*, *BD*, and *EG*. Some other line segments are line segments *AC*, *BC*, and *CF*.

A ray is a part of a line that has one endpoint and extends endlessly in the other direction. To name a ray, start with the endpoint and use any other point on the ray. For example, ray *AC* is the same ray as ray *AF* or ray *AH* since it starts at point *A* and extends endlessly along line *AH*. Some other rays are rays *CB*, *CA*, and *CD*.

Parallel lines are lines that will never meet, or intersect. Line *BD* is parallel to line *EG*.

Perpendicular lines are lines that meet, or intersect, to form a right angle. When you see a square in the corner it shows that a right angle is formed and thus the lines are perpendicular. Line *AH* is perpendicular to line *BD*. Line *AH* is also perpendicular to line *EG*.

Remember!
A right angle forms a square corner.

➡ You have defined points, lines, line segments, rays, parallel lines, and perpendicular lines.

Understand: Identifying right, acute, obtuse, and straight angles

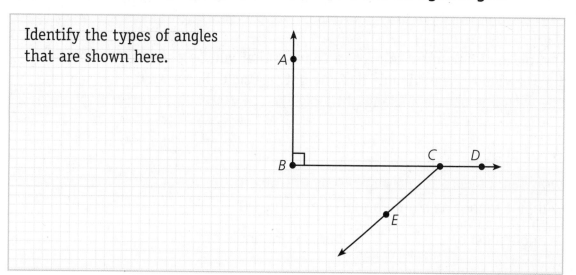

Identify the types of angles that are shown here.

An angle is named by its vertex, the point from which the two sides of an angle begin. The angle at *B* is marked by the symbol (⌐) so it is a right angle and measures 90°. It can also be named as angle *ABC*, or angle *CBA*. The letter naming the vertex names the angle. In a three letter angle name, the vertex is the middle letter.

Remember!

An angle is formed when two rays share the same endpoint, called the vertex. The two rays form the sides of the angle.

An angle that is less than a right angle is an acute angle. It measures less than 90°. Angle *BCE* is an acute angle.

An angle that is greater than a right angle is an obtuse angle. It measures more than 90° and less than 180°. Angle *DCE* is an obtuse angle.

An angle that forms a straight line is a straight angle. It measures 180°. Angle *BCD* is a straight angle.

➡ Angle *ABC* is a right angle, angle *BCE* is an acute angle, angle *DCE* is an obtuse angle, and angle *BCD* is a straight angle.

✏ How can you check that angles *BCE* and *DCE* are not right angles?

Guided Instruction

Connect: What you know about the language of geometry and geometric shapes

Pablo cuts a piece of blue glass to make a triangle that will be placed in a stained glass window. The triangle has one obtuse angle. Show what the triangle with one obtuse angle might look like.

Step 1

Understand what it means for an angle to be obtuse.

You know that it cannot be a right angle or measure 90°.

An obtuse angle must be _____ than a right angle but
                              greater or less
_____ than a straight angle.
greater or less

Step 2

Now draw an obtuse angle: from the same vertex point draw one horizontal ray and then another ray that is between the two rays representing 90° and 180°.

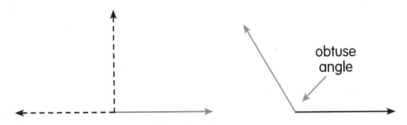

obtuse
angle

Step 3

Choose one point on each ray and connect the points to form a triangle with on obtuse angle.

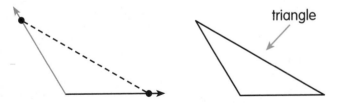

triangle

The triangle above is a triangle with one _____ angle.

Name another angle or angles that you see in the triangle formed in Step 3.

306 Unit 5 ■ Focus on Geometry

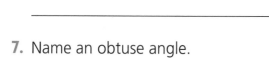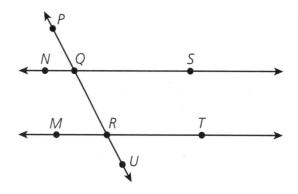

Guided Practice

For exercises 1–4, draw and label an example.

1. line *JK*

2. line segment *QR*

3. acute angle *CDE*

4. line *LM* parallel to line *ST*

For exercises 5–9, use the figure at the right.

5. Name three line segments.

_____

6. Name two rays.

_____

7. Name an obtuse angle.

_____

8. Name an acute angle.

_____

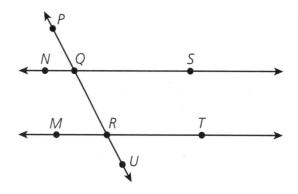

Solve the problem.

MP7 9. On a blueprint, a designer used two right angles to make a straight angle. Draw an example to show how two right angles can make a straight angle.

☆ Think•Pair•Share

MP3 10. Describe something in your classroom that reminds you of parallel lines. Explain why you think the lines are parallel.

Independent Practice

For exercises 1–10, draw and label an example.

1. ray *CD*

2. line *XY*

3. right angle *JKL*

4. line segment *AB*

5. line *EF* perpendicular to line *GH*

6. acute angle *PQR*

7. obtuse angle *DEF*

8. line *QR* parallel to line *ST*

9. straight angle *LMN*

10. line *AB* perpendicular to line segment *CD*

Independent Practice

Classify each angle as acute, right, obtuse, or straight.

11.

_____

12.

_____

13.

_____

14.

_____

For exercises 15–23, use the figure.

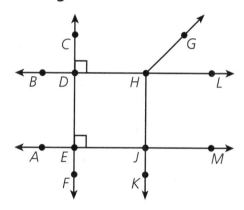

15. Name five points. _____

16. Name four line segments. _____

17. Name three lines. _____

18. Name four rays. _____

19. Line segments *DE* and *HJ* have the same length. Name a pair of

parallel lines. _____

20. Name a pair of perpendicular lines. _____

21. Name a straight angle. _____

22. Name an obtuse angle. _____

23. Name an acute angle. _____

Independent Practice

24. Draw a triangle with one right angle.

Classify the other two angles in your triangle as acute, right, obtuse, or straight. Explain how you classified the other two angles.

Solve the problems.

MP6 **25.** The window above a door is in the shape shown at the right. How many acute, obtuse, and right angles are in the window? Do any of the pairs of line segments used in the shape of the window look parallel or perpendicular?

MP4 **26.** Look at the stop sign at the right. How many acute, obtuse, and right angles are in the stop sign? Do any of the pairs of line segments used in the shape of the stop sign look parallel or perpendicular?

Independent Practice

MP4 **27.** The street my friend Craig lives on is parallel to the street Francie lives on. The street Francie lives on is parallel to the street Briana lives on. The street Briana lives on is parallel to the street Drew lives on. Describe the relationship between Craig's street and Drew's street.

Answer _____

✏️ **Justify your answer using words, drawings, or numbers.**

MP7 **28.** Taylor has two tiles shaped like the rectangle and the square shown below. She notices that some geometric characteristics of the tiles are the same and some are different.

What is something the same that Taylor might notice? What is something different?

Answer _____

✏️ **Justify your answer using words, drawings, or numbers.**

MP6 **29.** Travis draws a pair of lines on a sheet of paper. The lines he draws do not intersect. What can you say about the lines? Are they necessarily parallel, perpendicular, or neither? Explain.

Answer _____

✏️ **Justify your answer using words, drawings, or numbers.**

35 Classify Two-Dimensional Figures

Essential Question:
How do you classify two-dimensional figures?

4.G.2

Words to Know:
- **parallelogram**
- **adjacent**
- **rectangle**
- **trapezoid**
- **right triangle**
- **pentagon**
- **hexagon**

Guided Instruction

In this lesson you will learn how to classify two-dimensional figures using angle measures and pairs of parallel or perpendicular sides.

Understand: **Using parallel or perpendicular lines to classify two-dimensional figures**

> Dawn makes dog collars. She stamps the collars with two-dimensional figures to create decorative patterns. Two of the figures she uses are shown. Classify or identify by attributes the figures that Dawn uses to create the decorative patterns.
>
>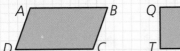

The figures that Dawn uses are quadrilaterals.

You can use parallel lines and perpendicular lines to further classify the quadrilaterals.

Parallel sides are sides that are parts of parallel lines. In quadrilateral *ABCD*, side *AB* is parallel to side *DC*. Side *AD* is parallel to side *BC*. Both pairs of opposite sides are parallel. So quadrilateral *ABCD* is a **parallelogram**. In quadrilateral *QRST*, side *QR* is parallel to side *TS*. Side *QT* is parallel to side *RS*. Both pairs of opposite sides of the quadrilateral are parallel. Quadrilateral *QRST* is also a parallelogram.

Remember!
Parallel lines never meet and are always the same distance apart. Perpendicular lines meet at right angles.

Perpendicular sides are sides that are **adjacent**, or next to each other, and are parts of perpendicular lines. In parallelogram *QRST*, side *QT* is perpendicular to side *TS*. Side *RS* is perpendicular to side *TS*. A parallelogram with two pairs of perpendicular sides is a **rectangle**. So quadrilateral *QRST* can also be classified as a rectangle.

➡ Dawn uses parallelograms and rectangles to create the decorative patterns.

You learned that a parallelogram with all sides of equal length can be classified as a rhombus. There is another kind of quadrilateral that has at least one set of parallel sides. It is a **trapezoid**.

Guided Instruction

Understand: Using angle measurement to classify two-dimensional figures

Dawn creates another pattern by stamping the same pair of two-dimensional figures several times. Classify the two-dimensional figures Dawn uses to create this new pattern for her dog collars.

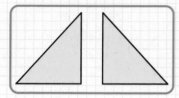 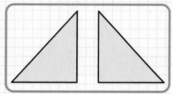 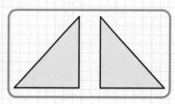

Each triangle has one pair of perpendicular sides.
The perpendicular sides meet at right angles.

Each triangle has exactly one right angle.
Notice that the other two angles in the triangle measure less than 90°, so they are acute angles.
A triangle with one right angle is called a right triangle.

Remember!
A right angle measures 90° and forms a square corner.

➡ Dawn uses right triangles to create the new pattern for her dog collars.

✏ Draw an example of a triangle that is not a right triangle.
How do you know it is not a right triangle?

Guided Instruction

Connect: What you know about classifying two-dimensional figures

Identify the polygons. Then identify any pairs of parallel or perpendicular sides.

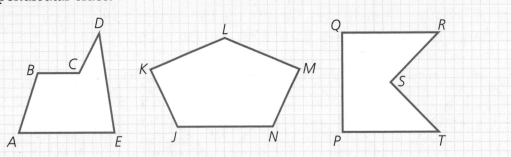

Each of the polygons is a pentagon.

A pentagon has _____ straight sides and _____ angles.

Do any pairs of sides of pentagon *ABCDE* form right angles? _____

Are any pairs of sides of pentagon *ABCDE* perpendicular? _____
In pentagon *ABCDE* side *AE* and side *BC* are always the same distance apart.

If the sides were extended, would the lines ever meet? _____

Are any pairs of sides of pentagon *ABCDE* parallel? _____

Which sides of pentagon *ABCDE* are parallel? _____

Do any pairs of sides of pentagon *JKLMN* form right angles? _____

Are any pairs of sides of pentagon *JKLMN* parallel? _____

Do any pairs of sides of pentagon *PQRST* form right angles? _____
Which pairs of sides of pentagon *PQRST* are perpendicular?

_____

Are any pairs of sides of pentagon *PQRST* parallel? _____

Which sides of pentagon *PQRST* are parallel? _____

▶ Polygons _____ each have one pair of parallel sides

and polygon _____ has two pairs of perpendicular sides.

A hexagon is a polygon with 6 sides and 6 angles.

Guided Practice

For questions 1–7, use polygons 1–5.

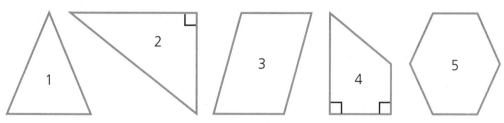

1. Which of the polygons have no right angles? _____

2. Which of the polygons have at least one pair of perpendicular sides?

   _____

3. Which of the polygons seem to have at least one pair of parallel sides?

   _____

4. Which of the polygons is a right triangle? _____

5. Which of the polygons are quadrilateral? _____

6. What is another way to classify each quadrilateral?

   _____

7. Classify polygon 5. _____

Solve the problem.

MP6 8. Julia says that she can draw a right triangle in which two sides have the same length. Is Julia correct? Draw an example to justify your answer.

Think·Pair·Share

MP5 9. Draw a hexagon with exactly two right angles. Explain how you drew the hexagon. Does your hexagon have any pairs of parallel or perpendicular sides?

Independent Practice

For questions 1–8, use polygons 1–5.

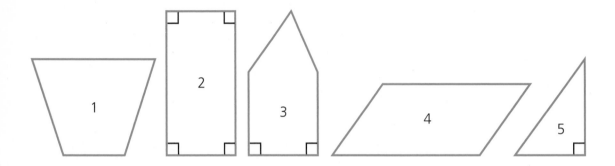

1. Which of the polygons have no right angles? _____

2. Which of the polygons have at least one pair of perpendicular sides?

   _____

3. Which of the polygons seem to have at least one pair of parallel sides?

   _____

4. Which of the polygons is a right triangle? _____

5. Which of the polygons are quadrilaterals? _____

6. Classify the quadrilaterals.

   _____

7. Classify polygon 3. _____

MP7 8. Choose two of the polygons. Tell how they are alike. Then tell how they are different.

Independent Practice

For exercises 9–15, draw an example of each. Then classify the polygon you drew.

9. A triangle with a pair of perpendicular sides _____

10. A polygon with 3 sides and no right angles _____

11. A rhombus with at least one right angle _____

12. A parallelogram with at least one pair of perpendicular sides

_____

13. A quadrilateral with no right angles and at least one pair of opposite sides that are parallel _____

14. A polygon with 5 sides, one pair of parallel sides, and at least one pair of perpendicular sides _____

15. A polygon with 6 sides and two pairs of parallel sides _____

Independent Practice

For exercises 16–20, use polygons 1–6 and the Venn diagram.

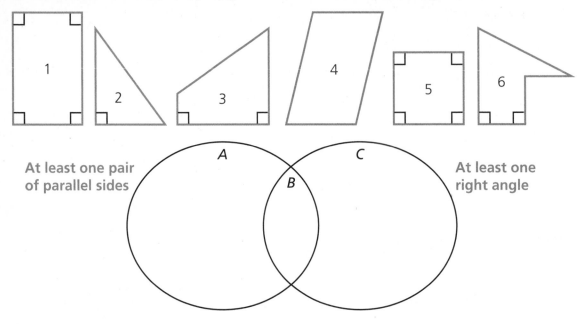

16. Write the numbers of the polygons in the correct parts of the Venn diagram (A, B, or C).

17. In which part did you place polygon 2 in the Venn diagram? Explain why.

18. In which part did you place polygon 3 in the Venn diagram? Explain why.

19. In which part did you place polygon 4 in the Venn diagram? Explain why.

MP3 20. Explain why you placed some of the polygons in the overlapping part of the diagram.

Independent Practice

MP7 **21.** Xavier says that he can draw a parallelogram with exactly one right angle. Is Xavier correct? If the statement is incorrect, how can you change it to make it correct?

Answer _____

➤ **Justify your answer using words, drawings, or numbers.**

MP8 **22.** Antoine says that every square is a rhombus. Is Antoine correct? If the statement is incorrect, how can you change it to make it correct?

Answer _____

➤ **Justify your answer using words, drawings, or numbers.**

MP3 **23.** Marisol says that every quadrilateral must be a parallelogram or a trapezoid. Is Marisol correct? If the statement is incorrect, how can you change it to make it correct?

Answer _____

➤ **Justify your answer using words, drawings, or numbers.**

36 Identify Lines of Symmetry

Guided Instruction

In this lesson you will learn how to recognize and draw lines of symmetry for a two-dimensional figure.

Understand: Identifying lines of symmetry

Theresa has a triangular piece of paper that she wants to fold so that the two parts will match. Which drawings show ways that Theresa can fold the triangular piece of paper so that the two parts match exactly?

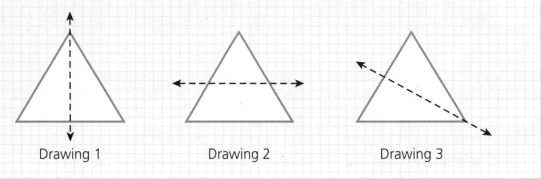

| Drawing 1 | Drawing 2 | Drawing 3 |

A two-dimensional figure has line symmetry if it can be folded along a line so that the two parts match exactly.

The line that represents the fold is called a line of symmetry. A two-dimensional figure can have one or more lines of symmetry. It can also have no lines of symmetry.

The dashed lines show different ways Theresa can fold the triangle. She must decide which of the dashed lines are lines of symmetry.

If Theresa folds the triangle along the dashed line shown in Drawing 1, both parts will match up exactly. The dashed line in Drawing 1 is a line of symmetry.

If Theresa folds the triangle along the dashed line shown in Drawing 2, both parts will not match up exactly. The dashed line in Drawing 2 is not a line of symmetry for the triangle.

If Theresa folds the triangle along the dashed line shown in Drawing 3, both parts will match up exactly. The dashed line in Drawing 3 is a line of symmetry.

▶ The two parts will match exactly if Theresa folds the triangular piece of paper along either of the lines of symmetry shown in Drawings 1 and 3.

Guided Instruction

Understand: Drawing lines of symmetry

Eric draws a pentagon. Each side of the pentagon is the same length. He wants to find all the lines of symmetry of the pentagon. How many lines of symmetry does his pentagon have?

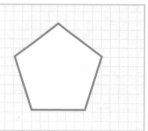

To draw a line of symmetry, decide where to fold the figure so that the parts match up exactly. If the pentagon is folded along the line from the top vertex to the center of the opposite side of the pentagon, the parts will fold over one another exactly. The dashed line shows a line of symmetry.

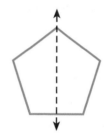

All of the sides of this pentagon are the same length. If the figure is folded along the line from any vertex to the middle of the opposite side, the parts will match. The drawing shows two more lines of symmetry.

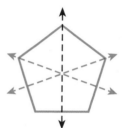

You can draw two more lines in the same way. Each line of symmetry goes through one of the vertices to the center of the opposite side. The drawing shows all the lines of symmetry of the pentagon.

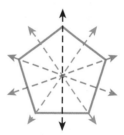

➤ The pentagon that Eric draws has five lines of symmetry.

✏ Will every pentagon have five lines of symmetry? Explain your thinking. Draw a diagram to support your answer.

Guided Instruction

Connect: **What you know about lines of symmetry**

Isabel is creating a design for a poster. The dashed line is a line of symmetry for the design. Draw the other half of Isabel's design.

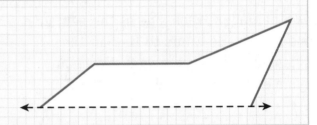

Step 1

The dashed line is a line of symmetry. When the top part of the design is folded over the line of symmetry, the bottom part will match it exactly. This means the part below the line is a mirror image of the part above the line.

There are 4 line segments above the line of symmetry. How many line segments will be in the other half of Isabel's design?

_____

Step 2

Draw the part of the design that will be below the line of symmetry.

Start with the leftmost line segment. Below the line of symmetry draw a line segment that looks like a mirror image of that line segment.

Continue to draw the line segments in order from left to right.

If you fold your completed design along the line of symmetry the parts match up.

Draw all the lines of symmetry for each figure.

1.
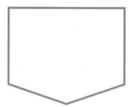

2.

3.

4.

Solve the problem.

5. Blake designs a circular invitation that shows a happy
face when it is opened. Draw the line of symmetry
along which Blake folds his invitation.

Think•Pair•Share

6. Use the dashed line below as a line of symmetry. Draw three sides of a
polygon above this line of symmetry. Then draw the other half of the
polygon below the line of symmetry. Explain why the completed polygon
has line symmetry.

Independent Practice

Is the dashed line on each figure a line of symmetry? Write *Yes* or *No*.

1.

_____

2.
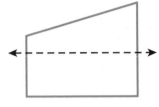

_____

3.
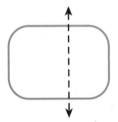

_____

4.
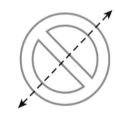

_____

Does the figure have line symmetry? If Yes, draw the line or lines of symmetry. If No, write *No*.

5.

_____

6.

_____

7.
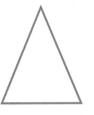

_____

8.

_____

Independent Practice

Draw all the lines of symmetry for each figure.

9.

10.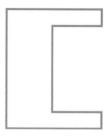

11.

12.

13.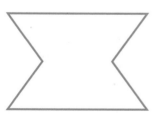

14.

15.

16.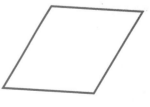

Independent Practice

17. Look at the circle. Does a circle have line symmetry? If so, how many lines of symmetry does a circle have? Explain your answer.

Solve the problems.

MP5 **18.** The logo for Zany's company is shown at the right. Does the logo have a line of symmetry? If so draw the line of symmetry.

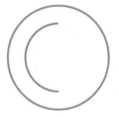

MP4 **19.** Alev drew these pictures of a shamrock, a leaf, and a flower that she saw while hiking. Do any of the shapes have line symmetry? If so, draw at least one line of symmetry on each shape.

Independent Practice

MP3 20. Jake says that the lines shown are lines of symmetry for the parallelogram. Is Jake correct?

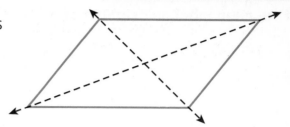

Answer _____

✏ **Justify your answer using words, drawings, or numbers.**

MP7 21. Think of the capital letters of the alphabet. Name three letters that do not have a line of symmetry. Name three letters that have exactly one line of symmetry. Name three letters that have more than one line of symmetry.

Answer _____

✏ **Justify your answer using words, drawings, or numbers.**

MP8 22. Each of the polygons below has sides that are the same length. Describe the pattern between the number of sides and the number of lines of symmetry for each figure. Use the pattern to predict the number of lines of symmetry for a polygon with 10 sides of equal length.

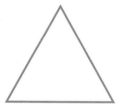   

Answer _____

✏ **Justify your answer using words, drawings, or numbers.**

Draw and label an example of each of the following.

1. line segment *AB*

2. line *CD* perpendicular to line *EF*

3. acute angle *GHI*

4. obtuse angle *JKL*

5. line *MN* parallel to line *OP*

6. ray *QR*

Circle the correct answer.

7. Which figure has a line of symmetry?

a.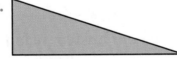

b.

c.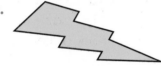

d.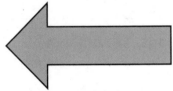

8. This triangle has all sides the same length. How many lines of symmetry does it have?

a. 0

b. 1

c. 2

d. 3

9. Draw a right triangle. Explain why your triangle is a right triangle.

10. What three kinds of angles can you find in the traffic sign? Label them.

For exercises 11–14, draw an example of each. Then classify the polygon you drew.

11. A polygon with 6 sides and 6 angles

_____

12. A triangle with a right angle

_____

13. A quadrilateral with at least one pair of parallel sides

_____

14. A parallelogram with 4 right angles and all sides the same length

_____

For exercises 15 and 16, one shape does not belong. Circle it. Tell why the shape does not belong.

MP7 15.

The shape I circled does not belong because

_____

MP7 16.

The shape I circled does not belong because

_____

Solve the problems.

MP6 **17.** The dashed line is a line of symmetry. Draw the other half of the shape to make a symmetrical figure. What shape did you make?

Answer _____

MP4 **18.** A bathroom tile is in the shape shown at the right. What kind of angles does the tile have—acute, right, or obtuse? Does the tile have any pairs of parallel or perpendicular sides?

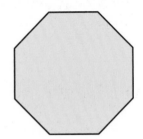

Answer _____

_____

MP3 **19.** Autumn drew the figure at the right to prove that a square has only 2 lines of symmetry. Is Autumn correct?

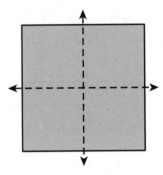

Answer _____

✏️ **Justify your answer using words, drawings, or numbers.**

MP6 **20.** Dominic says that every rhombus is a square. Is Dominic correct?

Answer _____

✏️ **Justify your answer using words, drawings, or numbers.**

4.OA.4, 4.NF.1, 4.NF.3a, 4.MD.1, 4.MD.2,
4.MD.3, 4.MD.4, 4.MD.6, 4.MD.7, 4.G.1,
4.G.2, 4.G.3

Performance Tasks

Performance Tasks show your understanding of the Math that you have learned. You will be doing various Performance Tasks as you complete your work in this text.

Beginning This Task

The next five pages provide you with the beginning of a Performance Task. You will be given 5 items to complete, and each item will have two or more parts. As you complete these items you will:

I Demonstrate that you have mastered mathematical skills and concepts

II Reason through a problem to a solution, and explain your reasoning

III Use models and apply them to real-world situations.

Extending This Task

Your teacher may extend this Performance Task with additional items provided in our online resources at sadlierconnect.com.

Scoring This Task

Your response to each item will be assessed against a rubric, or scoring guide. Some items will be worth 1 or 2 points, and others will be worth more. In each item you will show your work or explain your reasoning.

Performance Task 2

Building a Neighborhood Playground

1. The children and adults who live in Dan's neighborhood are building a playground. A team of children works together to tear down an old fence and take the boards away to a recycling bin.

    a. The team begins work at 3:30 P.M. Draw a point on the number line to show 3:30 P.M.

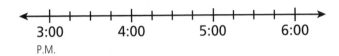

    b. The team spends $\frac{3}{4}$ hour tearing down the fence. What time does the team finish tearing down the fence? Show how to use the number line above to find what time the team finishes the task.

    c. Next, the team works $1\frac{1}{2}$ hours taking away the boards to a recycling bin. What time does the team finish taking away the boards? Show how to use the number line above to find what time the team finishes this task.

    d. How many minutes does the team spend altogether on the two tasks? Explain the method you used to find your answer.

A Lawn Area at the Playground

2. Rhonda is planning a lawn for a playground. The lawn will be a rectangle with an area of 60 square meters. The length of each side will be a whole number of meters.

   a. Explain how Rhonda can find possible side lengths for the lawn.

   b. Find all possible pairs of side lengths for the lawn.

   c. How do you know that you found all possible pairs of side lengths?

   d. Find the side lengths for the lawn that would have the least perimeter. What is the least perimeter? Explain your reasoning.

Future Shade

3. A tree nursery donates some trees for a new playground. Carlos and Nikki measure the heights of the trees and record the data.

   a. Use their data to make a line plot.

   Heights of Trees (ft)

$1\frac{2}{4}$	$1\frac{3}{4}$	$2\frac{1}{4}$	2	$1\frac{3}{4}$
$2\frac{2}{4}$	2	$2\frac{3}{4}$	$1\frac{2}{4}$	$2\frac{1}{4}$
$1\frac{3}{4}$	$2\frac{1}{4}$	$1\frac{1}{4}$	$2\frac{2}{4}$	$1\frac{3}{4}$

   _____

   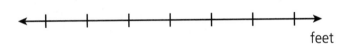

   feet

   b. Which Xs on the line plot represent trees that are $2\frac{1}{2}$ feet tall?

   c. How many inches tall is a tree that is 2 feet tall?

   d. What is the difference in height between the tallest tree and the shortest tree? Use the line plot.

A Gate for the Playground

4. Bernard works on a gate for a playground. The diagram shows that the gate should open to ∠ABC, but it only opens to ∠DBC.

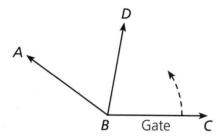

a. Use a protractor. Find the measure of ∠ABC and the measure of ∠DBC.

b. Explain two ways to find the measure of ∠ABD.

c. Find the measure of ∠ABD using both of your methods.

d. Which method do you prefer? Explain.

A Playground Game

5. Pedro and Derron are designing a playground game.

   a. Pedro begins by drawing a rectangle that is not a square. Draw a rectangle that could be Pedro's.

   b. Is the figure you drew a parallelogram? Explain.

   c. Next Pedro draws two line segments inside the rectangle. The line segments are perpendicular and are parts of two lines of symmetry of the rectangle. Draw those two line segments in your rectangle.

   d. Derron says that Pedro can draw two more line segments that are also parts of lines of symmetry of the rectangle. Is Derron correct? Explain why or why not.

A review of prerequisite mathematics needed to understand the concepts and skills of Grade 4.

A. Understand: The meaning of a product

A product is the result of multiplication.

The product of 4 × 5 is 20.

4 cards
5 dots on each card
4 fives equals 20.

factors → 4 × 5 = 20 ← product

B. Understand: Use multiplication to solve division

You can use related multiplication facts to solve division problems.
Knowing the fact family can help.

$$16 \div 2 = \blacksquare$$

| number in all | number in each group | number of groups |

Think: What number times 2 makes 16?

$$\blacksquare \times 2 = 16$$

| number of groups | number in each group | number in all |

Use the fact family for 2, 8, and 16 to help solve the problem.
2 × 8 = 16   16 ÷ 8 = 2
8 × 2 = 16   16 ÷ 2 = 8

Find the unknown factor in the multiplication: ■ × 2 = 16
Use the unknown factor to complete the related division: 16 ÷ 2 = 8

C. Understand: Round numbers to the nearest hundred

You can use a number line to round numbers to the nearest hundred.

Round 126 to the nearest hundred.
126 is closer to 100 than 200.
126 rounds to 100.

Round 271 to the nearest hundred.
271 is closer to 300 than to 200.
271 rounds to 300.

You can also use these rules to round three-digit numbers.
If the tens digit is 1, 2, 3, or 4, round to the lesser 100.
If the tens digit is 5 or greater, round to the greater 100.

Round 325 using the rules.
325 is between 300 and 400.
The tens digit is 2, so round to the lesser 100.
325 rounds to 300.

D. Understand: Multiplication Strategies

There are many ways to find a product. Here are two strategies you can use to find the product of 4 x 5.

You can draw an array.

The array at the left shows 4 equal groups of 5.
You can write 4 × 5 = 20.
You can also write

$$\begin{array}{r} 4 \\ \times\ 5 \\ \hline 20 \end{array}$$

You can also use the Commutative Property.

The array at the left shows that 5 × 4 = 20.

If you know that 5 × 4 = 20, then you know that 4 × 5 = 20.

E. Understand: Division Strategies

The result of a division problem is a quotient. Here are two strategies to find the quotient of 20 ÷ 5.

You can draw an array.

The array shows that 20 can be divided into 4 equal groups of 5.

You can write 20 ÷ 4 = 5.

You can also write
$$4\overline{)20} \quad 5$$

You can also use a related multiplication fact.

If you know that 4 × 5 = 20, then you know that 20 ÷ 5 = 4.

F. Understand: Find equivalent fractions on a number line

You can use number lines to find fractions that have different names but are at the same point on the number line. These are called equivalent fractions.

How many sixths are equivalent to $\frac{1}{3}$?

Find $\frac{1}{3}$ on the number line. Find the equivalent fraction in sixths directly below it on the number line on the bottom.

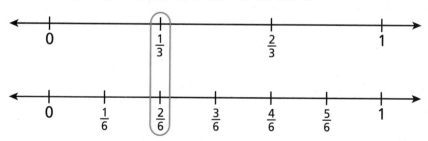

$\frac{1}{3}$ is equivalent to $\frac{2}{6}$.

$\frac{1}{3} = \frac{2}{6}$

G. **Understand:** Compare fractions on a number line

Compare $\frac{5}{8}$ and $\frac{3}{8}$.

Look at the number line.

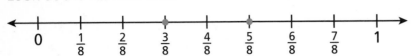

$\frac{5}{8}$ is to the right of $\frac{3}{8}$ on the number line, so $\frac{5}{8}$ is greater than $\frac{3}{8}$.

To show this comparison, write $\frac{5}{8} > \frac{3}{8}$.

$\frac{3}{8}$ is to the left of $\frac{5}{8}$ on the number line, so $\frac{3}{8}$ is less than $\frac{5}{8}$.

To show this comparison, write $\frac{3}{8} < \frac{5}{8}$.

H. **Understand:** The meaning of a unit fraction

A fraction is a number. When a whole is partitioned, or divided, into equal parts, a unit fraction represents the quantity, or amount, in one of those equal parts.

$$\frac{\text{numerator}}{\text{denominator}}$$

numerator ← number of equal parts in the fraction
denominator ← number of equal parts in the whole

A unit fraction has this form:

$$\frac{1}{\text{denominator}}$$

1 ← 1 equal part in the fraction
denominator ← number of equal parts in the whole

Each square has **1** equal part that is shaded.
Each square has **4** equal parts.

1 equal part in the fraction ⟶ $\dfrac{1}{4}$
4 equal parts in the whole ⟶

Read $\frac{1}{4}$ as "one fourth."

I. Understand: How to measure time intervals

The difference from one time to another time is called elapsed time.

Aaron swam from 8:45 A.M. to 9:35 A.M.
How long did Aaron swim?

Look at the minute hand on the clock.
Count time intervals of 10 minutes.
$10 + 10 + 10 + 10 + 10 = 50$

Aaron swam for 50 minutes.

Practice for the school play was from 3:00 P.M. to 4:30 P.M.
How long was play practice?

Use a number line. Count time intervals of 30 minutes.

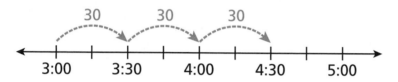

Play practice was 90 minutes, or 1 hour 30 minutes.

J. Understand: Multiply to find the area of rectangles

You can use different methods to find the area
of a rectangle.

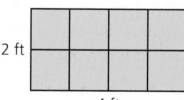

2 ft

4 ft

Method 1

Tile the rectangle.
Count the unit squares that will cover the rectangle.
The sides are measured in feet, so the area will be in square feet.

8 unit squares cover the rectangle.
The area of the rectangle is 8 square feet.

Method 2

Each unit square has an area of 1 square foot. There are 2 rows
of unit squares.

Each row has an area of 4 square feet.

Multiply the side lengths of the rectangle.
    $2 \times 4 = 8$
The area of the rectangle is 8 square feet.

K. Understand: How to draw line plots

The tally chart shows lengths of carrots from Anya's garden.

Lengths of Carrots	
Length (in.)	Tally
6	II
$6\frac{1}{2}$	I
7	III
$7\frac{1}{2}$	IIII
8	I

Use the tally chart to make a line plot of the measurement data.

Lengths of Carrots (in.)

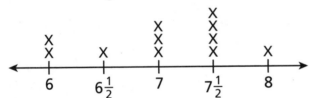

L. Understand: Use lengths of sides and angles to identify special quadrilaterals

To identify a quadrilateral, look at the sides and the angles.

rectangle
opposite sides the same length
4 right angles

rhombus
all 4 sides the same length

square
all 4 sides the same length
4 right angles

A square has the attributes of both a rhombus and a rectangle.

You can use this model to solve problems.

Read

Read the problem.
Focus on the facts and the questions.

- What facts do you know?
- What do you need to find out?

Plan

Outline a plan.
Plan how to solve the problem.

- What operation will you use?
- Do I need to use 1 step or 2 steps?
- Will you draw a picture?
- How have you solved similar problems?

Solve

Follow your plan to solve the problem.

- Did you answer the question?
- Did you label your answer?

Check

Test that the solution is reasonable.

- Does your answer make sense? If not, review and revise your plan.
- How can you solve the problem a different way? Is the answer the same?
- How can you estimate to check your answer?

An Envelope Problem

When you:	Use:
• Join like groups or quantities	$\Box + \Box = \Box$
• Separate, or take away, from a group. • Compare two groups or quantities. • Find part of a group. • Find how many more are needed.	$\Box - \Box = \Box$
• Join equal groups or quantities.	$\Box \times \Box = \Box$
• Partition into equal shares. • Share a group equally.	$\Box \div \Box = \Box$

Meg paints pictures and then puts them into envelopes. She puts 7 pictures into each envelope. How many envelopes does Meg need for 42 pictures?

Read

Visualize the problem as you reread it.
Focus on the facts and the question.

Facts: 7 pictures in each envelope
42 pictures

Question: How many envelopes does Meg need?

Plan

You are partitioning into equal groups.
The number of equal groups is unknown.

Divide: $42 \div 7 = $ ■
Think: ■ $\times 7 = 42$

Solve

$42 \div 7 = 6$

⇨ Meg needs 6 envelopes.

Check

Multiply to check division.
$6 \times 7 = 42$

344 Problem-Solving Model

A Recycling Problem

Tina, Maya, and Olga need to collect 200 aluminum cans to win a recycling contest. Tina has collected 57 cans, Maya has collected 76 cans, and Olga has collected 64 cans. How many more cans do the girls still need to collect?

Read

Visualize the problem as you reread it.
Focus on the facts and the question.

Facts: 200 cans needed.
Tina collected 57 cans.
Maya collected 76 cans.
Olga collected 64 cans.

Question: How many more cans are still needed?

Plan

Is more than one step needed to solve this problem? Yes.

Step 1: Find the number of cans collected. Add.

57   +   76   +   64   =   ■
Tina's cans   Maya's cans   Olga's cans   number of cans
                                              collected

Step 2: Find the number of cans the girls still need to collect.
Subtract the sum from 200.

200   −   ■   =   ▲
in all   number   number of cans
               collected   still needed

Solve

57 + 76 + 64 = 197
The girls collected 197 cans.

200 − 197 = 3
The girls still need to collect 3 more cans.

Check

Use addition to check your answer.

197   +   3   =   200
cans   cans   cans in all
collected   still needed

Common Core State Standards for Mathematical Practice

The Standards for Mathematical Practice, identified here, are an important part of learning mathematics. They are covered in every lesson in this book.

MP1 Make sense of problems and persevere in solving them.

- Analyze and plan a solution
- Relate to a similar problem
- Assess progress
- Use concrete objects or pictures
- Check solutions

MP2 Reason abstractly and quantitatively.

- Pay attention to all mathematical language
- Represent problems using symbols
- Consider units in problem solving
- Use properties of operations and objects

MP3 Construct viable arguments and critique the reasoning of others.

- Analyze a problem situation
- Share reasoning with others
- Explain an approach to a problem
- Construct arguments by using drawings or concrete objects

MP4 Model with mathematics.

- Relate mathematics to everyday problems
- Make assumptions and estimations
- Explain the relationship of quantities
- Use concrete tools to explain operations
- Interpret the solution in the context of a situation

MP5 Use appropriate tools strategically.

- Consider the range of available tools (e.g., place-value charts, graphs, clocks, etc.)
- Decide on appropriate tools to use for each situation
- Use tools carefully and strategically

MP6 Attend to precision.

- Communicate with precision
- Identify the meaning of symbols
- Use measurement units appropriately
- Calculate accurately
- Carefully formulate full explanations

MP7 Look for and make use of structure.

- Search for patterns or structure
- Evaluate the structure or design of a problem
- Discuss geometric shapes in terms of their similarities and differences

MP8 Look for and express regularity in repeated reasoning.

- Make generalizations in computation
- Obtain fluency using patterns
- Look for patterns with shapes and designs
- Use patterns to relate operations
- Evaluate reasonableness of answers

Key: MP = Mathematical Practice

A

acute angle An angle that measures between 0° and 90°.

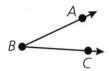

Angle *ABC* is an acute angle.

adjacent Sides of a polygon that are next to each other.

angle Formed when two rays share the same endpoint.

B

benchmark A known amount that can be used to compare or estimate other amounts.

C

compatible numbers Numbers that are easy to compute mentally.

complementary angles Two angles whose measures add to 90°.

composite number A number greater than 1 that has more than two factors.

For example, number 12.
The factors for 12 are 1, 2, 3, 4, 6, and 12.

customary units The measurement units used in the United States customary system of measurement.

D

data Facts or information.

decimal A number that uses place value and a decimal point.

decimal point Separates the whole-number part and the part that is less than 1 in a decimal.

decompose fractions Breaking apart a fraction by writing it as a sum of other fractions with the same denominator.

degree (°) The unit of measure for angles.

dividend The number being divided.

divisor The number by which the dividend is divided.

E

endpoint The point at either end of a line segment or the starting point of a ray.

equivalent fractions Fractions that have different names, but are at the same point on the number line.
For example, $\frac{1}{4} = \frac{2}{8}$

expanded form A number expressed in a way that shows the value of each digit.

For example,

2	9	,	0	3	5
↓	↓		↓	↓	↓
20,000	9,000		0	30	5

$29,035 = 20,000 + 9,000 + 30 + 5$

F

factor One of the two or more numbers that are multiplied to form a product.

factor pair Two numbers that multiply to give a product.

formula A mathematical rule that is expressed with symbols.

For example, $P = 2\ell + 2w$ is the formula for finding the perimeter of a rectangle.

fraction A number that names part of a whole, an area, or a group. It can be expressed in the form $\frac{a}{b}$.

H

hexagon A polygon with 6 sides and 6 angles.

hundredth Each part of a whole when the whole is partitioned into 100 equal parts.

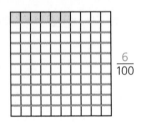

$\frac{6}{100}$

The figure shows $\frac{6}{100}$.

L

length How long something is.

For example, the measure of each side in the longer pair of opposite sides of a rectangle, is called the length of the rectangle.

like denominators The denominators of two or more fractions that are the same.

For example, in $\frac{3}{8} + \frac{1}{8} = \frac{4}{8}$ the fractions have like denominators.

line An endless collection of points along a straight path.

line of symmetry The line that is formed when a figure is folded into two parts that match exactly.

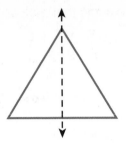

line plot A graph used to organize a set of data on a number line, with symbols to represent the data.

Maple Leaf Lengths

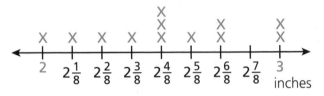

line segment Part of a line that has two endpoints.

M

metric units The measurement units used in the metric system of measurement.

mixed number A number that shows the sum of a whole number and a fraction but does not have a + sign.

For example, $4\frac{1}{2}$

multiple The product of a given whole number and another whole number.

N

number pattern An ordered list of numbers that follow a rule and repeat or change in some way.

O

obtuse angle An angle that measures between 90° and 180°.

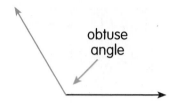

obtuse angle

one-degree angle An angle that turns through $\frac{1}{360}$ of a circle.

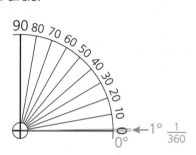

P

parallel lines Lines that will never meet, or intersect.

parallelogram A quadrilateral in which both pairs of opposite sides are parallel.

partial products Numbers that are formed by multiplying the value of each digit by a factor.

pattern rule Tells the term to start with and how to find the next term in a number or shape pattern.

pentagon A polygon with 5 sides and 5 angles.

period Every group of 3 places in a place-value chart.

This place-value chart shows the Thousands period and the Ones period.

Thousands			Ones		
hundreds	tens	ones	hundreds	tens	ones
	2	9	0	3	5

perpendicular Two lines, line segments, or rays that meet or intersect to form a 90° angle.

In the figure, rays *ED* and *EF* are perpendicular.

perpendicular lines Lines that meet, or intersect, to form a right angle.

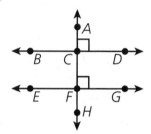

In the figure, lines *AH* and *BD* are perpendicular lines.

point An exact location in space.

prime number A number greater than 1 with only two factors, 1 and the number itself.

For example, 7 and 13 are prime numbers.

protractor A tool used to find the exact measure of an angle.

Q

quotient The result when two numbers are divided.

R

ray The part of a line that starts at an endpoint and goes on in one direction forever.

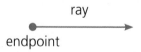

ray

endpoint

rectangle A parallelogram with two pairs of perpendicular sides.

remainder The amount left over after dividing.

For example, 52 ÷ 6 = 8 R4
"52 divided by 6 equals 8 remainder 4."
The amount left over after dividing is 4.

right angle An angle that turns through $\frac{90}{360}$, or $\frac{1}{4}$, of a circle. It measures 90°.

right triangle A triangle with one right angle and two acute angles.

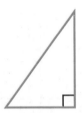

S

shape pattern An ordered sequence of shapes that follows a rule.

straight angle An angle that turns through $\frac{180}{360}$, or $\frac{1}{2}$, of a circle. It measures 180°.

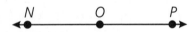

In the figure, angle *NOP* is a straight angle.

supplementary angles Two angles whose measures add to 180°.

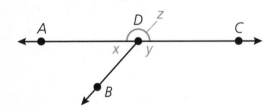

In the figure, angle *ADB* and angle *CDB* are supplementary angles.

T

tenth Each part of a whole when the whole is partitioned into 10 equal parts.

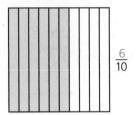

The shaded part of the figure shows $\frac{6}{10}$.

term Each number or shape in a number or shape pattern.

trapezoid A quadrilateral that has at least one pair of parallel sides.

U

unit fraction Represents the quantity, or amount, in one of the equal parts of a whole when the whole is partitioned, or divided.

V

vertex The shared endpoint of two rays that form an angle.

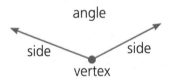

W

width How wide something is.

For example, the measure of each side in the shorter pair of opposite sides of a rectangle, is called the width of the rectangle.

Index

A

Addition
Associative Property of
Addition, 96–103
Commutative Property of
Addition, 96–103

Angles
acute angle, 282–289
angle, 274–281
complementary angles,
290–297
degree, 274–281
endpoint, 274–281
obtuse angle, 282–289
one-degree angle, 274–281
ray, 274–281
right angle, 274–281, 312–319
straight angle, 274–281
supplementary angles,
290–297
vertex, 274–281

Area
formula, 258–265
problem solving, 258–265
of rectangles, 258–265

C

Common Core Review, 50–52,
120–122, 222–224,
298–300, 328–330

**Common Core State Standards
for Mathematical Practice,**
346

Compatible numbers, 104–111

Composite numbers, 34–41

D

Data
line plot, 266–273
measurement, 266–273

Decimals
comparing, 214–221
decimal point, 214–221
use of, 214–221

Division
dividend, 104–111
divisor, 104–111
equations, 18–25
of whole numbers, 104–111,
112–119
place value, 104–111
properties of operations,
112–119
quotient, 104–111
remainder, 26–33

E

Equations
division, 18–25
multiplication, 10–17, 18–25

Essential Question—Unit,
9, 55, 125, 233, 303

Expanded form, 64–71, 96–103

F

Foundational Skills Handbook
compare fractions, 340
division strategies, 339
equivalent fractions, 339
draw line plots, 342
measure time intervals, 341
multiplication strategies, 338
area of rectangles, 341
round numbers, 338
meaning of a product, 337
meaning of a unit fraction, 340
identify special quadrilaterals,
342
use multiplication to solve
division, 337

Fractions
add and subtract, 150–157,
166–173, 174–181
benchmark, 142–149
compare, 126–133, 142–149

decimal, 214–221
decompose, 158–165
equivalent, 126–133, 134–141,
142–149
hundredth, 206–213
like denominators, 150–157,
166–173
mixed number, 166–173,
190–197
multiply by whole numbers,
182–189, 190–197, 198–205
on a number line, 150–157,
182–189
tenth, 206–213
unit fractions, 126–133,
182–189

G

Geometry
adjacent, 312–319
angle, 274–281, 304–311
hexagon, 312–319
line, 304–311
line segment, 304–311
line of symmetry, 320–327
parallelogram, 312–319
parallel lines, 304–311
pentagon, 312–319
perpendicular, 282–289,
304–311
point, 274–281, 304–311
rectangle, 312–319
rhombus, 312–319
right triangle, 312–319
two-dimensional figures,
312–319
trapezoid, 312–319

H

Home Connect, 8, 54, 124,
232, 302

L

Line of symmetry, 320–327

M

Measurement
centimeter, 242–249
cup, 234–241
customary units, 234–241
foot, 234–241
gallon, 234–241
gram, 242–249
inch, 234–241
kilogram, 242–249
kilometer, 242–249
liter, 242–249
meter, 242–249
metric units, 242–249
milliliter, 242–249
millimeter, 242–249
ounce, 234–241
pint, 234–241
pound, 234–241
quart, 234–241
ton, 234–241
yard, 234–241

Measurement and Data
angle measures, 274–281,
    282–289, 290–297
area, 250–257, 258–265
customary units, 234–241
data, 266–273
degree, 274–281
endpoint, 274–281
formulas for area and
    perimeters, 258–265
length, 258–265
line plot, 266–273
liquid volumes and masses,
    234–241, 242–249
metric units, 242–249
perimeter, 258–265
point, 274–281
protractor, 282–289
ray, 274–281
time, 234–241, 250–257
vertex, 274–281
width, 258–265

Multiplication
arrays, 10–17, 34–41
Associative Property of,
    96–103, 190–197
Commutative Property of,
    96–103
Distributive Property, 96–103

factor, 34–41
factor pair, 34–41
of fractions, 190–197, 198–205
multiple, 34–41, 112–119
place value, 88–95
of unit fractions, 182–189
of whole numbers, 10–17,
    34–41

N

**Number and Operations—
    Fractions**
add, subtract, 150–157,
    158–165, 166–173,
    174–181, 206–213
comparing, 126–133, 134–141,
    142–149
decimal fractions, 214–221
equivalent, 126–133, 134–141
multiply, 182–189, 190–197,
    198–205

**Number and Operations in
    Base Ten**
add and subtract, 80–87
divide, 104–111, 112–119
multiply, 88–95, 96–103
period, 64–71
place value, 56–63
read, write, compare, 64–71
round whole numbers, 72–79

O

**Operations and Algebraic
    Thinking**
division, 18–25
factors, 34–41
multiplication, 10–17, 18–25,
    34–41
multiples, 34–41
multistep problems, 26–33
patterns, 42–49

P

Partial products, 88–95

Pattern
number pattern, 42–49
pattern rule, 42–49
shape pattern, 42–49
term, 42–49

Performance Tasks, 225–230,
    331–336

Perimeter,
formulas, 258–265
of rectangles, 258–265

Prime number, 34–41

Problem solving
area, 258–265
fractions, 174–181, 198–205
line plots, 266–273
measurement, 250–257
multiplication and division,
    18–25
multistep problems, 26–33
perimeter, 258–265
time, 250–257
unknown angle measures,
    290–297

Problem Solving Model,
    343–345

Progress Check, 7, 53, 123,
    231, 301

Properties of Operations
Associative Property of
    Multiplication, 96–103,
    190–197
Commutative Property of
    Multiplication, 96–103
Distributive Property, 96–103

Q

Quadrilaterals, 312–319

R

Right triangle, 312–319

Rounding, 72–79

T

Time
elapsed, 250–257
hour, minute, second, 234–241
interval, 234–241